P O w

P O W
The Diary of a Prisoner of War

Ex-sergeant David Nell

of the 7th Battalion, The Green Howards

MechAero

MechAero Publishing
46 Lancaster Road
St Albans
AL1 4ET
UK
www.mechaero.co.uk

© MechAero Publishing 2004

Published by MechAero Publishing, 2004

ISBN 0-954-07343-6

Set by MechAero
Printed in Great Britain by Bemrose Booth Ltd,
Derby DE21 6XG, UK

To the strong amongst us whose example was the mainstay of the others, and to the loved ones at home – Evelyn in my case – whose concern for us was our hope for the future.

And to the International Red Cross without whose supply of food parcels many of us would have died.

Foreword

I had not really intended to keep a diary of my time as a prisoner of war. I think it evolved from a subconscious desire to be able to write articulately and reasonably grammatically, which had been smouldering in me ever since I had learned to read and write at the rather late age of almost eleven. Perhaps I had been considered to be uneducable as an infant. We had lived at Dunston on the south side of the River Tyne just across from Newcastle. I didn't see my dad until he left the army early in 1919 after the 1st World War when I was five years old. I didn't like him. It seemed to me that he had taken my mum from me. Until he returned she had been all mine. Now, apparently, she was all his!

I had always been regarded as a delicate child and my mum had pampered me but the return of my dad coincided with my having to start school. Because of my poor health my school attendance was very erratic and, also, I suffered from a chronic self-consciousness which caused me to blush when spoken to or even when I became aware that I was being looked at. I used to cover my face or even try to hide. However, in the class room I was eventually ignored. The teachers finally gave up trying to include me with the class and I simply dreamed my way through those class room hours. Each year I moved up with my class, nobody seeming to notice that I was not learning anything. During those early couple of years my mother fussed over me and kept me away from school when she had deemed me to be 'too poorly' to go to school. She, herself, was absolutely illiterate: couldn't read a word.

Then, suddenly, a few days before Christmas 1921, she died. Nothing since that has happened to me has devastated me so much. Dad was a miner, young, ex-army and bombastic, ignorant. And helpless! What could he do with me? My mother's family, less their dad who had apparently absconded to Australia, lived near us. But, apparently, Dad received no offers from them. For a short while we lived with his mother but this proved to be an unhappy period so, from a workmate he got the address of a young woman who was in domestic service but was looking for a husband. Dad wrote to her offering marriage. She accepted happily, and joined us, and she and Dad were married. But I wasn't the 'little Lord Fauntleroy' she had hoped me to be. I was unaware of any social manners and I simply refused to regard her as my mother and until I left home when I was eighteen our association was an unhappy one.

Soon after their marriage we moved to Scotland to the north side of the Forth Valley, a mining area. My speech at that time was coarse 'Geordie', understood only by other 'Geordies'. The speech in those mining districts of Scotland had accent and dialect equally as coarse but absolutely different from mine. Initially I understood nobody and nobody understood me. But a mutual understanding eventually seeped through and my new Scottish companions, the boys particularly, let me know immediately that they didn't like the English. They wanted me to know that the Scots had thoroughly thrashed the English at the Battle of Bannockburn. They were better fighters than the English. And they were better footballers too. They told me of all of their national heroes, some of whom I remember: William Wallace, Robert the Bruce, Bonny Prince Charlie, Rabby Burns (better than that English ponce, Shakespeare) and, although not a Scot, Jesus was included in a sort of special status.

Because of my chronic shyness and my 'funny' speech they 'took the micky' with me cruelly, so much so that at 'playtime', instead of going into the playground, I used to hide behind the coatracks in the cloakroom. One of the male teachers found me hiding there. "Get into the playground," he bawled at me, "and get some good Scottish air into your lungs and forget about your soft, warm, English air!" He appeared to have thought that I had been sheltering from the cold, as though the subtropics were just the south side of Hadrian's Wall! But my real torture was in the classroom. Even after I had been in Scotland a couple of years I still couldn't read a word and no one seemed to have bothered about having me taught.

For the Reading Lesson we stood up in turn to read a paragraph from our reading book. As I was at the bottom of the class, I was always last to 'read', when I would stand up holding my book but not knowing a word on the page, in an agony of selfconsciousness and blushing red hot, the silence broken only by suppressed giggles. And then, the impatient snap of our teacher: "Oh, sit down, boy!" or, "Sit down, you fool!" And this sort of pantomime went on until after my tenth birthday when, one day, our headmaster entered our classroom. I don't remember the lesson but I do remember his shock on learning that he had at his school a pupil, ten years of age, who couldn't read a word. And *he* had not been told.

"Why can't he read?" he demanded of our teacher: "Why?" I suppose our teacher offered some sort of reply, I don't remember that. But I do remember the headmaster's reaction. That nasty tempered old man grasped one of my ears between his finger and thumb and led me out of the classroom as though I was a foul piece of soiled cloth and dragged me along the corridor to the classroom where the five and six year olds were taught.

Unceremoniously he barged in with me, simultaneously addressing himself to the very young teacher: "Miss Kirk, this laddie canna read: teach him!" And he left the room as abruptly as he had entered. Temperamentally Miss Kirk was a lovely young woman, gentle and very patient and I loved her immediately as, quietly, she started to assess me as her latest problem. Why couldn't I read? she asked me.

"Cos nobody learnt us," I told her, believing this to be so. Gradually during the following days she taught me the alphabet, little letters and capitals. And then the phonetics followed by the construction of simple words and sentences and punctuation, with capitals, full-stops, and commas. She taught me to read and write sufficiently well to enable me to move up with the other eleven-year-olds at the start of the new school year in the autumn. But then I had only three years to go before leaving school at fourteen as nearly all working class children did in those days.

I had hardly started my final year when we moved to another district and, of course, a different school. Although also a primary school, its pupils in those final years, eleven to fourteen, were much further advanced than the similar age group I was leaving and I was shocked when I was introduced to more serious literature and poetry and, also, geometry and algebra. And French! This was my new class mates' final year.

I was absolutely out of my depth and was relieved when I was allowed to leave at the Easter break of that year, 1928. In common with most of my male ex class-mates I went to work down a mine and became known as the shy wee Englishman. When I was sixteen we moved back to Durham but I was still a miner.

At eighteen I became a soldier. I joined a Yorkshire regiment, The Green Howards. After serving in India I returned to England in time to go to France in September 1939 at the outbreak of the 2nd World war. But during my pre-war service the Army had educated me up to its 2nd class standard, its minimum educational standard for proficiency pay. Beyond that was optional, but to chance that the ordinary barrack-room soldier was likely to be regarded as 'big-headed'. Intellectual superiority was not accepted in the barrack-room. I was shy so didn't attempt it. But I became a very competent signaller (telegraphist). In those days communication in front-line units was in Morse code or telephone line.

Throughout my pre-war service and until I returned from France early in 1940 I had avoided promotion but, due to the rapid expansion of the Army, leaders and instructors were needed urgently – and immediately – and I was 'bull-dozed' into accepting promotion. Soon I was posted to an, as-yet, untrained battalion as its Signals Sergeant, that is, to train its untrained signallers, and to be in charge of the battalion's communications. This battalion had been recruited as a Territorial Army battalion, just a few weeks before the declaration of war, at Bridlington, the Yorkshire seaside town. The local grammar school master, who was a major in the Territorial Army, was initially its commanding officer. The Army, as best it could in the circumstances, provided him with a regular army major as his second in command, a couple of captains, the necessary regimental sergeant major, and a company sergeant major for each of the battalion's five companies for when they'd been enlisted. He was left to find his own junior officers and sergeants as best he could.

Naturally he thought of the most suitable of his school's 'old boys'. Apart from his senior officers and his sergeant majors, his new battalion was a very 'Tom, Dick, and Harry' organization which lacked the necessary discipline and soldiery skills so, initially, the unit was used as a labour battalion and even went to France as such, though for this posting an ex-regular army officer was put in command. After their return from France at the Dunkirque evacuation they had to be re-equipped and trained up to service standard. Despite their somewhat fluid and untrained state they were put on coastal command defence at Poole in Dorset. And this was where I joined them to find that my fellow sergeants were all ex-grammar school and whose speech was 'Bridlington posh'. My speech at that time was a sort of Tyneside-Scottish with a bit of a bias towards Edinburgh. At times I was addressed as 'Jock', 'Paddy', 'Taffy'. People had not travelled much in those days and regional accents were not heard much on the radio and films. Eventually it was established that I was, in fact, a 'Geordie'.

Although accepted by my new comrades, metaphorically, I regarded myself as a sort of weed in a flower garden: they had all been educated and I hadn't. An inferiority complex is a sad affliction.

However, I met Evelyn who, almost immediately, became my fiancée – provisionally – after all, there was a war in progress. I had always dreamed of marrying a girl who would be intelligent and articulate and without a regional accent. Evelyn personified this dream. But time and tide – and wars – wait for no man, or lovers. Our battalion, with all of the other units of our division, 50th Northumberland Division, were ordered overseas, so, in common with so many young lovers, our romance was put 'on hold' for the duration.

Our voyage was a long one because, Italy having now entered the war as an ally of Germany, the Mediterranean area was now infested by their submarines and their airforces and that was where we were destined. Our voyage was via the mid-Atlantic and South Africa, up through the Indian Ocean to Egypt. As this is essentially a copy of my prison camp diaries I shall not go into our military activities between our arrival in Egypt and being taken prisoner of war. Being a loner and frequently bored I decided that I needed some mental activity to while away, if any, the idle hours, so, in one of my letters to Evelyn, I asked her to send to me: a book on English Grammar, a book of poetry, and a dictionary. All mail, of course, was by sea and, where we were meant a passage each way of six weeks.

Eventually my book parcel arrived. From the time of my asking Evelyn for the books until my receiving them was about three months but this wasn't bad bearing in mind the long sea passage each way. And the books had to be shopped for when everything was war-time scarce. My parcel contained a large volume covering the whole of the Matriculation English Course; Palgrave's Golden Treasury of English Verse; an Oxford English Dictionary; and sundry other items of literature. During my pre-war service in India – almost five years – I had done a fair amount of reading: Galsworthy, Walpole, Rider Haggard, HG Wells, PC Wren, Baroness Onczy, Raphael

Sabatini, plus a few on travel and exploration, but now I was about to set about my English seriously.

It was now about a year since we had left England and the war, as we saw it, seemed to be jogging along quietly. Other people seemed to be doing the action. But it all changed barely a couple of weeks after I had received Evelyn's book parcel. We were ensconced in what was known as The Gazala Line, our western defence line in the Libyan Desert. The situation had been quiet for some time but then Rommel with his elite Afrika Korps attacked with the intention of wiping us off the desert. Sadly, and soon, our defence became a rear-guard action as we leap-frogged our way back towards Egypt. Unavoidably my academics were put on hold. And we didn't fare very well against our enemy. Sunday, 28th June, 1942, our battalion HQ and the remnants of two of our companies found ourselves 'hiding' in a wadi (a dried-up river bed which hadn't had water for thousands of years) a short distance south of Mersa Matruh...

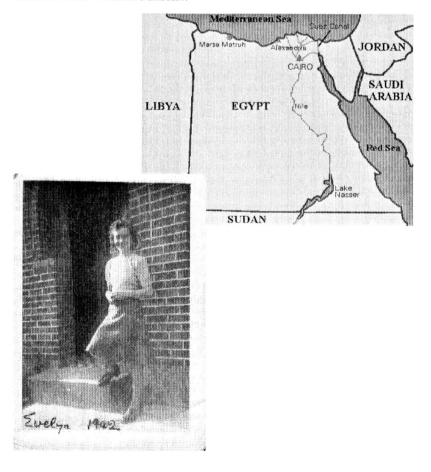

Surrender

I had a tommy-gun with an empty magazine, a loaded Webley .38 revolver and six spare rounds for it. I was alone.

A short while ago I had had a group of eighteen men: twelve of them were signallers, all that were left of my signal platoon, together with six men of the mortar platoon who had attached themselves to me and my lot for moral comfort.

Believing that we were about to be over-run by the Germans, my little band of reluctant heroes panicked and ran. My wild, indignant shouts to them to come back were mere cries in the wilderness: an infinitesimal addition to the multitude of battle noises of that desert night. They ignored me and disappeared into the darkness. For a few moments I stood considering my situation. The remnant of our battalion had been lying low in a 'wadi' a few miles south of Mersa Matruh waiting for darkness before trying to break through the enemy who had encircled us. But the Germans had seen us and had come to get us.

Altogether there were one hundred and thirty six of us, commanded by our colonel.

The only weapons we possessed in addition to our personal weapons were a two-pounder anti-tank gun, which had successfully knocked out several of the enemy's troop-carrying vehicles before darkness had rendered it useless, and a Bren gun for which there was only one magazine. There were several boxes of ammunition but only this one magazine. As a Bren magazine held only twenty eight rounds and the gun fired at the rate of about six hundred rounds per minute one magazine gave roughly three seconds of firing time. We could be said to have been at a disadvantage. Also, I had my tommy-gun, initially with three magazines, each holding twenty four rounds. It had not been my gun really. I had acquired it when it had been abandoned by a corporal of the R.A.S.C. who had been attached to us, when he decided that he no longer wished to take part in our conflict with the Germans. I don't know what happened to him but I picked up the gun and the spare magazines when the alarm was given that the Germans were advancing towards us.

I was directed to take my little group to a bit of high ground which overlooked that side of the 'wadi' from which the Germans approached.

They reached us just after darkness had fallen. We allowed them to come very close, hoping that they would miss us in the darkness and then go away. However, one of them wandered into a little bunch of our blokes. Someone, with a breezy friendliness, a little forced, said to him, "It's a lovely night, mate!"

Unfortunately the German was not of a friendly nature. Suddenly, all hell was let loose. My men, before I could control them, started to fire their rifles rapidly in the general direction of the enemy. 'Jimmy' Riddle, my dispatch rider, stood firing from the hip with his revolver until it was empty.

"Where's a spare rifle," he was shouting, "Anybody got a spare rifle?" With my tommy-gun I sprayed the vague silhouettes in the darkness. All of the shouting seemed to be, "Achtung, Britischer schweinhund," and "Bloody square-headed German bastards."

And suddenly, all was quiet. The shooting stopped. The Germans, having found us, seemed to be consolidating, and the British opposition on site were grateful for the break. But, obviously, we had had it.

I was facing the direction from which the shooting had come. My heart was pounding and my mind was in turmoil. What should I do?

The decision was made for me. A raucous, guttural voice screamed at us from a few yards to my left. Clearly silhouetted against the sky was a young German. Jack-booted legs apart, arrogant and sneering, he stood pointing his Schmeisser light machine-gun at us.

After weeks of insufficient food, water, or sleep; of being bombed, shelled and machine-gunned, my nerves were at breaking point. My reaction was crude reflex: I pressed the trigger of my tommy-gun. It jerked in my hands and made a devastating clatter. I saw the German's body shuddering under the impact of the heavy .45 bullets as he fell away backwards. Frank Inwood was the first to speak.

"The cheeky bugger," he said in an awed whisper, and then, more loudly, "Always knew you was a rotten bastard, Sarge."

I was given no time to reprove Frank or to ponder his accusation. My little fracas with their comrade had resuscitated our enemy's interest in us. They fired flares which lit up the whole landscape and their machine-gun tracer bullets converged on us from seemingly every direction. Mortar bombs dropped with terrifying crashes all around us. None of us was hurt but my fellows had had enough. To a man, they all took to their heels and left me with my dead German. I visualised myself being confronted by his bereaved comrades, hopefully offering the explanation, "It was like this, you see, my gun went off accidental like..."

I decided that I'd better find the colonel quickly. I reckoned that dealing with a situation such as I found myself was his prerogative. Years before when I had known him when he was a not so humble captain in India he had often told us that the officer's job was to direct; to lead; to be an inspiration in a crisis. I set off to find him.

I wended my way down the track into the 'wadi'. It was quite dark as there was no moon. A shadowy hulk I investigated turned out to be our only Bren-carrier, without a gun. A Bren-carrier was a sort of light tank. A young sergeant, Len Sharp, who had been a private until quite recently, and some men of his platoon were in it. He expressed relief on seeing me.

"Thank Christ you're here, Sarge. I thought we was the only buggers left," he said to me, "I'm bloody glad some bugger's still in charge."

I hadn't thought of it until he mentioned it but it was worth thinking about. I asked him had he had any orders about moving out. He said, no, all he knew was that we were going to move out and then the bloody square-heads had come and buggered it all up.

"Right, Len," I told him, "give me time to get my blanket and haversack from my truck and I'll give you all the orders you'll need!"

"I wish I knew what's bloody happening," he muttered.

"So do I," I answered over my shoulder as I walked along the 'wadi' to where my truck was where I had left my kit when the Germans had started their advance towards us. I found the truck, riddled with bullet holes, the woodwork splintered and the windscreen shattered. But I found my haversack, greatcoat, and blanket.

I was about to return to the Bren-carrier when I heard agitated whispers from behind some bushes. Then more loudly I heard some one say, "Christ! It's our sarge. It's the bloody padre." 'Padre' was their nickname for me.

I walked behind the bushes, and there they were: my charges, all squatting in the little holes which they had dug for cover. Several of them murmured greetings.

"Hello, Sarge."

"Pleased to see you again, Sarge."

"We thought we was all on our own, Sarge."

"Bloody glad you've found us, Sarge."

I looked at their worried faces. "A right shower of heroes you lot have turned out to be," I muttered viciously. "Talk about rats deserting a sinking ship..."

Jack Anderson, my second in command, who was with them now but who'd not been with them when they had panicked and ran, said quietly, "Don't be hard on them 'Padre', they're only lads and we've all had it bloody rough these last few weeks."

Jack and I were older than the men in our platoon. He was thirty two and I was twenty eight but he was not a regular soldier as I was. The average age of our platoon, of the whole battalion, in fact, was about twenty two or twenty three. And as Jack had reminded me, we had had it rough!

Since the start of the German offensive in May we had been tried to our limit. Repeatedly we had been encircled and had broken out. We had been dive-bombed, shelled, machine-gunned. Leap-frogging our way back to what was to be our main, and last, defensive position which was well east of the Egyptian/Lybian border, we had 'dug-in' during the day and had moved at night. Ours was a delaying action to give our troops time to prepare their defences. We had started as a battalion of five hundred men and now we were down to our count for that night: one hundred and thirty six. Our support weapons: Bren-carriers, Bren guns, anti-tank guns, mortars, had been taken from us. These, we were told, had been given to a composite unit who would put them to better use than we could. As our regimental sergeant major was heard to remark: "Poor buggers!"

Our water ration per day had been dropped from four pints, to two pints, to one pint, and we were in the middle of a desert summer. Our food was now that old army stand-by: bully beef and biscuits. Initially one tin of bully and one packet of biscuits per man per day. And now, even this had to be shared between two men. No one had had any proper sleep. We had been digging in or moving the whole of the time. And we had been shot at and bombed whatever we were doing.

I looked at the crouching figures who were staring at me, all hollow-eyed and sunken cheeked. A wave of pity surged through me. Their mothers would have cried had they seen them.

"Sorry, lads," I apologised, "I don't blame you."

But Len Sharp was waiting for me in his Bren-carrier.

"Jack," I said to Jack Anderson, "Sergeant Sharp is waiting for me with his Bren-carrier. I only came back to get my blanket and haversack."

Jack looked at me, shocked and unbelieving. "You're not going to leave us, Dave?" he whispered.

I knew then that I couldn't leave them. Now, after all of the years that have gone by I don't know whether I stayed with them because I regarded this as my moral obligation to them, or merely because I didn't want them to think of me as a coward running away and leaving them when they needed me most.

But Sergeant Sharp was waiting.

"Noddy," I said impulsively to 'Noddy' Milson, the youngest member of the group, a very quiet lad, "get your tackle and come with me."

Without a word, 'Noddy' picked up his rifle and haversack and followed me.

"Don't make a sound," I cautioned him.

Quickly and quietly I made my way back to the Bren-carrier with 'Noddy' at my heels. The Germans were making an awful din. Either a lot of orders were being shouted or else they were shouting to frighten us.

Len looked worried when we reached him.

"Thought you wasn't comin' back, Sarge," he began, and then, seeing 'Noddy,' remonstrated apologetically, "I'm sorry, Sarge, but there's only room for you."

"Take 'Noddy,' Len," I explained, "I'm not coming with you. I've found my platoon and I can't leave them."

Len looked at me in despair. "Christ almighty, Sarge," he pleaded, "we can't go without you. I can't find my way in the bloody desert."

"Look, Len," I started to explain to him, "go south-west for about twenty minutes, I shouldn't think the Germans will expect anyone to go that way – hell for leather – and then south for another twenty minutes, and then east. And don't stop for anybody or anything until you reach our defence line or you run out of petrol." I paused, and then added, "Go on, Len, don't waste time. Get moving."

"I can't," he argued, "I've not got a compass and I don't know which is north, south, or bloody east or west." He looked crest-fallen and added, "We'll just get lost in the bloody desert with no water."

If you've had no experience of navigating it the desert can be frightening. I appreciated his concern.

Looking around at the sky, I said, "Don't worry, Len, look: there's the north star!" Impatient and agitated, I tried to explain to him how to find it. He expressed doubt. He'd never be able to find it, he said. I explained it all again, while his men in the carrier, and 'Noddy', listened, apparently indifferent, accustomed as they were to having their moves decided by others.

Suddenly, Len grasped what I was explaining to him. "OK, Sarge, I've got it," he said. Turning to 'Noddy', he snapped, "Jump in, kid."

Quickly, 'Noddy' was pulled over the side by the men in the carrier.

Len turned to shake hands with me. "All the best, Sarge, and thanks," he said quietly.

"Best of luck, Len," I wished him.

He leapt lightly over the side of the carrier and slipped quickly down beside his driver. Suddenly the engine roared into life. The carrier spun on its tracks and accelerated away.

As I watched it go I tried to joke with myself, quoting 'tis a far far better thing that I do...' and then I dived for cover as a vicious stream of machine-gun bullets zipped along the 'wadi,' uncomfortably close. As I should have expected, the noise of the carrier engine had been heard by the Germans. One of the bullets hit the carrier and the musical spang of the ricochet trembled in the darkness. But the carrier didn't stop.

Wearily I made my way back to my men.

"Did they get away OK?" Jack asked me. He didn't seem surprised to see me.

"They've made it OK out of the 'wadi,'" I answered, "It's just a matter of their luck holding out now."

"Glad you didn't leave me to 'carry the can', Dave," he said. "we're in a bloody awful fix."

I agreed with him. "I'd noticed," I said.

There was no doubt about our being in a fix. Very soon after Len and his Bren-carrier had left us the enemy seemed to have infiltrated the whole length of the 'wadi'. Len had got away apparently with only minutes to spare. But he, somehow, got back to our main defence line. Whether or not he adhered to all of my advice I never got to know, but some months later in our prison camp, we learned from letters from home that he had been awarded the M.M. for getting away.

But, in the meantime, our situation had become increasingly dismal. The enemy were now all along the 'wadi' and also on the high ground either side. In fact, a motorized gun had been brought along the 'wadi' passing within feet of us as we squatted, cowering behind our bushes. Jack and I discussed our problem. We had no ammunition and we were effectively surrounded. I disliked the idea of cowering in holes waiting for the Germans to find us. And in the shock surprise of their finding us in the dark we would stand a fair chance of being sprayed with machine-gun bullets.

I got us into a little huddle to discuss our situation. Did anybody want to try to make a break for it, I asked. There was complete silence to this. Did anybody have anything else to suggest, I asked. Again there was no reply. They all felt beaten, weary, and helpless. Absolutely without hope.

I knew the only answer. Reluctantly, I voiced it. "I think we've got to surrender," I told them, "Does anybody object. Does anybody have anything else to suggest?"

There was silence for a few moments, and then Jack spoke. "You're the boss," he said simply. There were murmurs of agreement from the others.

I looked at them all for a moment, and then said, "Well, the best of luck to all of us," and without further ado, and afraid as I had never been afraid before, or have been since, I got up and walked over to the nearest Germans. They were very close and I reached them in seconds. There was a lot of shouting when they saw me and I was aware of countless weapons being pointed at me. Butterflies in the stomach does not describe adequately the sensation I experienced. Upright, and without putting up my hands, I asked for an officer.

I didn't recognize the rank of the officer by whom I was confronted. I had some men under cover, I told him, but I had decided to surrender.

He acknowledged my salute. He was courteous, and quietly he told me that our colonel had already surrendered. He relieved me of my revolver and binoculars. I had already dismantled and discarded the tommy-gun before surrendering.

Selecting half a dozen men or so, he motioned me to lead the way to where my men were and his surprise was obvious when he realized how close we had been to his lot, and it must have registered on him that had we been a determined and adequately armed little group the German victory over us would not have been nearly so easy. Apprehensively, I suppose, my lads must have been watching my return with the Germans. They emerged with their hands up when I shouted to them to quit their cover, but most of them, despite their despair, remained sullen and arrogant.

The German officer turned to me. Smiling, he said, "For you the war is now over." But it wasn't really. But that is a different story.

Between capture and eventual prison-camp life

With others of my unit, the 7th Battalion The Green Howards, I was taken prisoner on the night of Sunday, 28th June, 1942, somewhere south of Mersa Matruh in Egypt. The following morning we were marched to what were known to us as the 'prison cages' in Mersa Matruh. These cages were an area of open ground which had been divided into compartments by wire mesh. Sometime previously they had been constructed by our Army to accommodate enemy prisoners at the time of our Army's successes earlier in the war. Here we were given one tin of stew between two men and a half pint of water each.

Although we had been captured by the German Army – the Italians seemed to be singularly unsuccessful in battle and hardly ever captured any prisoners – we were then handed over to the Italian Army. In accordance with an Axis[1] agreement, all Allied prisoners who were captured in North Africa were regarded as prisoners of the Italians. We were all ashamed to think that the people at home would believe that we had been beaten in battle by the Italians.

On the afternoon of the same day we were all crammed onto large troop-carrying vehicles and taken on the two-day journey to Tobruk. During this journey we were give no food or water. At Tobruk, the Italians seemed to have no system in their feeding of us: a mugful of water per man per day and, perhaps, a tin of stew between two men. On a couple of occasions we were given some dry oatmeal and some margarine, but no additional water. I believed that this starvation was carried out with the deliberate intention of further lowering our morale and weakening us physically. There were about forty thousand of us prisoners in Tobruk at that time with only the Italian Army's second-best troops to guard us.

We were in Tobruk about a week before being shipped to Benghazi further west in Libya. The conditions here were more organized but little better physically. We were given very little solid food, and water amounted to only about a pint per man per day. We were kept in Benghazi about two weeks before being, literally, crammed into cargo ships which took us across to Italy. We were crowded into the ships' holds with sitting space only. The toilet arrangements were on deck and accessible only by a single ladder. Many of us were suffering from diarrhoea. Neither food nor water was issued. This voyage took two days. Some of the ships were sunk by the British Navy and there were no life-jackets. We were landed at Taranto.

---

[1] Axis – the combined German/Italian enemy.

At Taranto the Italian civilians came out in their thousands to view their prisoners of war. We were all starved and unshaven and none of us had had a change of clothing, or even a proper wash, for weeks and we were indescribably filthy. The good Italian people jeered at us as they threw stones and rotten fruit at us. They spat at us while their pompous little Italian soldiery strutted around threatening us with their rifles and bayonets. After this review we were taken by train to Brindisi.

Brindisi was a transit camp, or, as the Italians called it, a cleansing camp. Each of us was searched comprehensively on entering. The looting was bare-faced. Their soldiers took even tooth-brushes from the prisoners. I was lucky when I was searched. An Italian captain happened to be there when it was my turn. Amongst the articles I had in my possession, including my Army watch and a knife, I had a large text book on English, a dictionary, and a small souvenir bible which I had bought in Palestine for my fiancée. The captain looked at the bible, leafed through the English Grammar, shook me by the hand, and announced to the Italian soldiers present that I was not to be searched further.

All of us entered this camp free of lice. Two weeks later all of us left it, infested with lice. We learned then that all Italians were literally lousy. After Brindisi, seven thousand of us were taken by train to a prepared camp at Porto San Georgeo, which is south of Ancona on the Adriatic coast. We were still wearing our desert clothing and as autumn approached we began to suffer from the cold. It was winter before we received any additional clothing from the Italians. This turned out to be old Yugoslav uniforms. Dressed in them we all looked like players in the musical *Viennese Nights*. We were now established prisoners of war.

To paraphrase the story teller: Any resemblance between a Hollywood depicted prison camp and the prisoner of war camps which I have known is purely coincidental.

Unfortunately (?) many of the pages of the first book are missing.

I suppose PG70 was a haven after our weeks in transit. Obviously it had been built as a factory, indicated by the railway line which went into it. There were about eight large buildings each covered by a roof of three arches which were supported by pillars, there being no inner supporting walls. The floor was of concrete and the floor space was the area of the whole building now taken up entirely by 3-tier bunks. These larger buildings were divided by an eight foot high fence from the administrative buildings, guardhouse, hospital building, etc. There was a single stand-pipe water tap to serve these inner buildings which were to house the prisoners. At first there were no cooking facilities and no sanitary arrangements. A canvas covered lean-to was hastily arranged as a cookhouse and latrine trenches were dug. There were seven thousand of us.

Another very noticeable deficiency, as far as we prisoners were concerned, was food, which we had come to learn was far down on the Italian list of obligations to their captives. I am sure that in the period 1942-3 hundreds of prisoners died who would not have died had we been fed adequately. The usual cause of death was said to be pneumonia but, I believe, the real causes were starvation and lack of adequate medical attention. Other than a couple of British Army medical officers and Army chaplains there were no British Army officers. Their presence, of course, would have made little or no difference. The Italian military personnel made no secret of their delight in being 'in charge'. Their other ranks seemed to be down-trodden peasants turned bullies while their officers were as haughty as their leader, Mussolini.

For sleeping accommodation we were segregated, one of the buildings for sergeants and sergeant majors and the others for the lower ranks who were housed in the other buildings in groups of thirty. With another sergeant, I was put with a group of Durham Light Infantry men. As he, the other sergeant, was also of the Durham Light Infantry, they selected him as their group commander. This suited me: he knew all of them and I didn't. So I was second in command. We didn't have to work and there was little or nothing to read. Initially I think my three books were the only text books in the camp: English grammar, poetry, and dictionary. A few of the fellows had the odd paper-back which they had managed to hang on to. These were worth their weight in gold. Quickly we organized ourselves into friends of twos and threes according to temperament and intellect. I paired with Jerry, a New Zealander. Amongst us there was a fair variety of ability from university lecturers down to labourers.

Seriously I set about my *Oliphant's Matriculation English Course*. It started, 'It is assumed that the student has already had a grounding in English Grammar.' At that moment I doubt if I could have defined grammar. But I started. The first requirement demanded of the student being that he/she write something every day, be it only a single sentence, but, be it ever so brief, care must be taken to ensure that it could not have been expressed better. And here, right at the beginning, I was stumped! I had the intention and a good fountain pen – but no paper on which to record my thoughts and observations, most frustrating. And, as it seemed, the ordinary Italian of that time was not in any way a literary person, there was not a notebook available in the camp. At that time a very large proportion of the Italian Army was illiterate. But back to my own requirements: paper on which to write. And as my book directed me to write something every day I decided that this should be in the form of a diary. Some items were being allowed in to the camp for sale to us. We were paid weekly in 'camp' money. This was an agreement in the Geneva Convention. We were paid, in 'camp' money, the equivalent of a few pence of British currency. Some poor quality note pads were available and I managed to acquire one of these. For an equivalent sum in England I'm sure I could have bought a bound novel. But everything was 'black market' scarce in Italy at that time. But now I had my papers I could start my diary, my tentative journey into English grammar. Unfortunately, as there was no

cover on that first note pad, several weeks of those early entries were lost
a long time ago and the legible remainder is just prior to Christmas 1942.
Some of us had been discussing reading matter: newspapers, magazines,
etc. I had written '...Jerry thinks The Times and The Telegraph are reliable
newspapers and he favours the Argosy as a magazine, Only four days to
Christmas now. Hope each of us receives a Red Cross food parcel. (I'm sure
that without these Red Cross parcels of food thousands of us would have died
of malnutrition.)'
And so on, as I have written it:

22nd December 1942
Received a letter from Evelyn this morning. A very old one and it made me
just a bit love-sick. We've been issued with some old Yugoslav uniforms
to tide us over the winter. The previous occupant of mine must have been a
very big man; the breeches tend to chafe me under my armpits. I'll have to
cut about a foot off the top to bring it down to my waist. We do look a funny
lot. Like characters in that old Hollywood musical, 'Viennese Nights.' Surely
these uniforms weren't intended for real soldiers of a fighting army. That
they looked smashing in *Viennese Nights*.

Have gathered from fellow prisoners that I appear to be a cross between a
Mexican bandit and a Chinese general. Not very flattering. Have been told
that Christmas parcels (Red Cross) will be issued on Thursday. Hope that is
so. Thursday is going to be a big day: Christmas parcels, the ordinary Red
Cross parcel plus all of the buckshee stuff we're hoping to be receiving.
Jerry has given me a list of literature which I ought to read. Even after I have
returned to England I doubt if I'll have the time to read all of it. I wonder:
has he read all of it?!!

23rd December 1942
Didn't feel well when I got up this morning. Had my pulse and temperature
taken this afternoon: pulse 110, temperature 104°. Am going to bed, 1800hrs.
Haven't had a wash all day. Water was turned off all morning and felt too ill
when it was turned on again. Parcels tomorrow (we hope). Just my luck to be
ill at the only time we shall have lots of food. Perhaps I shall be OK by the
25th. Letter from Mr. Higginson.

24th December 1942
Didn't feel so bad this morning although I spent a rather restless night. As
a precaution I didn't go on roll-call. Went around to Jerry's place (he's a
corporal and is in one of the other buildings with the other ranks) and had
breakfast and then went to bed again. Christmas parcels issued. Bill Bailey
brought mine for me. Got up for skilly (soup), inspected contents of parcel
then went to bed again and stayed there until evening skilly when I got up,
spending the remainder of the evening in other barrack with Jerry and Reg.

26 December 1942

Was too ill to make any entries yesterday. Spent most of the day in bed and ate very little. Jerry didn't eat much either but what he ate had proved too much for him. He has been ill all day. I don't know what is the matter with me. Have an idea that it is merely a mild attack of flu but Jimmy Brown claims that it is diphtheria-malaria. My personal opinion is that he is talking through his hat... I haven't heard of such a disease.

Unconfirmed report yesterday stated that Sicily has fallen to the Allies. Confirmed report states that Tripoli (North Africa) is also ours now. Good show. Keep it up and we shall be home by spring!

28th December 1942

Have felt a bit wobbly all day. Put it down to my feeling not quite well yet. Hope that my ticker isn't going wonky. Got my watch back today. The thieving rat charged me 50 lires. Almost thirteen shillings in real money. Hope the RAF come and drop a bomb on his shop! The mechanical defect seems to have been remedied but the glass is now loose and a piece of enamel has been chipped off the face. Wrote to Evelyn today but forgot most of the things I had meant to tell her. Also wrote a card to Pam. I haven't heard from Pam since being taken prisoner. Can't imagine why she isn't writing. Perhaps she isn't receiving my cards and doesn't yet know my address.

29th December 1942

Got a letter from Betty this morning (Scottish cousin). Usual stuff: Good luck and God bless me. When will that girl learn to write a decent letter! It is just about time I had a letter from Evelyn. Perhaps I shall get one from her tomorrow. Got a Canadian Red Cross parcel today. We are rather well off for food these days. Wish that I were well enough to start eating normally again. Have been dreaming a lot today. I'm afraid I shall have to be very prosperous if my dream is to materialise. I pictured myself having glorious fun with a small yacht at Poole. It was a beautiful boat. White. Sails billowing as we scurried before the wind. It has always been my ambition to own and be able to manage a sailing boat. I wonder will I drown myself the first day I acquire one!

Even more bunks put in our billet today. Almost need a map to find your bed. Haven't had any authentic war news for some time now although rumour has it that the Russians are still going the right way. Keep it up, Joe (Joe Stalin) and it won't be much longer. The Italians are in a bad way, I think. They aren't being at all generous with the food they give us. They appear even to have run out of salt. I intend to sew a new waistband on my breeches tomorrow. Hope I don't weaken or forget. In one of her letters Evelyn said she and Doris had sent me some books. That was about two months ago. I wonder when I shall get them. The only time I have anything to read is when I borrow Jerry's book and I have to go to his billet to read it. No one in possession of a book will let it out of his sight. Roll on civil life again and with it a comfortable home with lots of books, an armchair, a cheery fire, and an adorable wife to care for me. Oh, how I will appreciate these when I have them. But here I am, dreaming again – may as well dream in the appropriate place: bed!

30th December 1942

This will probably be the last entry I shall make this year, the 29th year of my life. A lot has happened to me this year. I was very nearly commissioned but the colonel reasoned that an ex barrack-room soldier was the wrong person to become an 'officer and gentleman!' Kindly (!) he said he couldn't afford to lose me as his signals sergeant.

And then I went into hospital having been severely concussed. I have seen a fair amount of action and have even sprayed a horde of Germans with my 'tommy-gun', subsequently, with only a dozen men left, I walked over to the enemy and capitulated as though I were a general surrendering a city. And now, I am a prisoner of war in Italy awaiting our ultimate victory and subsequent repatriation to England. I think it will turn out to have been the biggest year of my life. And it has only one day to go, and then: roll on 1943 with the victory we are expecting. Roll on England!

I didn't feel at all energetic this morning but, remembering my resolution of last night, I set about rejoining the new waistband to my breeches. The finished job doesn't look at all good but perhaps it will last out the winter months. Surely I won't be wearing these decrepit old rags next winter.

Today I remembered something I had meant to tell Evelyn. It is something Mr. Higginson said about her appearance at a party. It was the first occasion on which he had seen her dressed for such an occasion. He had written: "...and I thought she looked lovely!" Of course he is a man in his sixties! But I must remember to tell her in my next letter. There has been no mail for two days. RAF to blame, I suppose. Good old RAF! But perhaps there will be some mail tomorrow. Surely I can have one more letter from Evelyn this year.

1943

1st January, 1943

My first entry in the year of our victory – we hope! My only resolution for the year is to remain cheerful until my return to England which I hope will be this year. To while away the last couple of hours of the old year Jerry and I tried to estimate the cost of setting up a home. He, Jerry, thinks it would require about £200, but my estimate is about £150. Jerry, of course, is reckoning on paying about £30 for records but I am not so keen on music. Anyway, I hope to start my home-making this year. Evelyn and I are going to get a lot of fun out of it. I hope she knows something about it. I don't. Perhaps her mother will help us. My future father-in-law too. We must get his advice. I will have to ask him about our garden. I know nothing about gardening. I don't seem to know much about anything. Well, I must start learning: everything the young married man ought to know. Must get some literature on the various subjects.

2nd January 1943

Was very tired last night so went to bed early. Today the weather has been lousy: cold, rainy, and windy. And it fell to me to make both of the 'brews' too (tea-making). Most unfortunate. Expected a letter from Evelyn today but didn't get one. Don't suppose there will be any more until Monday. Perhaps I shall get one then. Have been talking about houses this evening. I think Reg's ideas are a little bombastic. Maybe he has pots of money. If he has he ought to bear in mind that some people haven't. The house I could afford would be a very moderate place indeed: a small kitchen, a dining room, a lounge, two large and one small bedrooms. I would like to have carpets in all of the rooms but I'm afraid I shall be able to afford one for the lounge only. Linoleum will have to suffice for the other rooms.

But perhaps I'd better not have any ideas as Evelyn will most likely have her own way. Would rather not have any ideas than have them overridden. Had better not let her know this or I shall be a hen-pecked husband. I am wondering what would be better: a good reliable job, or a business of my own. I'm in favour of the former but perhaps I'm being too cautious. It would be much better to be my own boss and have some ambition. Perhaps I could create a big business. Have pots of money. A big house. A car and a yacht. As the old song says: 'I'm forever blowing bubbles...'

4th January 1943 2120hrs

Owing to the lights failing last night I was unable to make any entries. Got two letters from Evelyn yesterday, the later one dated 24 November. Letter cards have not been issued yet this week so I cannot send her my weekly letter. Was on the camp 'wood' fatigue today but the 'double' loaf wasn't forthcoming (non-workers receive only half a daily bread ration). Hope to receive it tomorrow night. Finished the novel *Rachel Moon* this evening. Had quite an interesting discussion with Jerry about it. Both of us are of the opinion that it is a good novel and extremely well written. Must admit though that my opinion doesn't really count for much as I am not very well up in literary appreciation. Still, Jerry didn't disagree with my views and interpretations so perhaps I am improving.

Had a further discussion with Jerry and Grif on love and marriage. I think perhaps I impressed Jerry with my philosophy and depth of thought on the subject. Although Grif is married I think he is a bit of an 'old woman' and rather petty. Quite a nice fellow really but he is apt to talk more than he thinks. Before his conscription he was an assistant in a grocery shop but his ambition is to be a window-dresser. His views, such as they are, are worth nothing. He can't keep on any subject but must go off at a tangent. Tonight he switched us over from the more interesting subject of love and marriage to an idiotic argument on the virtues of the practical gardener compared with those of the theoretical gardener. A chip off the old block, apparently: his father is a railway signalman!

I am still worried about my heart. I'm be coming a real hypochondriac. My pulse is beating much too fast. Hope my heart is not going to let me down. I'm still too young to be bothered with that but maybe it's just the cold weather causing it. Anyway worrying about it won't help. Time will tell.

Another batch of prisoners came in yesterday. Most of them were captured about the same time as I was. Four of my platoon were among them: Harry Lawson, Fred Scaife, Bentley and Wiffen. They are all much thinner but don't look too bad really. Despite my self-concern they tell me that I look really well! Today was our parcel day. It was 'bulk' stuff and we did fairly well on the deal. It struck me that it was too good to be true. My cynicism was justified: we were told later in the day that there will be no more issues until more supplies come into the camp. Rather disconcerting news but perhaps it won't be a long lapse. Fortunately Jerry and I have a good reserve.

5th Jan 1943

I am not in the mood for writing tonight. Nothing of importance has happened in the camp and we don't seem able to get any authentic war news. There are some very cheerful rumours but they strike me as being too fantastic. The Russians are said to have broken through the Germans in twelve places and the Italians are said to be asking for peace through the Vatican. I shall be home before summer if these stories are true. This morning Sgt Major Davis went to Porto San Georgeo to witness the transferring of parcels from the wide to the narrow gauge railway. We were all wrong. It was clothing and not parcels which turned up. Tonight I got my double loaf and a piece of cheese for my wood fatigue yesterday (a 'loaf' is only as big as a child's fist). Jerry and I have eaten half of the loaf and the cheese for supper tonight. The weather during the past few days has been good. There has been some frost during the night but we've had brilliant sunshine during the day. If it continues the ground ought to be dry in a few days.

6th Jan 1943

It has been a bitterly cold day and rather dull but fortunately it has been dry and the mud is gradually solidifying. It will soon be possible to have walks around the orchard. (The trees don't bear fruit!) The rumours about food parcels seem to have petered out. This is just as well: we get terribly depressed when they don't materialise.

7th Jan 1943

Jerry is reading something and Grif and Reg have gone to listen to a newly formed band. Some RAF prisoners were brought in the other day with the following 'news': Churchill, in a recent speech, said that there would be some very great changes during the ensuing six or seven weeks. Apparently he said that he is sorry that our army in the Middle East would have to go to the Far East instead of being repatriated to Britain when the European war is over. Apparently we will still have the Japs to contend with. Also, according to our RAF friends, Russia claims to have entered Poland. I don't believe this latter bit. If it were true we prisoners could find ourselves being repatriated in the near future. What a hope! But I get annoyed with these rumour mongers. Perhaps they are amused when they hear their nonsense being passed around as facts! Of course a lot of it may start merely as voiced hope. The Italians provide us with no news at all. We haven't seen a newspaper for weeks. Perhaps this is a good sign. I hope my optimism will be justified.

8th January 1943 2035hrs

When I went out for roll-call this morning it was raining and appeared to have been doing so all night. However the sun came out at about 9 o'clock making the aspect a little more cheerful and the weather remained good until about 6 this evening when we had more rain and it was still raining when I came in a few minutes ago. Gone are my hopes of a dry 'brewing ground' for at least another week. (We have no facilities for cooking. We must improvise with a little fire of twigs between a couple of bricks.) Looking at the *Barbed Wire*, our camp news sheet, today, I read that Generals Wavell and Gort have been promoted to the rank of Fieldmarshal. I wonder if they have done something exceptionally well. Something recently, I mean, that may have an appreciable effect on the war. I very sincerely hope that they have, but I thought that they had both effectively retired.

This morning Jimmy Wiffen, one of my platoon, asked me for my address. Perhaps he intends to write to me after the war. I gave him also the address of Bill Murray, our platoon commander, who asked me to give it to any of our lads who desired it. I wonder how many of us address collectors will bother to write? Not many I suppose. Looking at it sensibly there would seem to be little point in it. Perhaps it would be nice to have a reunion every few years again to meet old friends and to talk about old times: 'those were the days!' Talking of old times: I wonder what my lads thought of me when I was their sergeant? I shall never know. I know I made many mistakes in my dealing with them but, conscientiously, I can say that I always tried to do my best for them right up to our ultimate capture.

I had to summon up all of my courage for that show. The Germans were blasting everything and everybody before them. The party coming our way along the wadi in which we were quite inadequately 'dug-in' had a mobile artillery gun and light automatics. The gun passed within a few feet of us. We'd have been blasted to hell had they seen us. My lads were armed only with rifles and had used up all of their ammunition earlier that night and the 'tommy-gun' I had was now useless because I'd used up all of its ammunition and, in the circumstances, my revolver would have been no more effective than a pea-shooter. They stopped thirty or forty yards away from us.

Our predicament was most disconcerting: we weren't in a situation where we could fight: there was this large artillery blaster on one side of us and machine guns on the other. What should I do? I asked Terry Bray, my 2nd in command. He said: "I reckon we're finished – but you're the boss!" So, the ball was in my court. Surrendering seemed to be the only option, but first of all I got the lads into a little huddle to see if they agreed with me. One man, Frank Robinson, wanted to try and fight our way out. He actually sobbed as he pleaded with me to 'fight it out.' But fighting was out of the question. It wasn't cowardice on my part that made me refuse. It was cold common sense. We would surrender! There was nothing else for it.

But how were we going to surrender? That was a problem. If we shouted to the Germans they might open fire on us. If we got up out of our concealment they'd quite likely think we were about to attack them. They weren't at all reluctant to use their weapons in their excitement. The only possible way, as it seemed to me, was for one of us to go over to them and capitulate for the lot of us. As none of us could speak German I decided I must go myself. Carefully, I crawled out of the trench, stood up and trying to look much braver than I felt, I walked over to the Germans. It was a very short distance but it seemed a very long way to me. When about two thirds of the way towards them, one of them saw me. He swung his light machine-gun around to me and I felt an awful vacuum in my stomach. If he'd fired at that short range I'd have been cut in half. He shouted: "Come on, Tommy! Come on, Tommy!"

When I was amongst them I asked for an officer. They seemed to be saying they hadn't an officer but when I insisted a young officer who spoke English came. I told him that I would surrender my men to him if I had his

word that we would be treated decently, a pointless condition to ask for in
the circumstances. For what it was worth, he agreed immediately, adding
that there was no disgrace about our surrender as we were outnumbered
by a force whose arms were vastly superior to ours: rifles, a 'tommy-gun'
and a revolver. And, he added, our colonel had already surrendered! With a
number of his men he followed me to where my lads were still in hiding, all
the while covering me with his pistol.

I shouted to my blokes to come out. They came out from their hiding,
some with their hands up. It was all over. We were prisoners. I felt ashamed
but everyone told me it wasn't our fault: there had been no way out of
our situation. This attitude cheered me considerably. I hadn't failed them.
I wonder do they still think so? After seven months as prisoners of war
suffering cold and hunger, with the subsequent weakness, and having to wear
vermin-infested clothes that until recently belonged to the Yugoslav army
they may not be so well disposed towards me. I no longer feel cheered and
I wonder did I do the right thing when I surrendered. Perhaps I shall be told
one day but perhaps they'll be in a more charitable frame of mind when they
find themselves again in England and not names on a War Memorial.

9th Jan 1943

It has been very cold all day. We have had a little rain too. Hope we have
fine weather tomorrow. I am developing a cold. The rice today was terrible,
there seeming to be as many fleas as there were grains of rice. It was vile but
we must eat it or starve. We have had no mail for the past few days. I wonder
if we'll get any tomorrow. It is also time we were issued with lettercards. We
haven't had any for two weeks.

10th Jan 1943

I left the other billet, where Jerry sleeps, with the intention of going to bed
early but was intercepted and dragged into a conversation. There was a heavy
frost this morning but it thawed later in the day. The sun has been brilliant
but not at all warm. According to Cpl Tarantov[2] (our newspaper reader, he
speaks several languages) a puppet government in China has declared war
on the Allies. We hope this is not true but I don't suppose it matters much
anyway. I discovered today that the *Barbed Wire* news is censored by the
Italians before we are allowed to see it. In that case it isn't worth the time
it takes to read. There were about a dozen personal parcels received this
morning. I don't expect one as I don't think Dad would think of it. There was
also some mail this morning but there was none for me.

---

[2] Corporal Tarantov was a Palestinian Jew who had joined the Royal
Engineers. He had been a Russian refugee.

11th Jan 1943

There are some colossal war rumours about today. The Russians being in
Warsaw is one of them. This is obviously nonsense but we wish it were true.
I have a severe cold building up and my pulse is going rather rapidly. Cold
weather and lack of food, quite likely. A semi-official report has it that two
truck-loads of bulk Red Cross food have been dispatched to this camp. Some
clothing, too, is said to be expected. There was an earth tremor at about 7.30
this evening. We thought at first that it was perhaps the RAF on the job.
There was some mail this evening but none of it was for me. Some parcels
too have arrived but we don't know yet who are the lucky men.

12th Jan

I have felt better today and have made up my mind to stop worrying about
my heart. The shortage of food combined with the excessive cold may be
all that's the matter with me. Lettercards and post cards were issued today. I
wrote the letter to Evelyn and the card to Dad. Parcels and clothing rumours
of yesterday were true. Official circles have it that clothing and food parcels
have been dispatched.

Jimmy Brown tells me that warrant officers and sergeants are to be sent
from this camp to Germany on the 26th of this month. Naturally I hope that
this is not true. I'd rather stay here with Jerry and, anyway, it looks as though
the enemy thinks that there is a chance of an allied invasion and would want
to get us out of the way in time. Perhaps they think warrant officers and
sergeants are important. Naturally, we think we are. But is Jimmy talking
through his hat as usual?

There were some personal parcels arrived this morning. There was even
one from Palestine. Epstimas got it. I am wondering when I shall receive the
books which Evelyn and her sister Doris have sent to me. I hope I shall have
them before I'm moved away from here – if Jimmy's 'news' is true.

14th Jan

I had a headache last night and didn't feel well enough to write. But none of
us is fit really. Perhaps the cold weather and lack of food. There was nothing
of importance happened yesterday anyway. Some clothing arrived but wasn't
distributed. Jimmy Brown's tale of warrant officers and sergeants being
moved to Germany was just a load of bollocks as I should have known. Why
do I keep giving him the benefit of the doubt? A combination of pessimism
and wishful thinking perhaps. But as prisoners of war we are all 'sitting
ducks' for that sort of thing. The news (newspaper) has been good: the
Russians appear to be bashing the Germans fairly hard.

How I wish the war would come to a sudden end. We are all half starved.
Seeing fellows faint is a daily occurrence. We are all sick and weak and it
isn't any wonder bearing in mind that we are given less than half of that
issued to the Italian soldiery and they don't get a lot. According to the

Geneva Convention prisoners of war ought to receive rations equivalent to those of the detaining power's depot troops. Our rations for a day are: a mug of imitation coffee at 0700hrs, a scoopful of boiled rice or macaroni at 12 noon, a scrap of cheese at 1pm, a scoop of vegetable soup at half past four, and an issue of bread, the size of a small bun, at half past five. That's our lot. This amount of food falls far short of being sufficient. Our weakness, blackouts and fainting are ample proof. Still nothing can be done about it. We must wait, patiently or otherwise, for the end of the War. But when will it finish? The possibility of its ending in the near future heartens us but when we think of its going on for years the thought is unbearable. It is best not to think about it but there is little to help us to forget it. There is nothing to do: Very little physically. Nothing mentally. Personally, I keep bashing away at improving my English but it isn't all that helpful. Hopefully we think: perhaps it won't be long?

15 January 1943 2040hrs

Some clothing was issued today: 2 vests, 2 pants, 2 prs of socks, and a cap: clothing which will all be louse-ridden in a few days. There has been no war news today. To us that really means good news! I have still had no letters from Evelyn, or anyone else. It is now about two weeks or more since my last letter from Evelyn. I wonder what's the matter? It is most disheartening. Yet I know she will be writing. The blame must lie with the Italians. They are so finicky about their censoring. Her letters will eventually reach me – I hope!

16th January 1943 2105hrs

Some more clothing was issued today: one shirt and one pullover per man. Bulk food parcels have at last arrived. There are 600 cases we have been told. According to the last rate of issue that ought to be sufficient for about three weeks. Perhaps more will be delivered before we have finished this lot. Tonight we were given another rule regarding the censoring of our letters: letters whose writing is too small will be destroyed. I'd better be more careful with mine. Perhaps that is why Evelyn has received so few from me. Still no letters for me. Tomorrow, perhaps! Tonight the sky is beautifully clear and there is a moon. Very good for our bombers! There is a rumour afloat that peace-talks are taking place. It is supposed to come from Padre Thompson. Naturally I hope is true but I doubt it. All of our rumours are usually attributed to our camp clergy. Those illustrious gentlemen invariably deny all knowledge of them. The Russians are said to be still going the right way. That's the stuff, Joe. Bash them hard!

17 January 1943 1930hrs

I have retired early tonight: not because I'm tired but simply because time seems to be dragging. Some parcels were issued today but Jerry and I won't get ours until the fourth issue. The contents differ from what is usually issued but it is food and most acceptable. The weather was glorious today so I did a little walking around the orchard. My weakness surprised me – and I must stop moaning about my health. But we all do it. Reg has dropped out our tea-brewing partnership and has gone into partnership with Grif. Poor Grif! No mail. Left Kirkuk in Iraq a year ago today. What a year! ! !

18th January 1943 2125hrs

Yesterday evening I got involved in an argument which lasted well into the night and left me too tired to make an entry. I have been very despondent during the past couple of weeks. That is a lie – I always seem to be despondent! Perhaps it's because I'm not receiving letters from Evelyn. I wonder: are we still engaged? I'd be shattered were she to abandon me. I am a depressed character. Are all of us as I am, I wonder? I can't seem to get it out of my head that I'm almost middle-aged but I'm only twenty nine and at that age surely a man is still young. Comparatively! But I find that my self-assurance isn't so very reassuring. It must be this P.O.W. life I think. I walked around the orchard a few times today. Whenever I walk I think of home and good food and wish that I were back there. I walked until I was suddenly aware that I had blisters on both feet!

21st January 1943 l950hrs

Nothing of any consequence has happened today. Parcels were issued as was expected. I hope that there's sufficient for another issue on Saturday. Jerry and I are due for one then. I have walked miles today round and round the orchard. So many that my feet are sore. Must be out of practice. My skin is peeling off. The news from the Russian and Desert fronts is good. If the Russians can keep it up they will be in Poland in a month or so. The Desert front doesn't matter so much but even that will soon be over when the weather is more favourable. I wonder am I being too optimistic. I don't feel anywhere nearly so depressed as I was yesterday. I have still had no letters from Evelyn. I wonder shall I get one tomorrow? Tomorrow! Tomorrow! Tomorrow!

23 January 1943 l930hrs

There was nothing happened yesterday worth mentioning. Last night I attended a camp concert. I was depressed as I didn't get a letter from Evelyn. I was sure that she must have abandoned me but a bloke sang a song which cheered me up wonderfully: a song I heard with Evelyn on our first night out together: 'I'll walk beside you.' When I heard that song last night I told myself that I would get a letter from Evelyn today. However, when the letters were delivered this morning there wasn't one for me and I was depressed again. However a most unusual thing happened: the mail call sounded at 1 o'clock: two issues in one day! And there was one for me, from Evelyn! She says that she has received only one letter from me. I can't understand why. I have written to her almost every week I have been in this camp. It must be very disheartening for her not to be receiving my letters. I hope she will be receiving them more frequently now. The news is very good. Tripoli (North Africa) is said to be surrounded by our forces and the Russians are said to be still pushing hard towards Germany. It looks as though the Germans are about to evacuate Stalingrad.

25 January 1943 2020hrs
There was nothing in my mind that I considered mentioning last night. Red Cross food was issued to those whose turn it was to have it this morning. Now there is none left and there will be no more issues until more supplies arrive.

26 January 1943 2120hrs
The news is good today. Tripoli would seem to be ours. The newspaper states that a decisive battle for Rostov (on the Russian Front) is about to start. Lettercards and postcards were issued today. I wrote the letter to Evelyn and the card to Dad. Jimmy Brown has advised me to print my letters instead of writing them. This he ensures me guarantees their being passed by the censor. This morning I finished the novel, *The Lake*, by George Moore. A very good novel I think.

27th January 1943 l940hrs
I received two letters today – one from Evelyn and one from the Post Office ladies at Castle Cary. Evelyn says she has received the letter in which I asked her to make some enquiries for me. She is going to let me have this in her next letter. The Post Office letter was written by Margaret. She says that everything is going well and that we ought to be home by next Christmas. Famous last words! ! ! ! We have all hoped for this for the past three Christmases. She and her two sisters have sent Evelyn some money to buy something to put in the next parcel she sends me. I must write and thank them.

   The news is still fairly good. The Russians are still bashing the Germans fairly hard. They are said to be only about 800 miles from the German border. That isn't so far as it seems when it is considered how fast an Army moves these days. Now I'd like to see the British and American forces open up another front in western Europe. That would embarrass the Germans most certainly. Jerry and Reg had a battle of words this morning and fell out. I'd been expecting this for some time. Reg has been surly and rude for some time.

29 January 1943 1950hrs

A year ago almost to the hour I was regaining consciousness at the casualty clearing station at Tiberias on the Sea of Galilee. I didn't know my name or where I was. I didn't know my age. I was very soon reminded. I got a letter from Dad this morning, the first he has written for a long time. Bella has been doing all of his writing for him. He says I ought to be getting some parcels soon. Jerry has been working today. He couldn't get away for mid-morning or afternoon tea so I took it down for him. The Desert War is almost finished. A very cheerful aspect.

1st February 1943 2125hrs

Nothing worth mentioning has happened during the last two days. I received a letter from Evelyn this morning. Have written to her and to the Post Office ladies. We have run out of parcels again but Jerry and I have a small reserve.

2nd February 1943 2220hrs

There was no issue of parcels today but we have been told that 11000 have been dispatched to this camp but no one knows when they will arrive. Got my battle-dress today and look, and feel, much better.

We were told today that another consignment of parcels, 7000, has been sent to us, making a total of almost 18000. At the present rate of issuing that lot ought to last five weeks or so. It has been very cold today. There was a lot of rain this morning and, also, a very strong wind. It is quite warm this evening so perhaps tomorrow will be warm. It will be unpleasant frying our onions in a cold wind. The news is still good.

7th February 1943 2100hrs

I have made no entries during the past few days as there has been nothing worth mentioning. We are still waiting the arrival of the Red Cross parcels. Jerry and I have only a half tin of meat roll and that is for breakfast tomorrow. However we still have some butter and some jam and maybe we may be able to buy some onions. The news is still good and the Russians are still going the right way. The Italian Cabinet has been changed.

8th February 1943 2025hrs

A good day: Italian cigarettes issued, coffee issued, olive oil issued, and onions are available to be bought. We've bought 10 Lires worth. And the Red Cross parcels have arrived. Jerry and I ought to get ours on Saturday. News is still very good. Haven't had any letters since last Monday. Tomorrow, perhaps! Have just learned that two men tried to escape tonight. One of them was shot and killed. The Italian soldiery are rotten little bastards when they have you at the wrong end of their gun. They are inclined to shoot first and then think of an excuse.

9th February 1943 2015hrs
Parcels are to be issued at the rate of 1 per man per week until further orders.
We ought to get ours on Thursday now. 500 more prisoners were brought in
today. News is still very good.

10th February 1943 2110hrs
British cigarettes were issued today at the rate of 25 per man. Jerry and I
ought to receive our parcel tomorrow. There are two tobacco parcels for
Jerry. He's a pipe smoker. I don't smoke. I have still not received my book
parcel.

War News: The Russian front is now at Rostov and Karkov. There is still
some fighting in the North Africa desert. It seems the enemy is trying to
evacuate as much of his Army and equipment as possible. There are rumours
that an invasion of the continent is under way. This never happens but the
lads keep on rumouring. I am still waiting for some letters!

11th February 1943
(Watch having a glass put in.) A very good day indeed! Jerry and I got our
parcel – a good one, too! Jerry got a parcel of books and two tobacco parcels.
Wrote to Evelyn and Pam today. She has not yet received any letters. We
'lashed out' this evening and ate our apple pudding.

12th February 1943 (?hrs)
I overslept this morning so didn't shave. My left eye was troubling me so I
went to the camp hospital. There was a crowd waiting so I went back this
afternoon and was treated then. The staff is British. I have to attend every
evening until my eye is again OK. Still no mail. News is still good.

13th February 1943 2030hrs
I got my watch back today and gave the bloke 10 Players cigarettes. I got a
letter from Edith Hebden this morning but nothing from Evelyn. When am
I going to get my next letter from that girl? We are due for another parcel
tomorrow and are hoping that the present rate of issue continues. Parcels help
to keep us cheerful – and fed! But I am not very cheerful at the moment. This
existence is wearing me down.

16th February 1943 2010hrs
Feeling tired and not having anything worth mentioning I did not enter
anything last night. It has been made known that our camp intellectuals
intend to start education classes now that it is expected that the better weather
will soon be with us. I'm thinking of entering for English and a couple of
other subjects. I wonder how it is intended to overcome the lack of text
books. As far as I know the only text book in the camp is my book covering

the matriculation English Course. It looks as though I shall have to share it with whoever is to be the lecturer in English.

The Bible-bashers are at it again. They are claiming that *Revelations* predicts the end of the War so I decided to read it myself to see what I could make of it. A war is mentioned which lasts 42 months. If it is 'our' war which is predicted then it must end on the 13th day from now. Not very likely, I think, even though the Russians are still bashing the Germans very hard. In fact, today's newspaper states that Karkov has fallen to the Russians. Still I don't think it will all end 13 days from now. But if it does I shall no longer be an atheist.

I am still waiting for a letter from Evelyn. I am resolved in the event of her breaking off our engagement to re-engage to complete twenty one years in the Army. But despite this resolution, common sense would indicate that it is early days yet. Although the Germans are obviously beaten they are not prepared to admit this and it ought to be borne in the minds of those of us who are impatient that the German leaders are now literally fighting for their own lives.

17th February 2150hrs

I have just finished reading *Silk*, a legend of China. Some of it is very interesting but the author, I think, tends to be a little too flowery. I don't like literary embroidery: it takes the mind off the more important points. I am now occupying myself, mentally and physically, more than I have done in the past. Now I am spending my time reading, walking – around and round the orchard – or talking. It is also my intention to attend as many classes or lectures as I find convenient. I must not let myself slide. I want to leave this camp mentally alert and physically fit.

19th February 1943 1920hrs

I feel very tired tonight so I have come to bed early. I haven't yet had a letter from Evelyn but somehow I don't feel all that upset. Tomorrow, perhaps. The parcels have run out and there is not to be an issue tomorrow but our Red Cross representative is going to Porto San Georgeo tomorrow so perhaps we shall have them by Sunday. If this Red Cross food stopped there is no doubt we should all die of starvation.

20th February 1943

Some Red Cross sugar and cheese were issued today. Unlike the previous cheese we have had this issue was rather good! I received a letter from Evelyn this morning. She tells me her boss has subscribed 10 shillings towards a parcel for me. I must ask her to thank him for me. What a hell I have been in since I received my last letter from her. Letters and postcards were issued today. I sent the lettercard to the Misses Hebden at the post office. I have asked them to send me some books. Lights have gone out.

26 February 1943 1930hrs

I don't feel at all well tonight but I got some tablets from the hospital. Perhaps they will fix me up. Today's news is good. The Germans in Russia are continuing their 'ordered' withdrawal westward. Hope it remains fine for them!

27th February 1943

The tablets from the hospital worked well. I felt fine this morning and my cold has almost gone. We have again run out of Red Cross food parcels and we are hoping it won't be long before more arrive. The camp Education Scheme has, so far, worked without a hitch and my resolution to attend my classes regularly still remains intact. I can't claim to have learnt a lot but I have at least been occupied. I wrote to Evelyn and Dad today.

28th February 1943 2000hrs

I received two letters this morning: one from Evelyn and one from Pam. Pam says she couldn't write sooner as she didn't have my address. I don't know why the Hebdens could not have given it to her as she lives only a few yards from their post office. Evelyn tells me that Mr. Higginson is dead. I am very sorry. I owe him a lot.

Feeling industrious today. I washed a shirt. When we have the warm weather I shall be able to wash my clothes more frequently. There is a joke that somebody dropped a sock and it broke! But it isn't a joke really. Our clothes are crawling with lice.

1st March 1943 2010hrs

Nothing of importance today other than the arrival at Porto San Georgeo of some Red Cross parcels. I seem to be progressing quite well in English although I must admit that it is a somewhat intricate subject.

This morning I received an acknowledgment from the International Red Cross thanking me for the information which I was able to give them regarding Captain Webster. Today, the news is just the same as usual: the Germans are still sinking our ships and shooting down our aircraft. And also annihilating the Russians. We know we will be losing ships and aircraft. And we know also that the Russians will be losing thousands of men. But we know who is losing the war. What we would like to know of course is when it will end. Still it must end sooner than later. Jerry and I are going to have a 'Carlton' pudding for breakfast tomorrow (a canned solid pudding). We are both looking forward to it as we haven't yet sampled one.

I have thought about Pam since receiving her letter. She is an intriguing girl. Intelligent, witty, and likeable, but not in the least attractive. In fact, she could be described as frowsy! I am very fond of her. She is sincere, a quality lacking in many. I'd like to see her again.

3rd March 1943 2010hrs
Revelations is all 'hooey'! The war didn't end today as was predicted. Still, the news is good. So good in fact that perhaps the war may end in the very near future. The Carlton pudding we had for breakfast was very good indeed and I'll go so far as to say it was the finest we have had. Hope we receive some more. We are having a Yorkshire pudding for breakfast tomorrow and we are going to draw a parcel so I don't think I shall attend the English class in the morning.

4th March 1943 1910hrs
The Yorkshire pudding which we had for breakfast this morning would have been very nice – if Jerry had not burnt it. We spread jam on it. We are not short of jam.

5th March 1943 2030hrs
The news is still good: the Germans have evacuated two more places on the Russian Front. It is some time now since I had a letter from Dad. I ought to receive one soon.

6th March 1943 2015hrs
An uneventful day. The weather has changed and the rain has started. I hope it won't last long. There is a strong rumour that Naval Personnel in this camp are to be repatriated. This strikes me as being too fantastic to be true. Enemies don't hand over their able-bodied prisoners. There are no classes for me to attend today so I am going to do a little private studying.

7th March 1943 2150hrs
The weather has been terrible all day. It rained all last night and into this afternoon. It seems pretty definite that our sailors are to be repatriated. They are to leave us tomorrow. Good luck to them!

I borrowed a book from Danny Burnham this morning, *Our Mutual Friend* by Charles Dickens. I can't say I like Charles Dickens. For practice I have written an essay and have called it *A Shooting Leave in India*. I intend to have Jerry read it. No doubt he will pull it to pieces unmercifully. He regards himself as rather a purist where intellect is concerned. Basically, he is a nice bloke but he is such an intellectual snob.

8th March 1943 2155hrs
I have just been to a pantomime produced by my fellow prisoners. It is the best performance I've seen for some time. The interest in education seems to be waning. There were only five of us attended the elementary English class this morning.

9th March 2235hrs

An uneventful day. Jerry took so long to make the tea this afternoon that I missed the bigger part of the history lesson. Cpl. Davidson has set us an essay to write for next Monday: *A Shop Window* or *A Sea Port*. I think I shall try *A Shop Window*.

10th March 1943 2025hrs

It has rained almost incessantly since yesterday. Our wood is wet consequently making our tea is a bit of a problem. It takes almost an hour to an hour and a half to get the water boiling. The only fuel available is twigs and dry grass. Of course the rain has ruled out the latter. Some notebooks were offered for sale yesterday. I managed to get two. I'd liked to have had another but perhaps I shall manage to get that later. I have started my essay on *A Shop Window* but only reached the actual description of the display. Not knowing anything about shop-window displays I sought the assistance of Jimmy Harris. He was a window-dresser before he came into the Army. I shall see his effort tomorrow and build my essay around it.

I got a letter from Evelyn today. Unfortunately I lost it after reading it only once. She hasn't dispatched my next of kin parcel yet. She is still asking me what do I want? My fault!

The Red Cross parcel situation is becoming severe. There have been none for two days now. Hope they come soon. The Germans claim to have advanced a little towards Karkov. I hope they can't keep it up. Their success is not going to speed the end of the War.

11 March 1943 2245hrs

I got another letter from Evelyn today. In it she tells me of Mr. Higginson's death. It seems he died in his sleep. We had a visit by a Red Cross official today but so far we don't know what was said. We have been told today that we must have identifying patches sewn on to our clothes. This apparently is a reprisal because Italian prisoners in England have to wear them. I seem to have reached a dead end with my essay writing. I have tried both of those set by Cpl. Davidson but can't seem to be able to get anywhere with either of them.

12th March 1943 2125 hrs

I have been to our camp theatre and have seen the plays: *Who Killed the Colonel* and *The Monkey's Paw*. To me, they both seemed to have been put over rather well. I hope this sort of thing is continued. Excepting the absence of Red Cross parcels life is slipping along quite nicely. My book parcel has at last arrived and I hope to have it tomorrow. I hope they are books which have been selected by Evelyn and Doris (Evelyn's sister) and not those which W.H. Smith are trying to get rid of. Most of those which have arrived in camp are paper backs of the same old titles.

13th March

I got my book parcel this morning. They are bound books and not the usual paper backs as most of the book parcels seem to be. A good selection: *Letters of Lord Byron*, Palgravet's *A Treasury of Longer Verse*, *The Time Machine* and *The Wheels of Chance* by H G Wells, *The Romany Rye* by George Borrow, *Westward Ho!* by Charles Kingsley, *The Cloister on the Hearth* by Charles Reade, and *Lord Jim* by Joseph Conrad. These books should while away some pleasant hours. I must send a card to Doris thanking her for her share of the cost.

I have finished my essay on *A Shop Window*. It isn't by any means good but it's the best I could do. I'll let Jerry see it tomorrow and if in his view it's reasonable I'll let Cpl. Davidson have it and, subsequently, have it pulled apart by my fellow 'students'.

14th March

Sgt Major Davis went to Porto San Georgeo this morning and 5000 parcels have been delivered to the camp. Jerry has read my essay this morning and appears to believe it is quite good. Is he being diplomatic, I wonder? I shall give it to Cpl. Davidson tomorrow.

I've just had an argument with Cpl. Griffen. He is a communist and I can't stand their unreasonable reasoning. I think, perhaps, I allowed my dislike of their fraternity to bias me. I don't think I was fair. But he is an awful clot!

15th March

The Red Cross parcels, which I said arrived yesterday, didn't. Unfortunately there was a landslide which blocked the railway line and, consequently: no parcels! We have been told that they are due tomorrow.

16th March

Jerry has received another tobacco parcel and my essay was declared 'good' by my class-mates. But I'm inclined to be a bit suspicious: I think they are all ex-grammar school lads. Oh, well!

17th March

Postcards were issued today at the rate of two per man. I shall use mine to write to Doris and to Pam. I wanted to thank Doris for her contribution for my book parcel. I have used old newspapers to cover my books. It would be selfish of me not to allow them to be borrowed. The newspaper covers will afford them some protection although I can't see there being much demand for Palgrave's *Golden Treasury of Longer Verse*. The main inclination appears to be towards cowboy 'Westerns' and detective stories.

18th March

Nothing worth mentioning. The news isn't good. Apparently the Germans have re-taken Karkov. This was claimed a few days ago. The Russians are said to be pressing in the north but we don't know how effectively.

At present I am reading George Borrow's *The Romany Rye*. I have almost finished it having reached the appendix. However, I shall finish it tomorrow, I think.

19th March 1943

I have finished reading *The Romany Rye* this morning and have started on H G Wells' *Wheels of Chance*. Some news, said to be BBC news, admits to a Japanese attempt to invade Australia but, apparently, this was unsuccessful and they lost 25,000 men. The Russians are said to have by-passed Smolensk and are advancing on Karkov. In Tunisia the British and American forces have advanced 50 miles without opposition and there have been anti-German riots in the north of Italy. I can only hope that all of this is true.

I received a letter from Pam today but she mentions nothing of importance. Perhaps she was in a hurry at the time of her writing.

20th March

A miserable day. Very cold and windy. Perhaps it will be warmer tomorrow. In a prison camp there is always a 'tomorrow'.

22nd March

Our Parcel day. We drew a good one: a marmalade pudding which we had for tea, and other items of precious food which cheered us. We've been told that there is a consignment of parcels at Porto San Georgeo.

The Germans are claiming to have sunk 32 of our ships in the Atlantic.

A beautiful day but rather windy. I hope this rather good weather continues. Yesterday's tale of Red Cross parcels wasn't true and our present stock will run out on Wednesday. We hope more will arrive before then.

24th March

Lettercards and postcards were issued yesterday. I have written the letter to Evelyn and the card to Dad. Although these cards are sufficient for writing to most people – after all, there is little of interest to communicate about life in a prisoner of war camp that would pass our camp censors – but writing to close friends and fiancées requires more writing space than there is on a postcard.

We drew our 'parcel' today. Well, not a parcel really. Some of the Red Cross food comes in bulk, in crates, and is distributed amongst us as 'parcels.' We all prefer it to come to us as individual parcels but, regardless, it is food, much needed and we are grateful.

The newspapers have quoted Churchill's speech. His promise is that the Tunisian campaign will soon be over. However he doesn't promise an early end to what's left of the war.

26th March

I received a letter from Pam this morning. She invites me to ask her for anything she may send to me. It is kind of her but there is really nothing.

A fellow gave me some brown paper this morning and I'm using it to put covers on my books. There's a lot of wear and tear on books in our environment and some people just won't regard books as precious. I am still short of sufficient paper for one book. I must ask him to get me a little more.

Assistant group commanders are to be given a double ration of bread once a week! I am one, but I doubt if it will make me fat. A single ration of this Italian bread amounts only to a couple of slices of bread as we knew it in England.

27th March

There is some interesting news today said to be from the BBC. Of course it may be only rumour: Finland has capitulated and the Russians are said to have taken Smolensk. I thought the Russians had already done that! And they have crossed the frontier of either: Latvia, Lithuania, or Estonia. And the Germans are preparing to evacuate Tunisia. One day all of this will be true!

We are to draw a parcel tomorrow. The parcel situation seems to be very good at the moment. Let's hope it lasts.

29th March

The weather for some time now has been very dull. Today the rain started. We are pretty well into the year now so perhaps it won't last long.

1st April

The weather has been glorious today. What a pleasant change from the uncertain weather we've been having.

Last night I wrote an essay, *The Village*. I don't think it is very good but I've given it to Cpl. Davidson. He'll tell me what he thinks of it next time I see him.

The parcels have run out. It is a fact that our morale fluctuates with the delivery of the Red Cross food parcels and our letters. The news is still good but I've had no letters from Evelyn for a couple of weeks.

2nd April

We have had some rain today but the sky cleared this afternoon and we've had a period of brilliant sunshine. I've been to our camp theatre tonight. The plays were quite good but appreciation was difficult owing to some of the fellows walking about[3]. Most of us are not attuned to theatre plays. I think cowboy 'Westerns' at a Saturday matinee would be the limit of some of our lads here.

We are hoping for a consignment of parcels tomorrow.

4th April

The weather has been glorious today – large fleecy clouds racing across a sky the most beautiful blue.

With Jerry and Grif I went into the field where we sat down while Jerry read to us that part of the novel which he has written. He's been writing it for some months now and is about half-way through it. His actual writing – syntax, grammar, etc. – is good, of course, but I think his story lacks purpose. His leading character – himself, I think – works in an office and his story amounts to nothing more than his catty and supercilious psychoanalysis of his office colleagues. He sneers at their contentment with their lot and is cynical of their employer's parental concern for them. Of course I'm not going to tell him what I think of his 'novel'. It would shatter him – and our friendship!

Lettercards were issued today. I had intended to write them this evening but the lighting is so bad that I can't see the lines on the cards. I shall write them tomorrow: to the post office ladies and to Evelyn. There has been no mail for some time now. Has the RAF dropped a bomb on the Italian Post Office?

5th April 1943

Some RAMC personnel are to be repatriated. Cpl. Griffen is one of them. Good luck to him. I wish I were going.

6th April

Personnel for repatriation are going tomorrow, Wednesday. I have given Evelyn's address to Grif and have asked him to write to her when he is again in England.

7th April

I received a letter from Evelyn this morning. She tells me that she has sent off my next of kin parcel. Perhaps I shall receive it in a month or so. Also, she has told me that Mrs. Austin has written to me.

We've run out of Red Cross parcels again.

Grif went away this morning. I hope he remembers to write to Evelyn.

---

[3] There were no seats. We had to sit on the oor.

9th April

One of the lads escaped last night. No one knows how he got out and the Italians appear to be rather perplexed about it. Consequently we have had three very long roll-calls today. And now we have just been told that he has *not* escaped: he's been hiding in the Army food store: Eating!????

The weather has been very cold and windy today. Very unpleasant. There is still no information regarding Red Cross food parcels. We're hoping for some soon. Our stock is running out. But when isn't it running out.

10th April 1943 2045hrs

I received a letter from Pam this morning. She hasn't heard from me since Christmas she tells me. I shall let her have my next card, I think. If the Italians are running their Army as inefficiently as they do their postal service it is no wonder the Germans regard them as a liability. I have received two letters from her since I last wrote. Today is Saturday, the end of another week. Time is flying. Boredom is not troubling me at all. What a good thing is our Education scheme: classes, meals, roll calls, private study and reading leave no time to brood. I don't seem to be consciously learning anything but then, I'm not putting in a lot of effort. Still, I must be learning something I suppose. Anyway whether I'm learning or not doesn't matter so long as I'm occupied either mentally or physically. Regarding the English though, I am really keen to learn; to be able to write and speak good English is my aim. My inability to express myself effectively is the real cause of my shyness to speak when I'm confronted by someone I don't know, or even those I don't know very well. I must put more effort into my studying. Reading is enlarging my vocabulary and giving me an insight of good literature. Now I must put some effort into writing.

11th April 1943 2115hr

Jerry has finished reading to me his novel but I haven't yet formed an opinion. I don't know if I'll dare. He's as inflammable as petrol vapour where intellect is concerned. We have had glorious weather today and I've spent most of my time outside. Sitting in the sun I drafted a rough essay, swotted some English, read some poetry, and then I read a few chapters of Conrad's *Lord Jim*. I got a letter from Evelyn's boss this morning. She has been promoted, he tells me. There are three truck loads of parcels at San Georgeo.

13th April 1943 2153hrs

The news is good today. Tunisia ought to be all over soon. We expect to draw our parcel tomorrow. Roll on the day when we need no longer rely on them.

14th April 1943 2125hrs

A L/c Robinson was found dead in the field this morning. There is some doubt as to whether it is murder or suicide. Personally, I think it must be suicide. Life is easy here but it isn't worth anything. All that any of us has to live for is our repatriation. Perhaps Robinson thought that life here was too tedious to be bothered with. It's all a matter of opinion: expectation of the future, and how long must we wait for it. However, for the moment, I am happy, so long as I am receiving letters from Evelyn and home and the war doesn't last too long I shall hold on. Lettercards and postcards are late this week. For inconsistency and irregularity the Italians take the cake.

15th April 1943 2120hrs

The lettercards and postcards were issued today. I have written to Evelyn and Pam. There is nothing much in the news but what there is seems to be in our favour. But how much longer?

16th April 1943 2025hrs

I received a parcel of cigarettes today. It was sent by Rothman's. My address was given to them by a Mr. Thomas, one of Evelyn's office colleagues.

17th April 1943 2210hrs

Bill Bailey was taken on a trip to San Georgeo today. I was group commander in his absence. The news is still good but nothing startling. The Russian front seems to be almost stalemate at the moment. Of course they need time to prepare for each advance.

18th April 1943 2100hrs

I received a letter from Pam this morning. It was dated 5th March. Poor Pam, she must be so lonely. I wish she could find herself a good boyfriend. She needs one! We have been issued with Easter Greetings cards today. I have sent mine to Evelyn and worded it: Easter Greetings Darling to you and our families. Love David. There were no newspapers today and as there will be no newspapers tomorrow (Monday) we will have no news until Tuesday.

19th April 1943 2100hrs

I have just returned from a play rehearsal. Cpl. Davidson asked me to act as prompter. Not knowing anything about theatre prompting I was reluctant to take it on but everything went well. There was some Red Cross sugar issued today and some more parcels have arrived. Those we have now ought to last a few weeks.

21st April 1943 2230hrs

The weather was rather cold today and once or twice we had a few spots of rain. News is very scarce but there are some very cheering rumours current. I have borrowed Jimmy Brown's book of one-act plays. It will be of great help to me as prompter in our theatre.

23rd April 1943
Lettercards and postcards were issued today. I have written the letter to Pam and the card to Mr. Godsell (Evelyn's boss). Easter Sunday which I spent reading, writing and dreaming. A pleasant day. News is scarce but what we hear is good.

26th April 1943 2130hrs
I've just been to our camp theatre and seen the Musical *The Desert Song*. It was very good. I am still waiting for a letter from Evelyn but am not blaming her. The mail isn't coming through at all well at present – if it ever did!

28th April 1943 2050hrs
I received a letter from Evelyn this morning. It was dated 15th February. She tells me the wife of her brother Bill has produced a baby boy. News is still somewhat dead but still inclined to be in our favour. The Red Cross parcel situation is still good. We have a fairly large reserve.

29th April 1943 2045hrs
I have just written a lettercard to Evelyn and a postcard to her colleague who was responsible for the cigarettes I received. I don't smoke but my cigarettes are used as currency. The RAF seemed to be raiding a town west of our camp tonight. We could hear the anti-aircraft fire. Hope our lads bashed them well and hard.

30th April 1943
I have received another letter from Evelyn this morning, dated 22nd Feb. Her brother's baby is to be called David John – after me and Evelyn's dad. Some one stole my mug from the tea queue this evening. I'm rather annoyed about it as I bought it more than three years ago. Now I shall have to drink from an empty stew can.

3rd May 1943
I received another letter from Evelyn this morning dated 8th Feb.

4th May 1943
There was a lot of mail today and I got one from Mr. Godsell. He tells me he is a platoon commander in the Home Guard. Judging from his letters he seems to be a nice bloke. Perhaps I'll meet him one day. The activity on the Tunisian Front seems to be nothing more than local. We are all hoping for the start of the second front but when is it going to happen? The lads here are all talking about the 'big push' next spring. Well, this was next spring

a couple of weeks or so ago and it hasn't happened yet. I've been told by Jimmy Brown that some of the blokes here think I'm mad. They're a queer lot. All because I'm quiet and mind my own business.

6th May 1943

I received seven letters today: One from Mrs. Austin, one from Barkley's Bank, two from Evelyn, and two from Pam. Barkley's claim that I have no money to my credit with them. This will have to be sorted out after the war. I've written to Evelyn and Dad today. Margaret Hebden says that Sheilah would like to receive a card from me. Later, perhaps. Our issue of lettercards and post cards doesn't allow for pen-pals.

There are some very nice rumours of Tunis having fallen again and the Russians are maintaining their pressure on the Germans. Keep it up, Joe! (Joe Stalin.) Roll on the end!

7th May 1943

There was nothing in today's newspapers about Tunis. But, of course, in Italy, if it's bad news it's 'no news'. But Mussolini has made a speech which usually indicates that he is being more devastated politically But it is ever so cheering to know that the Russians keep going the right way. But what are our people doing in Africa? Time will tell. And we have lots of time at our disposal.

8th May 1943

I received two letters this morning: one from Evelyn and one from Pam. One of them posted in March and the other in January. Jerry got his next of kin parcel today and he has given me a tin of tooth powder. A 'next-of-kin' is allowed to send a personal parcel of clothing and toiletries once every three months. Some of the fellows have already received several. This was Jerry's first. I have not yet received any. Obviously they are being stolen in transit. Mainland Europe is destitute and these parcels contain goods which are not available in Europe. We are told that the ordinary Italian people don't have underwear. Their soldiers don't even have socks! Nuns from the nearest hospital visit this camp ostensibly to visit prisoners who are in the camp hospital which is situated in the outer compound. These men are dying. Quite openly these nuns come up to the inner fence to offer a bread-ration for a pair of Marks and Spencer underpants. These transactions are done quite openly. Having acquired her pair of 'St. Michael's' the exuberant nun simply turns her back on the man who has received her bread ration, and steps into her new knickers. Obviously delighted! This would be funny were it not so pathetic. They seem to know when these next of kin parcels are expected. What a country!

I managed to buy seven sheets of foolscap paper today. Even ordinary writing paper is scarce. But fresh air and lice are still in abundance.

9th May

I have been strolling around the camp with Bob Jackson. We had an interesting talk and have agreed to do this every evening. Today's news is good. Tunisia appears to be absolutely finished now but Mussolini vows THEY WILL RETURN! Who does he think he is kidding? Or should that be 'Whom'? – must watch my English!

It seems the Italians are short of workers and we have been informed that those prisoners who are selected for work and refuse will be taken by force. We are surely winning!

11th May

I have received a letter from Bella (my sister) and also one from the Paymaster. The latter informs me that I have in credit: £171, two shillings, and 5 pence. Per month I pay seventeen shillings tax and one shilling and six pence to the detaining power (Italy). Why? Also 6½ pence for something else. My pay is about ten shillings a day. Here I am, rolling in money and can't spend it. Like the Ancient Mariner, 'Water, water, all around, and not drop to drink!'

Soon? Perhaps?

The news is still good and 'Simmo' – Staff Sergeant Simmons – has made a wireless from old milk tins and radio parts which he 'acquired' when he repaired the camp commandant's radiogram. Now we won't have to rely absolutely on the unreliable newspaper.

13th May

We have just finished the dress rehearsal of *The Seventh Man*. It went wonderfully well and I had to 'prompt' only a very few times.

The news is still good and our enemy seems to be being bashed really hard.

14th May

The 'first night' of our production *The Seventh Man*. Its reception wasn't quite that given the earlier 'Dr. O'Toole' but nevertheless, it was considered first class.

I received three letters this morning: Evelyn, Edith Hebden, and Pam. The Hebdens have ordered some books for me. I am lucky to have so many friends.

Some rather good news came from the camp loud-speakers this morning. It was an American bulletin, I think, and we were not intended to hear it. The news is very good.

I've just finished writing for tonight. As an English exercise I am writing the story of the play *The Seventh Man*. I have spent about four days trying to make up my mind how to start it.

I received a letter from Pam today. Poor Pam! She thinks she loves me. I am very sorry but it isn't my fault. I think she is just fantasising. She and I have never been alone together.

The good news seems to have dropped off a bit but it still seems to be in our favour.

18th May

Today is the start of my twelfth year as a soldier.

20th May

I have written my lettercard to the Hebdens this week and the card to Evelyn. Hope she won't mind. Nothing in the news worth mentioning.

24th May

I've just received my next of kin parcel from Evelyn. I have everything in the way of clothing now other than footwear.

26th May

Cpl. Davidson has asked me to 'prompt' for the play *The Wicked Uncles*. His prompter has gone off 'sick'.

27th - 29th May

The Wicked Uncles dress-rehearsal and two shows. The acting was good but the play is rather weak in the third and fourth acts.

The enemy 'big push' started 28th May last year. Received a letter from Margaret Hebden dated 25th March.

Today I introduced Jerry to our camp 'Play Circle'. He has started to adapt the novel, *The Ragged Trouser Philanthropist* for the stage. If everything goes well it will be produced in August.

Boarded the troopship at Gourock two years ago today. My war 'proper' had started.

7th June 1943

I wrote to Evelyn and Pam today. I haven't had any letters from Evelyn for some time now. We have had heavy rain all day but it has cleared up considerably tonight. There is a dearth of news at the moment. I wonder how long the lull will last? *(a few sentences in my notebook too faint to read).*

5th June

Received two letters today: one from Evelyn and one from Denis Hebden, a nephew of the Misses Hebden. He is still a boy and his aunts have told him that I would like to send and receive letters. This is really not so as our issue of postcards and lettercards is very limited. I have asked his aunts not to volunteer me to anyone else. However, I have sent him a card.

The weather has changed today and is now lovely. We are still short of news but there are some fantastic rumours about the situation in Greece. I wish I could believe them but I've been here long enough to be able to 'separate the wheat from the chaff'.

It is a year ago today that we put in an attack at El Sahdri, the site of the perimeter occupied until then by our 150 Brigade until they were overwhelmed by the enemy when they had run out of ammunition. A couple of weeks later, our local high command had decided that they must redeem the situation. Believing the site to be now occupied by the enemy's 'soft stuff' i.e. reserves, field workshops, stores, etc. it was decided that the position could be re-taken by one battalion, supported by a minimum of tanks. 'Ours was not to reason why' but we, the 7th Battalion of The Green Howards, were selected for the task and I, a humble sergeant, was forewarned of its futility: on our approach to the start-line for our attack (overnight a white tape of several hundred yards had been laid for this) the staff car of our brigadier was abreast of my signals truck for a while. When, momentarily, the vehicles in front stopped, I distinctly heard the brigadier and the accompanying staff colonel discussing our project and one said to the other: "...we'll fail, you know, but we've got to put on a show." They looked worried. And then I felt worried. And I felt immediate concern for our lads who would be some way ahead of me 'going in with the rifle and bayonet'.

A little while later when we were lined up for our attack I was 'briefed' by our adjutant who, for some reason or other, had become very irritable and nasty with me. Finishing his briefing, he continued: "and I want no heroics from you, sergeant," he emphasised, "your job is to keep out of the way until we're properly in occupation of the perimeter and then you'll set up your signals office and establish communications!" Walking away from me he suddenly shouted back over his shoulder, "And understand, sergeant, it's the equipment I'm concerned about: not you!"

And our attack commenced. Our lads went forward expecting to be opposed only by mechanics, storemen, and clerks. But we had been misinformed. There were units of Rommel's 21st Panzer Division in residence and alert. A little terrier dog attacking a Doberman Pinscher.

I was at the back and really saw nothing of the action but, in my blissful ignorance, waiting to go forward, I decided that my four signallers, driver and I use the lull in brewing and enjoying a mug of tea. It could be some time before another opportunity came along. While we were having our tea one of our tanks rumbled back from the battle area and stopped alongside us. The turret opened and one of 'the crew shouted to us: "Got any spare, lads?" I beckoned them to join us. Three of them alighted: a lieutenent and two of the crew. Expecting there to be four of them, one of my chaps, addressing the officer, asked: " what about the other bloke, sir?" The officer shook his head and shrugged.

"He's dead, poor bugger!" While they were drinking their tea one of the crew, addressing me, said: "It's absolutely bloody hell back there, sarge!" Thanking us for the tea, they left us, but they had told us nothing about the conflict they had come from. I was in doubt.

The adjutant's instructions had not been very clear: "…keep out of the way until we're properly in occupation of the perimeter," he had told me. So I decided that we would, tentatively, go forward, but I had barely made that decision when we saw our battalion's troop carrying vehicles racing back towards us from their action. A raggle taggle, tail-between-legs exit from the battle, and we tagged on! We reassembled in a hastily decided perimeter a couple of miles to our east. A tank battle was in progress near by and our area was being swept by missiles all day.

In our brief conflict with the enemy we had lost 190 men: about a third of our force, and a larger proportion of officers. In addition to being in charge of our battalion's communications I now found myself in command of our HQ Company. A couple of our senior officers and our sergeant majors had been left in our old perimeter with our brigade HQ.

I don't know where the adjutant was. The only officers we had at our battalion HQ were our Army chaplain and our medical officer, both non-combatants, leaving our colonel with only me: his signals sergeant, and Vin Bailey: his sergeant clerk. While our depleted force was arranging our defences as best they could, I was called to the phone. A telephone line had been laid immediately we'd established our new position. It was the commanding officer of East Yorks battalion of our brigade. He explained that he was anticipating an action against his position by the Italians and without our help he was going to find himself 'up a well-known creek with no means of propulsion'! "Would we help him?" And our colonel was nowhere available. Vin Bailey didn't know where he was. And there was this cry for immediate help from the East Yorks! So I sent the help they were asking for: a section each of: bren carriers (light armoured vehicles), mortars and anti-tank guns.

And then our colonel was suddenly in control again and he was told by Vin Bailey of my agreeing with the East Yorks' colonel to loan them some of our bren carriers, anti-tank guns, and mortars. He sent for me immediately. Rather apprehensively, I reported to him. He had worked himself up into an incandescent rage by this time. He was almost speechless with fury.

He shouted at me: "Who the hell do you think you are?" he bawled, "you've given away half of my bloody defence weapons. If the bloody Germans attack us at this moment we may as well ask the buggers in for tea!" In charge of men, he thundered at me, you're not fit to dig bloody latrine trenches! And he went on and on until he had run out of steam. A sergeant can't reason with an irate colonel. Of course he had come through a traumatic experience! He'd been directed to take his battalion into a futile attack against, at that moment, an impregnable position and in doing so had lost a third of his battalion and many of his officers. And then he'd had to set up this 'make-do' defence on this barren, rocky ground which was too hard for picks and shovels to dig for trenches. And I had 'given away' an effective part of the remnant of his battalion. I stood there in front of him, silent.

He stopped bawling at me, and then, quietly, he said: "Just get out of my sight, sergeant. I'll deal with you later!" I was a very unhappy sergeant. But all turned out well for the moment! The East Yorks' anticipatory action proved to be wonderfully successful, foiling the Italian attack and taking most of them prisoner without any loss by our side. Our colonel, because of *his* 'instant appreciation of his neighbouring battalion's situation and his immediate cooperation', shared in the honours with the East Yorks' colonel!

When he saw me later, as I thought, to be dealt with for my stupidity and incompetence, though he didn't apologise for what I regarded as his unwarranted verbal thrashing of me earlier his manner on this occasion was rather that of a vicar conversing with one of his favoured parishioners. Memories! But a few weeks later he and I and most of our battalion became prisoners of war. And here I am, with some of them, languishing in a prison camp in Italy.

11th June 1943
Today Jacky Barras gave me his lettercard and postcard. He doesn't read or write and he receives no mail. I've used these to write to Evelyn and to Sheilah. I have written to the paymaster and have asked him to transfer £100 from my account to Evelyn. After all, she is acting as my next of kin. And she is sending me parcels which are an expense – even though I'm not receiving many of them. I have asked her to send me some text books: *A First Course in Wireless*, also, two pamphlets, *Definitions and Formulae for Students* (*Radio* and *Telephony & Telegraphy*).

14th June 1943
Exactly a year ago today – to the hour, 2245 hrs – we were formed up just east of the Italian defences. The remnants of our brigade were surrounded and we were preparing to smash our way out: westward, then south, and then east, to form a new defensive line somewhere near the Egyptian border. We were successful but it was an experience which I shall never forget.

I have been with Jerry to see Fred Hindle's production, *Gypsy Rose*. It was a wonderful show: the best we've had so far. Good work, Fred!

15th June
Today's news is good: the two enemy island bases, Lampadusa, and Pantalerio, are now in Allied hands, and it is said, unofficially, that our forces are attacking Sicily. If this is the case then surely the Italian mainland must be next!

17th June

No news of importance during the last couple of days but I feel that something big is about to happen soon.

I have written to Evelyn and I've told her about Jacky Barras: that nobody writes to him and consequently he's such a lonely man. I've suggested her friends might like to send him an occasional cigarette parcel.

18th June

I've written to Dad and I've asked him why I've had no letters from him. I am aware that a lot of letters addressed to us don't reach us but I'm receiving letters from other people.

19th June

Received my second inoculation this morning – also two letters from Evelyn, dated 6th April and 18th May. She says my second parcel has been prepared, and suggests that I write about some of my experiences. Is this a sort of occupational therapy she's suggesting? I think I'll leave that – writing – until I'm safely ensconced in a comfortable home with her!

22nd June

Received a letter from my cousin Betty this morning, dated 23rd May. I have not seen her since the summer of 1939. She was on holiday from her home near Alloa in Scotland. Sixteen, fresh-faced, blue eyes, and a natural blond. A plump girl, but with a nice natural shyness. I'm dreaming again! But when am I not?

28th June 1943

I became a prisoner of war one year ago tonight: just before midnight, 28th June 1942. It's been a long uncomfortable year. We've been filthy, cold, starved, uncomfortable, and louse-ridden. If Italy was ever the idyllic place described by Byron, Shelley, and Browning, it has gone through a terrible change. Or perhaps it is only the Italian people, though I've seen only their soldiery, and they *are* a miserable shower of humanity: like vicious, bullying schoolboys when they have a victim at the wrong end of their gun but miserable whining peasants otherwise. I don't like Italy!

29th June 1943 2130hrs

I received a letter from Pam this morning. She says that the letters she had written to me after I became a prisoner have all been returned to her. Apparently one of them had been opened and some one had written on it: 'I'm surprised at you!' Pam says the signature wasn't legible. I have no idea. Again she says she's in love with me. I wonder? But I can't do anything about it. Poor Pam! But I do wish she could meet a nice bloke to whom she could transfer her affection.

3rd July 1943 2300hrs
Received letters from Pam and Bella today. Bella says that Dad hasn't received any cards from me for some time. It's about a year since I last had a letter from him.

6th July 1943 2125hrs
I received letters from Bella and Betty this morning. Bella says that she thinks Dad isn't writing to me because his writing isn't clear enough. The news is very flat these days. I wish that something would happen. Of course this starving us of news usually indicates that the war is going badly for the enemy.

7th July 1943 2150hrs
Received another letter from Bella today, dated 24th June. She is studying hard, she tells me, and that I will be surprised when I find out what she is doing! Actually, I think, perhaps, she is learning wireless telegraphy.

8th July 1943 2220hrs
Have just been to the *Pygmalion* dress rehearsal. Not too good but perhaps it will come over OK. Wrote to Evelyn today and told her I've not received anything from her for some time. Today's news is good. I wonder what tomorrow will bring?

9th July 1943 2330 hrs
Pygmalion first night. Fairly good but could have been much better. Wrote to Dad and Pam. Some rather good rumours about Sicily today.

10th July 1943 2320hrs
The show was much better tonight. Creenstein, playing 'Doolittle', was superb. Sicily news (rumours) gaining strength.

11th July 1943 2130hrs
Newspapers announce that Sicily was invaded by the Allies Friday night and reported to be going strongly. Received another letter from Bella this morning.

12th July 1943 2330hrs
Tonight's *Pygmalion* was interrupted for a roll-call. Two men have escaped.

13th July 1943 2210hrs
The news is still good. Our forces in Sicily appear to be doing well. Received two letters from Pam this morning.

14th July 1943 2250 hrs
Received two letters from Evelyn today. The news is good. Our troops in Sicily are doing well and also there is a tale that we have landed a force in Sardinia. Not long now – I hope!

19th July 1943 2140hrs
Nothing at all today. Yesterday's news was good. There seems to be a lot of defeatist talk in the newspapers. Leaflets have been dropped over Rome by our aircraft and there is a rumour that Rome has been bombed. I wonder what tomorrow's newspapers will say? Our camp is very crowded now there being 10,000 prisoners here. Rumour has it that there will be, eventually, 21,000.

21st July 1943 2310hrs
Received a letter from Evelyn yesterday. There have been no newspapers for three days. We are regarding this as a good sign. Our Red Cross parcels are getting low so they are to be issued now at the rate of one per ten days.

23rd July 1943 2125 hrs
Received two letters from Evelyn and two from Pam today. Have written to Evelyn and the Jameses. The news is still good.

25th July 2315hrs
Great news in the camp today. Mussolini is said to have done a bunk to Spain and Italy has become Royalist. Everyone (we) expecting an Italian capitulation soon. Got a letter from Sheilah this morning. She's a nice kid.

1st August 1943 2130hrs
I am a very disappointed man tonight! ! ! Somebody told me that the war (with Italy) would end at 1200hrs today and it didn't. But perhaps it won't be long. Sicily can't last out much longer and obviously Italy must be the next item on the agenda. Rumour has it that the Germans are establishing a line across from Trieste. If this is so then apparently they are expecting Italy to capitulate. Arrived in Italy a year ago today.

3rd August 1943 2255hrs
Received two letters today: one from Sheilah, and one from Jenny. The latter has not written to me before. I wonder why she is starting now? She says that Evelyn is going to spend a holiday at my home. The thought of this shocks me. I'd have thought that Bella would have tried to put her off. I can just imagine what 'home' is like!

4th August 1943 2250hrs
Wrote to Evelyn and Jenny. Apologised to Evelyn for not having had time to warn her of the conditions she shoul d expect at my home.

5th August 1943 1730hrs

The newspapers are reporting expected peace terms. Also rumours about a peace conference supposedly taking place today. Don't set much store by it. We must just wait and see – and hope!

6th August 1943 1545hrs

Have received three letters today: from Evelyn, Betty, and Pam. Evelyn's letter dated 18th March. I wonder why? Her letters appear to be so erratic: old letters arriving after those which have been written more recently. But they're letters and very welcome regardless of dates. In her letter today she says I should soon be receiving my 2nd next of kin parcel and also a book parcel. The 'peace-conference' amounted, as usual, to nothing more than rumour. Nothing but rumours. Oh well, it can't last forever.

8th August 1943 1310hrs

Have just received three letters: from Dad, Evelyn and Betty. Dad says that all at home are well, excepting himself. His doctor's told him it's ulcers. Hope it isn't anything serious. Evelyn's is a very nice letter, one of the nicest I've received. She has sent off another parcel for me. I wonder who's receiving these parcels? I'm not. I shall never be able to repay her and her people for what they are doing for me. She said she was due to go to a wedding the following day and jokingly grumbled that it was time she were going to her own. That's what I think. Betty's letter was, as usual, airy nothing.

We finished the last of Shaw's *Pygmalion* last night. It has run for two weeks now. After the first week we had some new arrivals in the camp so it was suggested it be put on for another week. Well, the audiences have justified the extra performances. Even though I saw it every night from the wings I didn't tire of seeing it although it must have been rather a strain for the cast. Oh well, they can have a rest now.

Italy has not yet capitulated. So near and yet so far. How much longer? We are all so deadly sick of it all. And those poor fellows who were captured at Dunkirk have had three years of it. A few more months, perhaps!

11th August 1943 2200hrs

There is little or no news at present and there are no newspapers allowed in the camp. The 'Free English,' as we sneeringly call them, are no longer working in Fermo, a nearby town. They have been sacked. These are fellows who volunteered to work in an Italian factory. A bus took and returned them to the camp each day. And all they received for helping the enemy was a daily double ration of bread. Some of the principal towns in the north and Naples in the south have been bombed heavily and there have been thousands of civilian casualties. What a rotten business this war is! Still, worse is to follow, I suppose. How much longer I wonder?

14th August 1943 2345hrs
Received five letters today: from Evelyn, her boss, from Dad, and two from Pam. Dad tells me that Emma has become engaged. At seventeen! For some unknown reason we have had an extra roll-call tonight. We have had access to no newspapers today and rumour has it that Rome has been heavily bombed. And it is assumed that the news is very good.

15th August 1943 2330hrs
Milan and Terni have been bombed heavily. Milan is said to have been bombed almost flat. There go our future letters and parcels for some time to come – if we get any more at all. Tonight is a beautiful night for a bombing: a full moon and a clear sky!

16th August 1943 2115hrs
Have been listening to the letter news from England tonight. It was interesting and amusing. Apparently we prisoners of war are not forgotten. A repatriated sailor writes that he was given seven days leave. I wonder if Evelyn will marry me if I am given seven days leave? She can't have any idea of how much I want her. Or does she? And does she want me as much as I want her? My Evelyn! Only two words but what a lot they mean. I am indeed a lucky fellow.

17th August 1943 2110hrs
Received and answered a letter from Evelyn. She says she wants to marry me as soon as I arrive in England: poor girl! But I'd marry her on the ship which takes me back to England if I could. According to a letter a repatriated sailor got seven weeks leave. If I'm allowed that much I shall have ample time to marry Evelyn and, also, to visit friends at Bath and Castle Cary. In her letter today Evelyn says she is not going to Pelton to spend her holiday. That's an immense relief to me. I hoped she wouldn't. She can go with me when we're married. I shall be very proud when I present her to my Dad, sisters and brother. And my cousins, too. All of them girls. I don't think she realises it but she is now almost all of my life. I haven't really had any; that is going to start with her. Am I blowing bubbles again: 'pretty bubbles in the air'?

18th August 1943 2250hrs
I've just been to see PG65's production *Philadelphia Story*. (These are prisoners who have recently joined us at PG70. Their camp is apparently too close to the area which is of current interest to our bombers.) I can't say whether or not it is a good play because I'm not qualified but I found it interesting and amusing. And there was some unique philosophy in it.

There are some very good rumours afloat today: Messina is said to have been evacuated and Kharkov (Russian front) is said to have fallen to the Russians. Well, perhaps it is true! But it must happen some time. Sicily has been taken again but I think it must be really true this time. Marshal Bagdolio (took over from Mussolini) has made a speech about it. How long now before Italy collapses?

22nd August 1943 1730hrs
Received a letter from Evelyn this morning. At the time of her writing it she had just returned from a holiday in Kent. Our mutual friend, Freda, has just produced a baby girl.

25th August 1943 2230hrs
Received a letter from Evelyn and one from Betty yesterday. I've written to Evelyn and to Mr. Godsell today. Today's news is very good: Kharkov has been evacuated by the Germans and the stage is set – we've heard this before – for the final effort!

28th August 1943 2130hrs
The news during the past few days has been very good. There is a rumour today that Naples has been invaded, but there is nothing in the newspaper about this. However Naples has been bombed. A prelude! I wonder? Red Cross parcels won't last much longer. It looks as though we are in for a thin time. Roll on the collapse of Italy.

Start of 2nd notebook

Wednesday 1st September 1943

I've just written a lettercard to Evelyn and a postcard to Dad. In a letter which I received yesterday Dad tells me that Emma is going to be married at Christmas. The news came as a shock: I have always regarded Emma as a child but she has been in the air force a year and she is eighteen. A couple of days ago I gave Johnny Riles some money so that he could buy some communist literature for the camp communist party. My benevolence apparently entitles me to borrow their books if I would like to do so.

The war seems to have slipped into neutral gear again. We are all waiting for the Allies to invade Italy – but will they? We all thought that the collapse of their fascist government would mean the collapse of Italy. What is their government holding out for? I wish the invasion would start: I'm sure they would surrender immediately. Everyone seems to expect it. All of their prison camps in the south have been evacuated. Capt. Webster (our battalion medical officer) came through this camp a few days ago. He told us that according to the people he passed he is of the opinion that Italy can't possibly last much longer. Everyone seems to be of the same opinion. Will I be home for Emma's wedding at Christmas? ! !

Thursday 2nd September 1943

Have just darned some socks and done some washing. The socks I have will have to last until I've been repatriated because there are no next of kin parcels arriving. It is rather hard luck on us that Milan was the Red Cross dump. The Red Cross stuff will have gone the way of the rest of Milan. May the remainder of Italy go with it soon. I have just learned that Jeff Usher has been killed in Sicily. He was transferred to the East Yorks when he was commissioned. He was one of three of us who were recommended for commissions by Major Girling. Poor old Jeff!

There wasn't much in the news last night. The Russians still seem to be doing well. At present our own part in the war (British-American) seems to amount to no more than the bombing of Italy and Germany. The Pope is said to have made a speech on 31st of last month. It hasn't yet appeared in the newspapers but we expect to see it today. According to what we hear, Churchill has been going to make a speech for some time now: it has been postponed time an again. What's he waiting for? The invasion of Italy? Perhaps the invasion will take place when the moon is more suitable. In that case we will have only a few more days to wait.

There are only two more issues of Red Cross food left. When we have had these we will be on Italian rations until Italy surrenders. Hard times are here again it would seem. Four years ago this evening I reported back to my regiment as a reservist.

Friday 3rd September 1943

War was declared four years ago today. Waiting for it to begin I was sitting on the barrack room steps at Richmond feeling a little strange in my new uniform. Now I'm looking forward to the strange feeling I'll experience when I again don civvies. Churchill's speech was in yesterday's newspaper but it didn't amount to much. He said that there would be no 2nd front until he was certain that there would be no lives lost unnecessarily. Italy wasn't mentioned so perhaps it has been written off virtually. Yesterday one of the British medical officers gave a lecture on the activity on the Northwest Frontier of India. He was very interesting and it was nice to hear of old times. They were hard times of mountain and cold, desert and thirst, hard marching and hard digging. But it was adventure, something which most people are privileged only to read about.

Saturday 4th September 1943

Some fellows have been discovered trying to tunnel their way out. It is a pity they were caught. They had tunnelled right beyond the wall and had actually intended to make their break last night. It is thought that somebody gave away their secret to the Italians.

Last night we heard some more extracts from Churchill's speech. He says: Italy need no longer be regarded as a military adversary; Berlin and other German towns will be razed to the ground within the next few weeks; the Balkans will soon be freed of the Nazi yoke. There is a rumour afloat that the 'toe of Italy' has been invaded and that our forces are doing well. I am wishing as I have never wished before that this is true.

Had an interesting conversation last night with Ted Warman and Norman Milson, both RAF men. We talked, that is, they talked and I listened, about flying and navigating. The latter subject fascinates me.

Sunday 5th September 1943

The weather has broken. We have had continual rain for about twenty four hours. Yesterday's rumour is true: Regio Calabria is now occupied by the Allies. The newspapers didn't admit much but there was sufficient to boost our hopes. We are said to have a front of 120 kilos. Today's rumour has it that our troops are advancing with little or no opposition. The landing is said to have been made in the early morning of 3rd September. If that is so our forces should be well into Italy now. May they reach us soon. Our food is low and winter is only two months away. Another winter like last would just about finish off some of us.

Monday 6th September 1943

The rain has stopped but I don't think it will be long before it starts again. The air is very chilly and the sky is cloudy.

Last night's newspaper was very encouraging for us. Friday's reports are the latest: Axis troops have evacuated four towns in the Calabria area but they claim to have inflicted heavy losses on our forces. Well, they would, wouldn't they? From the Italian point of view the newspaper must have seemed rather depressing. It said that the Italian people had now only hope and concord. The Italian soldiery are not showing much of either. Eighteen of them deserted from the camp guards two days ago. But those we see seem to be quite cheered by the Allies' success. It is expected that Portugal will declare war on Japan. The latter has apparently taken over some Portuguese islands. The Japs will be trembling now!

Portuguese hitting power must be just about negligible. Of course if the intention of the Allies is to pass through Spain into France then Portugal would be the ideal starting point. Wait and see! There are no newspapers today so we shall have to wait until Tuesday for further definite news. Until then we will have to exist on rumoured wireless reports.

Last night Ted Warman gave me an interesting talk on the theory of navigation. Before he became a prisoner, Ted was with the Coastal Command, a branch of flying which requires a special type of navigating. Although knowing little or nothing about the subject I have always been interested in it and wish that I could have been a navigator.

The last letter I received from Evelyn was on Sunday, 29th of last month. I wonder if I shall get any more. It doesn't take much to upset the Italians and they must be in rather a turmoil in Rome. How much longer?

The latest rumour: The allies are reported to have landed at Brindisi. Of course we are all hoping that this is true.

Tuesday 7th September 1943

'News from Home' last night (little bits of news which get past the censor), an amusing tale – obviously a load of bollocks, as most of the lads agree – a woman whose husband was serving in the Middle-East wrote to Churchill and said she wanted a baby. Her husband was repatriated. Another story dealt with medals: the 'Africa Star' is to be awarded to all men who have served in Africa between May 1940 and June 1943. Apparently there is also to be the '1939-43 Star', but in the meantime I'm feeling rather worried about our present situation. While we believe that our troops will sweep through Italy quickly there is the obvious likelihood of the Germans grabbing us prisoners while they have the chance and simply moving us further north. That would just about drive us insane. I wish the Italians would surrender then there would be little or no chance of our being taken to Germany. We just wait and hope.

Wednesday 8th September 1943

Yesterday's newspaper reports were quite satisfactory for us. In the south of Italy our forces are continuing to push back the Axis troops who say they are outnumbered. They claim, also, that the Allies' equipment is superior to theirs. We are hoping that our troops will move up quickly and embarrass the enemy so much that they won't have time to move us prisoners. The Russians also are doing well. The Germans are talking about their own 'elastic' defence. This would indicate that they are being pushed back! Budapest has been declared an 'open city'.

Autumn is with us again. There is a noticeable nip in the morning and evening air. I have had to take my blanket into use. Have just written a lettercard to Evelyn and a postcard to Pam, and I'm hoping that it won't be long before I'll be with Evelyn again. Optimism!

2030hrs Rumour! ! ! A bloke has just told me that an armistice has been signed between the Allies and Italy! I wish it were true.

2100hrs It's not a rumour! We have just been informed officially that an armistice between the Allies and Italy was signed on 3rd September but was kept secret until the admission of it would be advantageous to the Allies.

2300hrs The BBC News was read out to us. The Germans are evacuating the Donetz (Russian front) and Stalino has fallen. And the Italians are said to be fighting the Germans. Good for us! – but what a shower of rats to have as an ally!

Thursday 9th September 1943

There was no roll-call this morning but at nine o'clock we paraded under Major Parks, our senior medical officer. We were told that a military mission is on its way here. Yesterday morning this camp was a hell of depression but today everyone is jubilant and we are all wondering how long it will be before we are all in England. Evelyn's birthday is on 30th October: Will I make it?

Friday 10th September 1943

Sailed for France four years ago today. Last night there was a nasty rumour that there are German troops in Porto San Georgeo. I'm rather worried. Some of the lads have panicked and have left the camp. Some of them have come back of their own accord. My own emotion is now back to normal but it is a worrying time. Our own guardsmen prisoners are now doing the guard duties in the camp. Apparently it was necessary to put our own men on guard duties as the Italians have given up all control. We are still very much in the dark regarding the situation of the Germans and our own troops but it will be a great relief to us when our own troops reach us – if they do!

Saturday 11th September 1943

The war situation in Italy would still seem to be favourable. The Germans, however, are fighting hard for the country and obviously it will take some time to overcome them. But in the meantime I don't think we prisoners have anything to worry about as the Germans will have sufficient trouble attending to their own army. The Brenner Pass is said to be held by the Italians but we'd all feel safer if it were held by British or American troops. Yesterday it was reported that British naval units were sighted off Ancona. I wonder are we going to land troops in the north. Ancona is only about fifteen miles north of us.

It is now many days since we received any letters. I wonder when the next batch will arrive? I don't suppose there will be any next-of-kin parcels or book parcels. Milan used to be the depot and I'm sure there must be too many Germans in the north to allow much in the way of road or rail communication. Well, we can do without the luxuries of letters and parcels if we have the hope of being freed by our own forces. When we first received the news of the Armistice I immediately thought that I might even be in England for Evelyn's birthday, 30th Oct. but I don't see much chance of that now. Christmas perhaps?

Sunday 12th September 1943

Received a letter from Evelyn yesterday, dated 25th of last month. I shall never be able to repay her for her loyalty to me. She has stood by me nearly three years now and during the last two years she hasn't seen me. Perhaps it won't be much longer.

Major Parks talked to us last night. He advises us not to panic: there is nothing to worry about, so he tells us! Perhaps there isn't but we are very much in the dark and we are not going to feel comfortable until our own troops reach us.

Monday 13th September 1943

According to the news the war in Italy is progressing slowly but surely in our favour. The British 8th Army is said to be coming up the east coast (our side). They may be with us in a few days. It gives me a very pleasant feeling to know that my battalion is with them. Some more men left the camp last night. I think we are much safer in the camp and anyway their efforts won't be appreciated.

Tuesday 14th September 1943

More men have gone and our freedom has been curtailed. We are to have two roll-calls per day and until our own forces take over we are still to regard ourselves as prisoners of the Italians. But the news is very good: the 8th Army had reached Bari and is going well. Perhaps they will be with us by the weekend. The American 5th Army isn't doing so well. The Germans are

showing them strong opposition. Our 8th Army is going all out to link up
with the American 5th. Our hope is that when they do between them they
will sweep all of the German opposition before them. The Russians are still
doing exceptionally well.

Wednesday 15th September 1943

The restrictions imposed on us yesterday have been cut down a little. There
are to be organized walks, ie, for those inclined, groups of a sergeant and
six men may go out to walk locally. While the news isn't bad there is no
improvement on yesterday. The Americans are still facing stiff opposition
and our 8th Army hasn't yet linked up with them but we are told that our
little 8th are facing opposition on the eastern side. I wonder will they
continue to advance on the east side or wait until the Americans have
effectively dealt with their opposition in the west.

The sooner our people advance up the east coast the more comfortable it
will be for us. Although Italy has capitulated we are still virtually prisoners
while we are in enemy territory. I have written to Evelyn and Dad this
morning. I wonder how many more letters I shall write from this camp? It is
now a week since I received my last letter. It was from Evelyn and dated 25th
Aug. I don't suppose I shall receive many more as both Rome and Milan are
occupied by the Germans. According to the news – rumour, perhaps – the
Pope has been taken hostage by the Germans.

Thursday 16th September

The situation is tense. Literally hundreds made a break from the camp
yesterday. Although the accusation 'desertion' is being used I don't really
believe it amounts to that. We are in a political darkness and panic is
showing its frightened head. Should we simulate calm and wait in hope that
our Army will come and rescue us or should each of us take his chance and
hope to disappear into the Italian countryside until the Germans move north
and leave us to be collected by our own army? Extrapolate! Extrapolate!
Extrapolate! If a herring and a half costs four pence and friction causes heat
how long would it take to fry a rasher of bacon by rubbing it between two
bricks?... But our situation is really serious: our own troops must be at least
150 miles to our south and we are now into autumn with its chilly nights and
the attitude of the Italians towards their ex-prisoners could be expected to be
nothing better than ambivalent.

It's a perplexing situation and, having given it some thought, Jerry and I
have decided to stay here just as long as there are rations issued. We have
checked up on the Red Cross food which we've saved during the past few
weeks and it's Jerry's opinion that we could survive at least three weeks on
it. We have 3 tins of butter (about 1½lbs), 3 packets of biscuits, 3 packets
of raisins and 3 of prunes, 2 tins of powdered milk and 2 of condensed, and

a quantity of tea, cocoa, coffee, and sugar. There is plenty of water in the country and vegetables would be available from the farms we pass through.

Last night's news wasn't bad regarding the war in general but our 8th Army doesn't appear to be coming our way: they appear to be going all out to link up with the American 5th Army which is still in difficulties around Salerno. However we are not in any danger here so long as the Germans don't come over to the east coast. The latter is the eventuality which we are all dreading. If, or when, they do come, it is my, and Jerry's intention to leave this camp and do our utmost to find our 8th army. I am now going to pack my haversack with the articles I don't want to lose.

1720hrs I've just come back after a walk with Sgt Milson viewing the high ground to our south. It seems to be pretty hard going and I think that in the event of a break being necessary ten miles a day would be about as much as we would manage. On our return to camp I was told the latest BBC news. The Americans would seem to be holding their own and our 8th Army still seems to be going all out to meet up with them. In the east the 8th seems to be consolidating at Bari. If that is the case it will be some time before they will reach us – if they do reach us in time! The BBC also reports that the Germans are aware of the British and the American prisoners who are roaming the country and state that they, the prisoners, must give themselves up to the nearest German HQ. That is asking a lot: men surrendering their hope of freedom!

Personally I am going to 'stay put' until Major Parks advises us otherwise. When I move, if I have to move, I shall do so in British service clothing then the Germans can't claim that I'm a spy. To continue my sojourn as a prisoner would seem to be the worst that could happen to me. The Germans won t treat us badly so long as we do nothing to hinder their war effort and to try to do that wouldn't be worth the effort on my part. I am going to remain strictly neutral until I am again safely with the British Army.

Friday 17th September 1943

All our hopes of escape have evaporated: a few minutes ago while we were on roll-call parade German soldiers mounted the sentry boxes. We are prisoners again! Information from the office would have us believe that the Germans are keeping us imprisoned merely to prevent our getting in the way of their own troops. I very much doubt this. I think it is merely to maintain our docility until they have moved more troops to maintain our captivity. With the will and leadership 7,000 men could seriously embarrass the few Germans who are now holding us. Naturally we are all shattered but there is no point in our crying over spilt milk: we are no worse off than we were a couple of weeks ago. Our hope now is that our own troops will move up the country fast enough to prevent the Germans evacuating us.

The news of last night was good: the Americans had managed to make a good advance. This morning's news is that our 8th Army is now only 18 miles from the Salerno battle area. The Russians, too, are also doing well. If we are sent to Germany it surely won't be long before the Russians swamp Germany. I am very sorry for Evelyn's sake. She has waited so long for me and just when it looked as though her waiting was coming to an end I find myself 'in the bag' again. Roll on the 8th Army! Roll on the 5th American Army! And Roll on the Russians!

Saturday 18th September 1943

There is rather a good rumour afloat this morning: all of the Germans who were in Fermo and Monturano are said to have moved out and those in this camp are supposed to be following shortly. As fantastic as this may seem there may be some truth in it. According to the news from our secret radio the 8th and the 5th have linked up. Also the 5th Corps, coming up from the 'toe' of Italy, have joined them. Since by this time the news will be 48 hours old it would account for the German eagerness to evacuate. Oh, if it is only true! But last night we were informed that we are now prisoners of the Italian Fascist Republican Government. Apparently the Italians in this camp were given the option of joining the Fascist Republican Army or of becoming civilians. A lot of them – most of those we considered to be pro-British – have turned against us. If the Germans do move out these Italians had better move with them!

Sunday 19th September

Yesterday we were told, unofficially, that the Germans were going to move out and leave us. It was wishful thinking or somebody's idea of a joke because we've just been told that we are to be moved to another camp. Sgt Young has just told us that trains have been laid on for us. Our hopes are dashed again. The war news isn't bad generally but our forces don't appear to be moving very quickly although they are still maintaining a line from Bari to Salerno. But they had that a few days ago. I wonder how long it will take them to drive out the Germans? And will the Germans evacuate us to Germany? I am depressed. I had so hoped that I might spend part of the autumn in England. Another Christmas deadline. By Christmas! Always Christmas! Everything comes to he who waits. We waited and the blasted Germans came. And it's Major Parks' fault: he said we'd be regarded as deserters if we left the camp without authority. So we waited. And now we are properly in the soup and we'll have to wait until Germany has been absolutely crushed. Oh, well, I suppose he was handling the situation as he thought best.

Monday 20th September

There is still tension in the camp. No one seems to know what is going to happen. Yesterday the Germans brought us thousands of Red Cross parcels from other camps which have been evacuated. Their explanation is that they can't take the Red Cross food for themselves and they won't allow the Italians to have them. The only alternative was to bring the stuff to the British prisoners they are holding. THEY HAVE A GREAT RESPECT FOR THE BRITISH, they say! ! !

The news is fairly good. On the Russian front the German defences have been beaten back from Smolensk to the Aegean Sea. The Russians are rolling forward. In a few months they ought to be in Germany. In Italy, our forces are said to be doing well. Everything is being set for the battle of Naples. Corsica and Sardinia have been evacuated by the Germans and are now being used by the Allies as air bases and are being referred to as 'our unsinkable aircraft carriers'. On the Italian east coast our 8th Army is said to be advancing but we don't know where our furthest advanced troops are. We hope they are very close. There is a rumour that they have made a landing a few miles south of Porto San Georgeo. Fear of further disappointment forbids us to believe this. Yesterday the Germans laid aside three days of rations for each of the four compounds here. We are all wondening what this means. Are they rations to be used when they move us? Or are they rations to be used when the Germans have left us? We are hoping for the latter. We must wait and see. Every prisoner received a Red Cross parcel this morning.

Wednesday 22nd September

There was nothing worth mentioning yesterday. We are still waiting and wondering. Unofficial information from the German soldiers is that it is not their intention to take us to Germany. Naturally we hope this to be the case. We have been told that each of us is to receive a medical parcel tomorrow. These 'medical' parcels are intended only for those prisoners who are recovering from illness. We seem to be receiving rather a lot of food! There is a tale that the Germans are trying to procure transport for us. This suspense is demoralizing.

Thursday 23rd September

The Germans were present on the roll-call this morning. A different unit took over the camp yesterday and it would seem that they intend to out-do the others in efficiency. The promised medical parcels have not yet been issued. Just as well, perhaps. I don't feel well this morning. I have a severe cold. It wasn't possible to sleep last night. Our Germans seemed to be celebrating by blasting the sky with machine-gun and rifle fire. Perhaps they are new inexperienced troops destined to reinforce their comrades who are battling with the British and American forces in the south. There was also the blaring of music from the camp's loud speakers. We are still in doubt regarding our future. Germans are coming and going all of the time and there is a strong feeling in the camp that we will ultimately be moved north. The suspense is demoralising. We clutch at straws. Not a word of our secret bulletin is missed. Our 8th Army is said to have been advancing since the

Italians capitulated but as far as we know they are still no further north than Bari. Where are they now? But our impatience will avail us nothing. We are unimportant and consequentially unfortunate.

1545hrs No. 4 Compound, plus 300 men of No. 3 Compound, have received instructions that they will be moved out in one hour. We don't know where they are going but believe it to be Germany! When will the remainder of us follow?

Friday 24th September 1415hrs

I am writing this in the railway station at Porto San Georgeo. Groups 1 to 26 were ordered to parade at ten o'clock this morning. It looks as though we are on our way to Germany.

Thursday 29th September

Somewhere in Germany. After four days and nights of travelling we arrived here Tuesday 28th and are at present in an old concentration camp previously occupied by Jewish and Russian prisoners. We are no longer with our own groups but are mixed with men from camps in Italy other than ours, PG70, in Italy. So far I've been able to stay with Gerry so our food partnership still holds. We've had no news for a week.

Friday 1st October

The remainder of Nos. 2 and 3 Compounds plus 1000 Italians (workers, I believe) arrived yesterday. These are unfortunate as there are no buildings in which to house them. We still have no further news of the war and we are concerned about the people at home who will be worrying about us. And I wonder what Evelyn is thinking?

On our rail journey to Germany we were uncomfortably crowded into cattle vans and we were hungry and thirsty after we had left the prison camp in Italy. On occasions we were allowed out of our trucks so that we could perform our natural body functions but otherwise we were locked-up during the whole of the journey. We had a brief frightening spell when our train was stationary at the large railway junction at Verona. (Rather different I think from when the Merchant of Venice lived there.) A large number of American aircraft selected the junction as a target and for a few minutes created a fairly life-like hell for us as they dropped their bombs. I don't know if they did any real damage but they frightened the lives out of us prisoners. In the truck where I was there was panic. Through the grille on our truck side we could see lots of anti-aircraft guns but none were being fired at the American aircraft. The gun crews were taking cover in the gun trenches. One chap, a paratrooper, north Yorkshireman from his accent, screamed hysterically through the grille, "Fermez la bloody rotten porte, you rotten bastards," indicating a weakness in his ability with the French language (I'm sure he meant 'open' rather than 'close') and navigationally, too, he was rather wide of the mark: Verona is hundreds of miles east of the French border with Italy.

He continued: "Get them bloody guns firing, you cowardly bastards!" Reasonably I tried to point out to him that the bombing aircraft were American, and fighting on our side.

"Bollocks, mate," he shouted at me, "I don't care a monkey's whose bombers they are: when they're dropping bombs on me they're the bloody enemy!" Actually, I think the bombing lasted only some minutes and we, though terrified, didn't see any effect because of our very restricted view. Eventually our train moved, and here we are: somewhere in Germany.

Friday 2nd October
My pen has run dry so I shall have to do the best I can with a pencil. I don't know when I shall be able to get some ink. This camp is desolate, and holding 3 or 4 times the number of inmates for which it was intended. The food is reasonably good and sufficient but we are receiving only one issue of hot water per day for making a hot drink.

Sunday
Another day...! And we are all fed-up. There is nothing to do and nowhere to do it. 4000 men in accommodation intended for 1000. And another batch came in last night, including 500 Americans. How much longer are we going to be kept here? It is most depressing.

Wednesday 6th Oct
The Italians have been moved out, it is believed, to be used as workers. But we are wondering where we will be in the near future. On checking up this morning I've noticed that I have lost all of my razor blades. This is a sad blow because it looks as though there will be none available here. I have been using the present blade in my razor for over a month but it seems that it will have to last a while longer.

Thursday 7th Oct
Since yesterday I have found my missing razor blades: they had become stuck in a fold in my wallet.

One postcard per man was issued this morning. I have used this to write to Evelyn and I've asked her to let Dad know that I'm OK. I intend to try to do some washing today: all of my clothes are filthy and the thought of getting more lice horrifies me. And I have not had an all-over wash for some weeks. My hair hasn't been cut for five weeks. I am missing Jimmy Brown. He was one of the camp barbers when we were in Italy. He claimed to have his own barber shop in Filey before the army claimed him. But he was stretching a point, really! According to one of my signallers who has known him for a long time, Jimmy's 'Barber Shop' was merely an attic over somebody else's little sweet shop. He, Jimmy, tells some awful whoppers – but he's ever so good-natured with it!

Monday 11th Oct

We are expecting to be moved during the next ten days. According to information brought into the camp we are to be disinfested and have all our hair cut off. Also we are to photographed.

RUMOUR! received yesterday: the Russians are on the Polish frontier. Today, they are only 80 kilos from Warsaw. There may be some truth in this as British prisoners of war who were working in eastern Poland have been brought westward into Germany.

Thursday 21st Oct

Still here! However the news is good, but vague. There are no newspapers. Last night our bombers were over a town south west of us. We don't know for certain but we think perhaps it was Dresden. But I must write that the tale of the Russians nearing Warsaw was untrue. But perhaps they will be there soon. Life here is steadily sliding past and conditions are not unpleasant. I find it cold at night as I have only one blanket and my greatcoat for bedding. We have a daily issue of bread and margarine and some days we are given some meat paste or jam. Daily we have a hot meal of boiled potatoes and vegetable, which some people say isn't fit for a pig – I think it is! – but there is plenty of it. Coffee must be scarce in Germany just now. We have had it only twice. Morning and evening we get a mug full of German tea, a mysterious weak concoction. But we mustn't grumble: things could be worse. The arrival of Red Cross parcels would cheer us immensely.

Wednesday 27th Oct

We were moved into a different camp yesterday near a town called Mulberg which is about ten miles from where we were. Of course we had to walk. At present we are in a sort of quarantine camp awaiting disinfestation and the complete removal of our hair. We are sleeping 200 per hut. There is a rumour that there may be an issue of Red Cross parcels.

Saturday 30th Oct

Evelyn's birthday. And what a day for me! I've had all of my hair cut off; had a shower and been dried by hot air; had certain intimate parts of me swabbed with iodine by a Russian prisoner; I've been inoculated, vaccinated, had my clothes disinfested by cyanide gas; I've been registered as a prisoner of the Germans, been finger-printed and photographed and am now waiting to be X-rayed. We do have fun as prisoners of war! We have had lettercards issued and I'm going to write again to Evelyn to let her know that I'm OK. If she receives it I'm sure she'll let Dad know. I shall send him a card as soon as I have one. As in Italy, the issue of lettercards and postcards is very

uncertain. It is also my intention to write to the Engineer in charge of Post
Office telephones to have myself registered for employment with them.

Thursday 4th Nov

We were X-rayed this morning. A charming German girl operated the
apparatus. A curious thing about this camp is the scarcity of German soldiers.
All of the administrative staff appear to be Frenchmen, Dutch, or Czechs.
All of the manual work is done by Russian prisoners. Educational classes are
about to be started. I have enrolled for Electricity. It may help me to get on to
the Post Office engineering staff.

Sunday 7th Nov

The last few days have been very cold and there was some snow this
morning but only for a few minutes. We are wondering will we get any food
parcels tomorrow. Since coming to this camp we have had two weekly issues
of ½ parcel per man. There are not sufficient of these ordinary parcels in the
store to allow another ½ per man tomorrow but apparently there are several
thousand 'medical' parcels. Perhaps an issue of these will be made.

Monday 8th Nov

Lettercards were issed today and I have written to Dad. It was my intention
also to write to the post office ladies at Castle Cary but only one card was
issued.

Sunday 14th Nov

The weather has broken and it has been raining since last night. In his latest
speech Hitler says he is winning the war and is not going to capitulate. That's
funny because we reckon we are winning the war. He's in a panic and he's
obviously trying to build a shell around so much fresh air. He's not fooling
us and we are mere prisoners.

Tuesday 16th Nov

Lettercards were issued today. I have wrtten to Evelyn and I've enclosed a
small photo of myself. I hope she receives it. Perhaps I ought to have told
her it was taken 18 months ago in the Western Desert. That, however, would
have defeated my object: I want her to see me as she last saw me. I suppose it
was dishonest of me but: 'all's fair in love... etc.' Looking in my mirror and
visualising the photo I'm afraid I've been untruthful. While, for the moment,
I feel happy and healthy, my mirror tells me my youth has left me. Perhaps
I'll have a second youth when I'm again with her! But when is this blasted
war going to end: I can't keep the poor girl waiting forever.

Thursday 25th Nov

Two postcards were issued yesterday and I've written to Margaret (Castle Cary Post Office) and Pam. I can't write to just one of them, they live virtually next door to each other. The war news isn't bad: the Russians are advancing slowly and the RAF is bombing Germany to Hell, the right place for it.

Thursday 2nd Dec

Today 1500 of us were moved back to Jacobsthal. What a dump! Although we had been told that it had been improved we have found it in no way changed. It is just as bad as ever. Roll on peace! Lettercards were issued yesterday and I have written to Evelyn. Very selfishly I pleaded with her to wait for me. Now, having done that, it is up to me to keep myself fit. It wouldn't do for me to go back to her an old man. I hope she won't be shocked by my bald temples. Oh Evelyn, if you only knew how I worry about losing you. I am now a section leader and in charge of 20 other NCOs.

Monday 13th Dec

Lettercards were issued today and I've written to Evelyn. Wonderful girl. How patient she is. Some more letters have been received here. I wonder when I shall get some? I have just had my second haircut since the whole lot was whipped off. It is only about a ½ inch long but it's going to have time to grow apparently. But a ½ inch would be long enough were the war to end now! A Russian prisoner came round today selling mirrors, gloves, knives etc. for cigarettes. I bought a mirror. He asked for 20 cigarettes. I gave him 30. I don't know where he got the stuff. Perhaps he had stolen it. Or perhaps he was commissioned by a German.

Tuesday 14th Dec

Have just had a shower and at the same time I had my clothes disinfested by hot air. I forgot to take my watch and my fountain pen out of my pocket but they don't seem to have suffered by the heat. My watch, although too hot to hold, came out ticking merrily. And my pen: although smelling of burnt rubber appears to be OK.

Tuesday 21st Dec

I've been ill for some days but am slowly recovering. I had a pulse rate of 144 but our British doctor told me that hearts behave in this manner for no apparent reason. Anyway I'm beginning to feel fit again so it doesn't matter. Postcards were issued on Thursday. I wrote one to Sheilah and one to Jenny. I got another card from 'Sailor' Haynes so I wrote to Evelyn. There is some wonderful bombing being done by our aircraft and the Germans seem to be perplexed. I don't blame them. Leipzig is twenty or thirty miles from us and we can hear the bombing. It must be sheer hell. Oh why don't they call off this horrible war.

Christmas Day 1943

Postcards were issued yesterday and I was also given an extra card. I have written to Evelyn and have used the other two cards to write to Dad and Evelyn's mother. My appetite has improved but it's not much better than it was last Christmas. A year ago I said my next Christmas would be in England. I was wrong! Next one, perhaps? This life is so deadening and I get awful fits of depression. I look back and see an endless arch of wasted years. Looking ahead I see no release – just a tunnel of time broken by roll-calls and meals which have become so automatic that they have, insidiously, become time. The monotony and futility of it all is maddening. When will I break out of this darkness into the light?

It reminds me of a recurring dream which I have occasionally: I find myself struggling up a vertical shaft in the earth until I climb into a horizontal tunnel along which I crawl until suddenly I emerge through the side of a hill. Then I see before me everything clean, bright, and green and a wave of happiness surges through me. And then I wake up! ! Is that how my life is to be, I wonder? Is the end of the war to be my breaking through the side of the hill? Or is my subconscious mind doing a bit of wishful thinking. Christmas day 1943, the 30th Christmas of my life, 2nd Christmas as a prisoner, 12th Christmas in the Army, 9th Christmas abroad ... Christmas day 1943, my sister's wedding day, according to one of Dad's letters. Are they thinking of me, I wonder! Little Emma who was a child last time I saw her will contentedly sleep in the arms of a man tonight: a girl today, a woman tomorrow. My 30th Christmas and I'm still single. Will my 31st see me married?

Friday 31st Dec

My last entry this year, the year of our victory, we all hoped. Well, our victory is in sight even though it may be in the far distance. We believe the end to be sure – no one doubts the final outcome – but when will it be? The lot of a prisoner of war is a hard one. Conditions here are not really bad but this idle useless existence of ours rots the whole being. I shall never allow myself to be taken prisoner again. I shall be forever grateful to Evelyn for what she means to me: the light in my darkness; cheerfully twinkling; beckoning me onward. What a miserable wretch I would be were I to give up hope now. This morning I was showing an old photo to a friend. He saw the little photo of Evelyn among my collection. How proud and happy I was when he admired it! Will 1944 put her in my arms?

1944

Saturday 1st 1944

New year's day and it is snowing as I have never seen it snow before. Last night we saw the old year out – English style, that is, the old Scottish style. Entertainers were performing in our billet from 9 o'clock last night until 3 this morning. Some of the fellows dressed up as girls – and what charming pieces of femininity they looked, too! However they sang songs which no lady would sing: incongruous, but funny. Of late there have been very cheering rumours of our '2nd Front'. The Allies are said to have landed at Calais but up till now the Germans have not mentioned it although for some time now they have admitted that they expect it. If the rumour is not a rumour then we ought to hear something definite about it in a day or so. Roll on the Allies! And roll on my repatriation!

Wednesday 5th Jan 44

It was just a rumour. What we heard a few days ago was nothing more than a rumour. Somebody's idea of a joke. However the RAF seems to be bombing steadily and heavily. When will the Germans wake up? They can't win. Hitler is having his population killed for nothing. A beaten man, he appears to be dragging the war on out of pure spite. We heard yesterday that the Russians had launched an offensive of 3,000,000 men: the Russian 'steam-roller!' May it roll everything before it. Our own western offensive ought to start soon. Perhaps they are waiting for favourable weather. We are still waiting for letters from England. A few arrived a few days ago so it is hoped that more may arrive soon. I'm longing to hear from Evelyn again. And I must not forget Pam, Sheilah, Margaret, and Dad.

Friday 7th Jan

Our group was moved into No 8 compound today. Two postcards and one lettercard were issued today. Despite their war effort, the Germans seem to try to be fair in their dealings with British and American prisoners. As usual, I have written the lettercard to Evelyn. The cards I have written to Dad and Jenny. We heard some newspaper reports yesterday. They were quite encouraging. The Germans are having hell knocked out of them. How long now?

Sunday 9th Jan

An educational scheme is afoot. At first I enrolled for English, Electricity, and Psychology, but have since changed over to the London Matriculation Course. I wonder: can I do it? It's a large mouthful! Can I chew it? But anyway the studying can't do me any harm and if I should pass it may do me a lot of good. I'm not yet certain but I think my subjects will be: English, Mathematics, History, and Electro-magnetism. Currently, students over 25 years of age need do only four subjects instead of the normal five which would include a foreign language.

Thursday 13th Jan

I was interviewed by Padre Day re the Matric Course. Apparently Electro-magnetism may not be taken as a science subject. My subjects now will be: English, Maths, History, and Physics. Recently I have learned a little about English but I know really nothing at all about the other subjects. I'm afraid the Matric will be beyond me but the effort ought to be good for me.

Sunday 16th Jan

We are going to be moved again. Just after we've got nicely settled they decide to move us. But we don't know where we are going. We are being kept in suspense: blasted unsettling suspense. Our Education scheme is now up the spout. Also there will be trouble with our letters. Just when we ought to be receiving them. It is now about five months since I received my last letter and now there is going to be more confusion. How much longer is it going to last? I put up quite happily with the action in the desert but this endless turning over of days in a prison camp waiting – waiting – waiting... When is it going to end? A lettercard and a postcard were issued yesterday. I have written to Evelyn and to Sheilah.

Thursday 20th Jan

Still here! Our move has been postponed for a couple of weeks. There is a rumour that we are only going back to Mulberg. I hope that this is so: I hate travelling long distances in cattle-trucks. The news is very encouraging just now. The Germans admit that they are unable to check the Russians and that they are awaiting an invasion by the Allies in the west – Normandy, we all think. But when are they going to throw in the towel? And when is our promised invasion going to take place? I am running out of socks and this is quite serious in this cold weather. And when will I get another next-of-kin parcel? Or will the war end first? I'm feeling very tired. I haven't slept at all well recently. The RAF is overhead and we can feel the ground shaking. Some of the fellows are showing fear – of the bombing! Yellow rats!

Sunday 23rd Jan

The latest news regarding our move is that it is to be soon. Still waiting for letters. Several fellows have already received some but they are coming in very slowly. But when am I going to get mine? We have had no news for some days now but there are some good rumours afloat. The RAF is doing well – no rumour, we can feel the bombs dropping. One rumour has it that Hitler has handed the reins over to a General. There may be something in this but I doubt it. We shall know when we get a newspaper. Postcards were issued today: one per man. I have written to Evelyn. I scrubbed my trousers yesterday. They were rather greasy and shabby-looking.

Wednesday 26th Jan

The other compound has moved this morning and we have had orders to pack our kit ready for our move. Oh well, as it has to happen let it happen soon. There has been little or no news recently. It seems the Germans are getting ready to announce another loss. May it be the biggest yet!

Saturday 29th Jan

At Mulberg again. We were moved out of Jacobsthal yesterday morning and after a search of our kit had been made we were marched here. The Germans were confiscating private blankets but I managed to bribe the bloke who searched my kit. On arriving here we had a hot shower and had our kit disinfested. There is a rumour that we are still in transit and will be moving again soon. We are all hoping that this is not so. Today I had a reunion with Terry Bray and Jimmy Brown. They both look well and have been receiving letters.

Tuesday 2nd Feb

Lettercards were issued today. 'Sailor' Haynes gave his to me. He doesn't write to anyone so I have written to Pam as well as Evelyn. There was some mail brought in today but there was none for me. I received my last letter last September. The war still appears to be chugging along merrily. When is it going to end? I am going to run out of question marks! The news is good but it has been good for the past year. But why doesn't someone kick that black-moustached square headed Austrian bastard to hell out of it. Thousands of people are losing their lives daily because that squealing hysterical rat is afraid for his own skin. I've heard that Colonel Macdonnell, Major Girling, and Lieut. Murray are back in England again having escaped from their camp in Italy. And I am here! But the war can't last forever. Neither can I!!

Friday 5th Feb

Moved again today but not far this time. We have been moved from the transit compound into Compound D North. We accept this as meaning that we are here on a semi-permanent basis but there is no knowing what the Germans will decide. They seem to be as erratic as a butterfly. And I am waiting for some letters.

The Germans are getting annoyed about the wireless they think we have and are offering 5000 marks to any informer. What a hope they have! We have a good camp theatre here and I was there this evening and saw the play, *Boy Meets Girl*. It was very amusing and the acting was very convincing. When a young man is dressed as a woman he can be made to look astoundingly like the authentic article. But none of us has been on speaking terms with a woman for a long time. Perhaps that has something to do with it. It is almost two years since I last spoke to a woman. That was when I was in hospital in Palestine. Roll on peace.

Friday 11th Feb
Two postcards per man were issued yesterday so I wrote to Evelyn and Dad. Many of us have still not had any letters addressed to us in Germany. Those received were re-directed from Italy. Soon, perhaps?

The other day Jimmy Brown told me that Peggy, his fiancée, had told him that she was still writing to Evelyn and that Evelyn had told her I am safe. This indicates that Evelyn must have received some of my letters from this camp. Our camp newspaper tells us that three men in the camp dreamt that the war would end on 3rd March. All three are in the same billet and all had that dream on the same night. I wonder…!

Thursday 17th Feb
Lettercards have been issued. I have written to Evelyn. At long last I have received a letter but this was from Bella. She wrote it on 21st Jan. She says that Dad has received nothing from me from Germany. I wonder why? I have written to him about ten times while I've been in Germany. I hope he has received some since Bella wrote her letter. Now all I want is a letter from Evelyn. I do long for one! Soon, perhaps. The war is progressing satisfactorily. Finland is expected to capitulate soon and the other lesser nations must follow. What it amounts to, of course, is that Russia is swamping these countries with their victorious troops. Russia says that their offensive proper has not yet started but is due to do so when the Anglo-American invasion of the continent takes place. But when is that going to be? The Germans are terrified so evidently they expect it.

Friday 18th Feb
Letters at last! ! ! three of them, two from Evelyn and one from Dad. At long last I have got letters from my darling Evelyn. Oh, Evie, my sweet, if only you knew how happy they have made me. But what a lone time I have had to wait! Nearly six months. But they are coming now. Perhaps I shall get one almost every week. No more months of waiting. Dad's letter didn't cheer me so much. He had not heard from me when he wrote. But apparently my cousin Jenny received a card from me and Dad is hurt because he believes I wrote to her before writing to him. Actually I wrote to him several times before I wrote to Jenny. I hope he's received something from me since he wrote this letter.

Tuesday 22 Feb
My 30th birthday but I'm not telling anybody. Congratulations and best
wishes always embarrass me. I haven't received any more letters since
Friday but it's too soon to start moaning and grumbling and worrying. But
we are still waiting for our invasion of the continent to take place and are
hoping it to be in the near future. Ever hopeful! But the Germans are having
a rather rough time on the Russian Front: so rough that I genuinely feel sorry
for them. Why don't they capitulate. Irrespective of who's right and who's
wrong the Germans can't possibly win now. Everything is against them. I
wish Germany would capitulate before our invasion could take place. But
they won't!

Wednesday 23rd Feb
I received three letters this afternoon: Evelyn, Pam, and Mr. Godsell. It's
wonderful to be receiving letters again. And I was very pleased when I got
Pam's letter. She is a nice girl and I'm very fond of her – after Evelyn, of
course – but, anyway, I don't suppose I shall ever see her again.

Thursday 24th Feb
Lettercards were issued today and I've written to Evelyn. The news is still
good but surely our invasion is due to happen soon.

Tuesday 29th Feb
Received letters from Pam, Sheilah, and Jenny. I'm afraid the affection of
my sweet cousin tends to be more than cousinly though she veils it well.
Poor Jenny! Does she at such an early age – about twenty – believe herself
to be fated for the shelf. Silly girl. She is young and attractive even though
she tends to plumpness. Pam's case is entirely different: she's physically
unattractive though she's a very nice person, witty, straight forward and
sincere. Why doesn't somebody appreciate her good points and marry the
girl. It is now a week since I received my last letter from Evelyn and it seems
such a long time. Evelyn if you only knew how I long for you. But I keep on
saying that. I look about me and think: all of these blokes are the same. What
a highly charged battery of love! ! !

Wednesday 1st March
Lettercards were issued today and I've written to Margaret. I haven't
received any letters today. I'm beginning to worry about Jerry. He seems to
be falling to pieces because, in his view, he has failed as writer. Since June of
last year he has been working on a novel and now he feels that he can't carry
on. Personally I feel that this is nothing more than his lack of knowledge
of people and life's experiences. Brought up in a New Zealand village his
experience of life is very limited. He had a boyhood dream of becoming a
writer and he has lived in a dream-world of Shakespeare, Jane Austin and

the nineteenth century poets until he migrated to London, the Mecca of the intelligentsia, the writers, the artists: the aesthetes of the world. And Jerry considers himself an aesthete, and is boastful of it, too. He is an atheist: Shakespeare is his god.

Once I saw him almost hysterical when one or other of our camp's intelligentsia dared to suggest that the plays attributed to Shakespeare were actually written by Francis Bacon. What does it matter, I tried to reason with him: what matters is the quality of the work. Temporarily he sent me to Coventry for that bit of reasoning. But back to the moment: I am concerned for him. He and I are both 'loners' and I believe I'm the only person here who is anywhere near his temperamental 'wavelength'. All of the other fellows tend to regard him as just a harmless eccentric while he regards this as their acknowledgment of his intellect. So I'm worried about him and feel so helpless.

Friday 3rd March

I have arranged with Eric Hurst, who edits our 'Times' (camp wall-newspaper) to pay Jerry a visit, supposedly spontaneously, to ask Jerry's advice on something intellectual. I've explained my reason to Eric. I hadn't spoken to Eric before but I'm sure he understands the situation. He seems to be a very nice bloke although I think he is away up with the 'airy fairies'! He, Eric, may be able to boost up Jerry's spirits by asking his advice on matters intellectual. Eric, in civil life, is in the publishing business. I hope it works, my bit of intellectual artificial respiration!

Saturday 4th March

Jerry was agreeably surprised when Eric Hurst paid us a visit today. Introducing himself to Jerry, he turned to me and said in a joking tone, 'I've come to pick Jerry's brains about things literary and intellectual so if you don't mind you may as well bugger off for a while!' I grinned and sniffed and said, 'I know when I'm not wanted,' and left Eric to carry on with his spiritual resuscitation. They talked some hours and Eric did a good job. Jerry's spirits are now in the stratosphere. His knowledge had been tapped and some of his answers written to be used in an article. Jerry is delighted. Over the moon. Chuffed beyond description. He, Jerry Souster, has been asked by no less a person than our camp editor for opinions and advice. If he ever learns about this while we are still in this camp he will murder me – or die of embarrassment. It's a certainty that he'd never speak to me again. He's very proud and sensitive is Jerry.

We have just been informed that we in this hut are in quarantine. One of our number has gone into hospital with diphtheria. Typhus is suspected. Add nostalgia, of his roommates, and you have a real bargain. But it is no joke, really. We are not allowed outside our hut for anything – not even to visit the latrine. We must use the night latrine which is part of our building. Not a very inspiring prospect. There are 220 men in the building. If each man requires only two minutes per visit it will require about ten hours for each man to pass through. A long time to stand in a queue!

Friday 10th March
Still in quarantine! I've had no letters since 29th of last month. The news is still very good but our invasion has not yet happened. Some time ago the Russians said that their offensive would not start until the Allies started their invasion of western Europe. But the Russians have started their offensive and appear to be doing well. What are the Allies waiting for?

I've not been feeling too well recently. Physically I'm as fit as I've ever been since becoming a prisoner but my nerves are bad and I jump at the slightest noise and lose my temper for any silly little thing. I am really concerned because I've always been very even tempered. But I suppose this prison camp life is having a similar effect on all of us.

Saturday 11th March
A fellow has gone into hospital today with Typhus. We had all thought that tomorrow would see us out of quarantine but it now looks as though we're in it for some time. What an existence. There was a lot of mail today but I didn't get any. Perhaps I shall get some next week. The news is good but our invasion doesn't seem to be any more imminent than it was five months ago. We have all believed that Churchill said the middle of March: 4 days to go! Will it happen.

Wednesday 15th March
We are disappointed: today is the middle of March and our expected invasion doesn't seem to have happened. There were some cheering rumours afloat last night but I'm afraid they were just rumours. Perhaps we shall get some news soon. I received two letters this morning: one from Evelyn and one from Pam. Evelyn says she is forever thinking of my home coming. So am I. Oh for that glorious day! She wonders will I have changed much. I must have changed. But, Evelyn I wonder how much she has changed? I take for granted that she is, will be, attractive. But can she cook. And when will I experience her efforts in our kitchen?

The sentry has been taken away from our door but we still don't know if we are yet out of quarantine. Our sentry is with us again. Apparently we are out of quarantine for Diphtheria and then it was remembered about the Typhus. What a life!

Thursday 16th March
I've just received a letter from Pam. She hints at a possible romance between her and a boyfriend in India. I wish her the best of luck. Despite her lack of physical attraction she is one of the nicest girls I know.

Friday 17th March
Have just received another letter from Pam. Her last three letters have been dated: 13th, 20th, and 27th Feb. so it would seem that she is writing regularly every week.

Saturday 18th March
Two letters today: One from Evelyn and one from Bella. Bella says that Dad had not received anything from me. That was on 25th of last month. I've been writing to him. Where are my cards going? What's happening to them. I could understand Dad worrying if he had no news of me but he seems to think I'm neglecting him as others are receiving cards from me.

Monday 20th March
Received three letters : two from Dad and one from Evelyn's mum. Dad's was dated 1st of this month and he had not then had anything from me. I don't know why Mrs. Randall (Evelyn's mother) wrote unless perhaps because of my recent birthday. It was nice of her to remember me. We are still in quarantine and are likely to be so for some time. But we are allowed out for exercise one hour each day. I look forward to this hour every day and hope it continues.

It *has* been stopped! The Germans are getting awkward again. Must be because they are losing the war. But it's rather hard on us.

Tuesday 21st March
They have relented and have let us out for an hour this afternoon. It was raining, snowing, hailstoning and blowing but I was determined to have my hour in the open. I had it and then returned to find that we are no longer in quarantine! We are still winning the war. The Russians are now in Rumania and are about 150 kilos across Poland. Everything comes to he who waits, Adolf, and the Russians are surely coming for you!

Wednesday 22nd March
Lettercards were issued today. I have written to Evelyn. I still owe letters to many people: Dad, Mrs. Randall, Mr. Godsell, Sheilah , Jenny and Pam, have all written to me and are waiting for answers.

The issue per month – sometimes – is only two lettercards and four postcards. This makes it very difficult if several people write to you. The Germans must be worrying about the war: they have issued three blankets to every Russian prisoner and issuing to them fuel for their hut stoves. A little late however to be human. Thousands of Russian prisoners have died of TB as a result of malnutrition and neglect. Do the Germans actually hope that their bad treatment of their eastern European prisoners will be forgotten? We prisoners of the western Allies are treated fairly well but those of other nationalities are given no more consideration than animals. But the day of reckoning is approaching. But it is unfair that the many Germans should pay for the wickedness of the few.

Saturday 25 March

The RAF was over last night and created a most life-like ersatz hell. The raid lasted almost an hour and although Leipzig, about twenty miles away, appeared to be the target, we could feel our buildings shaking. There was an explosion quite close to this camp but everybody here thinks it was merely a crashed fighter. The sound didn't seem loud enough to have been caused by a crashed bomber, or even a bomb. As I lay listening to the drone of our aircraft I thought of the children and old people, terrified and being maimed and killed and made homeless. Why does this man-made hell have to continue? It is so stupid – and at the same time so bloody and cruel. How much longer have these people got to be so cruelly destroyed. How much longer?

Sunday 26th March

Have just written to Dad and Jenny (postcards). I've told Dad that I've written to him several times. I hope Jenny doesn't get her card before he receives his.

Wednesday 29th March

We're in quarantine again: Diphtheria again. Oh well, we've had a week of fresh air and exercise. We expect to be cooped-up for at least ten days so we'd better not get depressed yet. During our isolation perhaps our invasion will take place and break the monotony – also the German heart!

I have not had any mail for over a week now and I'm looking forward to receiving Evelyn's next letter. What would my life be like without her letters to look forward to? Receiving one is like a rest after a long climb: a drink after a long thirst – but I'm beginning to wax monotonous. Most of the other blokes obscure their dreams and longings in card-playing and verbal reminiscing : 'who can tell the biggest'? And I've heard some 'big' ones.

Friday 31st March

Have just received three letters: two from Pam and one from Ruth. Ruth has just married Norman Metcalf. Really it doesn't seem so long ago that she was sobbing on my shoulder, sad and broken hearted apparently. I put my arm around her and hugged her and told her how sorry I was that she was so unhappy because of me. But I don't think I was really very concerned. She could have been no more than seventeen and, I believed, in search of romance. I was on leave and visiting the area only because Evelyn lives there. Oh Evelyn, if you knew this terrible longing I have for you! A little boy may cry for what he wants but a man must suffer and want in silence. But I am not alone: there are countless others waiting and wanting. But our time is coming: some day, Evelyn, you and I will be together and I shall spend my life trying to make your wait worth while.

Sunday 2nd April

There is a lot of unrest in the camp today. W.O. Meyers has suggested that from 15th of this month – when the issue of fuel ends – we will go on communal feeding with the food from the Red Cross parcels. We are all cynical. We know what a racket it will become. There will be a black market trading with the Germans and all of those who can barter with the racketeers. Without fuel, we are aware that tea, coffee, and cocoa will have to be prepared in the central cookhouse, but the other Red Cross food, which is already cooked, we would rather have straight out of the can. These food parcels are individual and are intended to be issued individually. Meyers means well but he is an RAF pilot who has not been a prisoner long enough to know about camp racketeering. The cooks and committee he has appointed are experienced food racketeers. They learned how to do it in the Italian prison camps.

I've just received a letter dated 13th March from Evelyn. I wish it were possible to express my feeling for her. There is insufficient space on the issued lettercards but if they were larger there would be more censors on the camp staff than there are guards. Roll on the day when I may write as much as I like to her and to have only her read it. In this last letter she says she had been with Ruth. Ruth, she tells me, wasn't looking very bright. I wonder why? Is she not happy with Norman? But I wonder what Evelyn would think if she knew the nonsense that's going through my head! Poor Evelyn! She doesn't know it but for some time I'm going to be her baby. Evelyn, my darling – or should I say, 'Mummy'!

Tuesday 4th April

I've just written to Evelyn and Pam. I was at first undecided whether to write to Pam or to Evelyn's mother but finally decided on Pam because Eve's Mum will be told by Evelyn that I've received her letter where as Pam may only hear of me direct and the last time I wrote to her was on 2nd February. I like Pam and mustn't neglect her.

The news in general is good but we are said to have lost 90 bombers in a raid on an industrial town. Apparently over 900 bombers took part in the raid but 10% is a large loss. If our offensive doesn't take place soon we will be talking of our offensive next spring! We have learned that a large part of the southern coast of England has been cleared as from the 1st of this month. Surely this means that the stage is being set!

There is a rumour that we will be out of quarantine tomorrow. I hope that this is so: this being continuously cooped up is getting on everybody's nerves. The typhus has been checked. There have been 15 British cases but none was fatal and there is only one still ill.

Yesterday a RAF fellow died of a bullet wound. He was shot by a sentry whilst trying to steal coal. The RAF lads have been considering this coal stealing as bit of a lark. It is no longer a lark!

Wednesday 5th April

The news is very good. The Russians are well into Rumania proper and there is little opposition. General Tito with his Yugoslav force is doing well and has established contact with Bagdolio's Italian guerrillas in the north east of Italy. Bagdolio has advised the Hungarians and the Rumanians to capitulate.

Armistice terms have been offered to them by the Allies. Bagdolio (Italian) has offered them his assistance. This latter item evoked a rousing cheer from the lads in this hut. Bagdolio was in command of the Italians when, with 300,000 men he attacked the British 30,000 in the Libyan desert. Nearly all of his army were captured. But he escaped. But his heart is in the right place: he's not a fascist. These poor unwanted Italians. No one has any time for them. Education, decent government and time are what they need. But who am I to rant about another nation: the British working class have been as much puppets as the Italians, only a little more educated. Most of us can read and write. Well, nearly!

It has been said that the Germans, to combat one of our raids, sent out old obsolete fighter aircraft. Apparently many of these were shot down. And we lost 30 bombers.

As good as the news is we believe the whole of the situation has not been told to us. Major White, British medical officer, I've been told, censors the news before we get it. Indiscriminate blabbing on our part would upset our prison camp Germans if they have lost relatives in our bombing raids. Most of 'our' Germans are aware that the end can't be far distant and are inclined to be easy with us, but some of them show a vicious hatred toward us, after all Hitler told them they were the best! It would be silly to taunt them: here, at least, they still hold the weapons. Major White's action is a commonsense precaution.

There are rumours about that our Camp Government has, in secret (in this camp!!), everything prepared for the end. R.S.M. Carr is said to have been appointed OC troops as we have no officers in camp other than padres and doctors. When the collapse does come we will need a good leader to prevent confusion occurring. Most of us are worried about the apparent tension between the Allies and the Russians. We are afraid the Russians might reach us before we can be evacuated by Allied troops. To anyone who doesn't understand, this attitude of ours would seem silly, but as we have had one great disappointment in Italy another couldn't be stood by any of us, hence the necessity to have some sort of organization planned before the Germans abandon the reins. Our spirits are high. We think the war could end any week. Well, the sooner the better. Every week is a week too long.

I've just received a letter from Evelyn, dated 21st March. This is the quickest I've received so far. At the time of her writing it, the latest letter she had received from me was dated 16th Jan. She has told me that an announcement has been made advising that only next-of-kin and those really close should write to prisoners. This is a bit of a blow but it won't be bad so long as she writes to me. She is my acting next-of-kin. But I believe really that this is merely an appeal to ease the work of the censors.

We have just been let out of quarantine.

Thursday 6th April

I've just received two letters from Sheilah, dated 6th and 14th March. She thanks me for the lettercard which she has received but after checking up I find that I haven't sent her any lettercards while I've been in Germany. She must be alluding to one which I sent from Italy but if this is the case it must have taken a long time to reach her. Jimmy Brown has just received his first next-of-kin parcel since he's been in Germany. He gave me a massive chunk of chocolate: good stuff, too. Rowntrees milk! An announcement was made last night that 170,000 parcels were destroyed by fire at Geneva. Mine would be in that lot I suppose!

Saturday 8th April

Postcards have been issued and I've written to Evelyn's mum and to Sheilah. The weather is glorious today – there isn't a cloud in the sky. The news is still favourable but our invasion has not happened yet. Soon, perhaps! Surely it must happen soon. There is a tale going around us prisoners that the invasion is being held up because of the striking miners. I don't believe this. The British miner has never been noted for his intelligence but neither is he without loyalty to his country in its hour of need. And also to the miners – hundreds of them – who are in the Yorkshire, Durham and Scottish regiments. But I'm sure this is only a stupid rumour.

Sunday 9th April

Three years ago I was at Castle Cary. How I wish that I were there now! It is one of the nicest places I have been stationed as a soldier. Quiet and pretty – and reasonably close to Poole, too. One day I shall have to go back there on a visit. Perhaps it would be nice to go there to spend a few days of my first leave. Also, of course, I could visit Bath. I must, of course, spend some time with my Dad at Pelton in Durham, but I want to be with Evelyn as soon as possible. However, my arrangements will be dictated by circumstances. But that's all in the semi-indefinite future. Our weather is still holding good. it would be awful if operations were held up because of bad weather. I was talking to Harry Simmons today – he's a wireless engineer – and I tried to sound him out on the news situation. All I learned was that the situation is still good but he, Harry, doesn't think anything spectacular will happen until the Rumanian business has been finally settled. Also, he 'suggested' that we may hear something about raids on the French coast in a few days' time. Is this merely surmise on his part or does he know something? I wonder!

Tuesday 11th April

We've been on fatigues all day. We've been moving barrack fittings, blankets and palliasses from the outer to the inner perimeter. Some Italians have been living in the hut and consequently the blankets etc. are alive with fleas and lice. When we'd finished we were allowed a bath and our clothing was disinfested.

Last night's news was good: the Russians have entered Czecho-Slovakia and are going forward. Today's rumour has it that Odessa has fallen. I've been talking to Jimmy Brown and he tells me that the German newspapers admit the fall of Odessa. The article states that they, the Germans, have their backs to the wall!

Monday 17th April

Lettercards have been issued and I've written to Evelyn. It is more than a fortnight since I received my last letter but as there were few letters last week I can't really complain. The news is good and there is a rumour that Sevastopol has fallen to the Russians. We were re-registered this morning. The Germans believe that some privates are masquerading as NCOs[4]. They're right – but failed to find any!

Tuesday 18th April

The news has it that there is fighting in the streets of Sevastopol. Since the news must be two days old when we get it, I think it is safe to say that Sevastopol has already fallen. Another step towards victory. The air of expectancy that was over the camp a week ago has gone. What brought it into the camp? Perhaps it was the spring: Easter! New hopes for old, and Easter has gone – and with it our hopes for an early end of the war! For months we waited for the spring, feeling that something spectacular would be done by the waiting force in England. Now we are in the middle of our hoped-for period and nothing has happened and now we are in a hell of depression. We are winning the war and we know it, but when! I am thirty; getting older and looking older. And my hair has been going for some time. My poor Evelyn will be shocked, I'm sure, when she sees me. And disappointed. But her disappointment will be mine also. Who am I feeling sorry for: Evelyn or myself? Stone walls do not a prison make... Sound philosophy perhaps. If you are on the outside!

---

[4] Geneva Convention: NCO prisoners must not be compelled to work.

Saturday 22nd April

There has been very little mail this week. And none of it has been for me. Next week, perhaps? There is nothing spectacular in the way of news. Sevastopol has not yet fallen – but must very soon. It is a sort of German 'Dunkirk' and they are trying to evacuate as much as they can. Our expected invasion from England is mentioned in almost every bulletin but not a hint of the date or place. Meanwhile we are still waiting: where? when?

Monday 24th April

There has been no news today owing to there being a technical problem with our secret wireless. Our next bulletin will be read tomorrow. And what will it be? It has been so consistently good for the past year that it takes something really big to boost our feelings. But the Armistice will stir us – when it comes.

Tuesday 25th April

Postcards were issued today and I've written to Dad and to Evelyn. It seems ages since I received any letters but we are all in the same boat. However some mail has come today so perhaps I shall be lucky.

At the bath-house today I saw some Russians who had just come out of the shower. They were naked and were waiting for their bodies to dry in the air (they have no towels). What a disturbing sight they were! Nothing but skin and bone; impossible to describe on paper. Skin stretched tightly over their ribs; stomachs distended like bladders. No flesh where their buttocks should have been. No one would believe that any human beings could treat their fellow men as the Germans are treating these Russians. But, so we are told, it is simply tit for tat as far as the Germans are concerned.

Saturday 29th April

Some days ago 'Sailor' Haynes managed to scrounge some ink from somewhere and he gave it to me. (Many years ago 'Sailor' came to our regiment from a Dr. Barnardo's Home so I have known him a long time.) Now I can make my entries in ink again. But I'm feeling depressed again: I've had no letters and we've had no news as our wireless isn't functioning.

Nearly everyone has had his next-of-kin parcel but I'm still waiting for mine. Jimmy Brown thinks he stands a good chance of being repatriated. Some medical staff are going and Jimmy was our battalion medical sergeant. I hope he will be lucky enough to go. He'll be able to visit, or at least write to Evelyn. I would like him to let her know that we were captured by the Germans and not the Italians as she may believe as we were first of all prisoners in Italy. It may appear to be a trivial thing but all of us have some pride! He could send my photo to her. Also to my Dad. And, perhaps, to Pam. I don't suppose Evelyn would mind. Oh when is this blasted war going to end?

Sunday 30th April

A very sad thing happened today. With Jimmy Brown and John Vincent I was walking around the football ground while a couple of German aircraft were manoeuvring rather dangerously. For some time now these planes have been diving over the camp and we've been nervous and expecting something nasty to happen. The pilots seemed to think it was great fun to skim the ground and frighten us. Well, it happened today. The aircraft swooped over the field a few feet above ground level. When it started to rise its tail skimmed the ground. Two RAF lads who were walking just in front of us were hit by it. The head and shoulder of one of these lads were taken off and the other lad was left in a writhing heap. One killed and the other with multiple fractures. As we were so very close we were naturally very shaken. Jimmy went to get stretcher bearers and I took John back to his barrack room. He was very upset. He's only twenty and though he was one of a crew of a shot-down bomber, he'd never seen anything so ghastly as this.

Today is a National day of prayer for the Germans. Apparently they believe God could do much more for them than he has so far done. They are out of luck because if God exists then surely he is on our side. That must be so – we are winning! Tomorrow is a German holiday celebrating the National Socialist Party's coming to power. It will be their last celebration.

Wednesday 3rd May

I received a letter from Jenny today. It was nice and jovial and she finished it off with love and a few kisses. Cousinly affection! I wonder? This evening I've been given a Ticket for a Personal Parcel. I wonder if it's the next-of-kin Evelyn has sent or is it cigarettes from somebody. I'm hoping it will be a next-of-kin.

Thursday 4th May

The parcel is a next-of-kin from Evelyn. In it are just the things I need: socks, razor blades, tooth paste, tooth brushes, and other much needed articles. Lettercards were issued today so I am able to acknowledge receipt of the parcel immediately. I had a spare postcard which Ron Briton gave to me so I've used it to write to Ruth.

Saturday 6th May

We have just had the news: Although it is good our invasion seems to be as far off as ever. But they are talking of the feint attacks which will be made before the invasion proper takes place. But this is all so frustrating. We know we are winning but the thought of having to stay here another year which seems quite likely to be the case is most depressing. I am thirty years of age and going bald. What will Evelyn think when she sees me? If she waits that long and she's waited three years already. There is nothing now but a spiritual link and I'm so afraid the war is going to stretch it to breaking point. What then?

Tuesday 9th May

I've just repaired my pen. That is, I've had it in pieces and have washed and cleaned all of the bits. It appears to be working very well, too. I wonder how long it will last. I'm still waiting for some letters. A few days ago I received one from Bella, a very old one. It is now five or six weeks since I received my last letter from Evelyn. I wonder when we'll receive the next batch? The stopping of the airmail is rather a blow. The news is very good and the weather has changed for the better. Perhaps we'll have the invasion soon.

Wednesday 10th May

Another glorious day. There isn't a cloud in the sky this morning and there is a gentle breeze blowing just sufficient to keep us cool. It seems the German people believe that our invasion will take place today! I hope they are right. Apparently they base this fear on today being the 4th anniversary of their march into Belgium. Well, the weather is ideal for a channel-crossing. We in this camp are all hoping that advantage is being taken of it.

Postcards have been issued and I've written to Evelyn and Margaret.

Thursday 11th May

There was no news read out last night but it seems definite that Sevastopol has fallen at last. I've received a letter from Dad dated 30th March. At the time of his writing he had received three cards from me. One of these was written before Christmas.

According to today's newspaper a State of Emergency has been proclaimed in this country. People are no longer being allowed to move from place to place without permission. And there is a 10pm curfew. The war is gathering speed. How long now?

Sunday 14th May

We don't have the news read out in this billet now. The last night he was here our news reader noticed a Dutchman amongst us and it is a ruling, in the interest of our secret wireless, that no bulletins will be read if there is a 'foreign body' present. It doesn't really matter: the news will be passed to us from the other billets. Last night's news was good. The Russians have just seen off 150,000 Germans. The Allied forces in Italy are on the move and, according to neutral observers, the German defence in Italy is broken. In the Far East 250,000 Japanese face annihilation as they are absolutely cut off. Roll-on!

Monday 15th May

I was on fire-watch duty last night so I went back to bed after breakfast.
The weather changed suddenly during the night and we had a down-pour of
rain which lasted several hours. It was cloudy and windy until after four this
afternoon and then the sun started to shine. The news is still very good but
there are no letters.

Tuesday 16th May

Lettercards were issued so I've written to Evelyn.

Wednesday 17th May

The camp was visited today by the Protective Power's representative.
He inspected our billet and asked about tea-making facilities. He was
accompanied by several senior German officers. Tomorrow I start my 13th
year in the Army. I mentioned this to some fellows today and one of them, a
Canadian, said, "Say, fellah, you haven't been in the Army that long – you
aren't old enough!" Perhaps I'm looking younger than my years.

Thursday 18th May

Have just received a letter from Sheilah. She doesn't tell me much but it was
nice of her to think of me. I wonder why Sheilah, Pam, and Jenny are so
kind. They all know I'm engaged to Evelyn and therefore out of matrimonial
circulation. Have I charm? or are they just sorry for me! ! ! But when I am
back in England I must try this 'charm' lark. It's unknown territory to me
– I've been out of circulation since I was twenty.

Friday 19th May

The weather has changed again and we have had beautiful weather all day. I
prefer hot weather. I feel very tired tonight. I didn't sleep well last night so
intend to make up for it tonight. I am just waiting for the news and then I'm
going to bed.

Wednesday 24th May

Yesterday and today the weather has been very cold. The wind from the
north has made it too unpleasant to spend much time out of doors. There is
nothing much in the way of news. Everything seems to be going well but not
spectacularly so. The latest news is that the King has inspected the parachute
regiment and the commandos. Perhaps something is going to happen soon.
He inspected us before we left England. A sort of a 'Fond farewell'! Also
he made a speech concerning us just before we were captured. But is the
invasion about to happen? And if so, when. We are all so tired of it all.

Saturday 27th May
Nothing much happening and still no mail. The news: According to last night's news our troops in Italy have broken through at Anzio and the Canadians have broken through the Hitler Line, wherever that is, and are pouring masses of armour through. The Italian Patriots, with British officers, and the French Patriots are doing well. The Russians are lined up with the largest force they have had in the war so far and are well equipped and ready.

Sunday 25th May
Three years ago I had my last phone call with Evelyn. She wasn't aware of it but she was the last civilian I spoke to in England. Neither did she know that while I was speaking to her my battalion was all formed up ready to march off to the station. And that was three years ago. What an age of time it has seemed.

Some of our bombers were over today: about forty. Dresden appeared to be their target. They all flew over in formation and all of them dropped their bombs on a signal from the leader. What a wonderful sight it was! And what a deliciously devastating rumble of exploding bombs we heard! Even the French prisoners here were impressed – and those jelly-spined latin bastards are pro-German. The other nationalities in the camp were jubilant. These poor Germans: does anybody like them? And I don't think the Frenchmen like them all that much.

Monday 29th May
Embarked at Greenock three years ago today. We've had some more of our bombers over today – several hundreds of them. A lot of 'flak' was thrown at them and one was shot down. One of the survivors, an American, is in our camp hospital. He can't believe his luck. Tonight's news is good but other than the heavy bombing there is nothing of importance. However our side seems to be building up for a big event. Surely it must come soon.

Thursday 1st June
I've just received two letters from Evelyn and one from Pam. Evelyn's latest is dated 1st April and Pam's 2nd April. Evelyn's is a wonderful letter. So loving and sweet.

Friday 2nd June
I've just written to Evelyn. It is so much easier to write a letter after receiving one. The news is quite good but it seems there's some disagreement between Britain and America regarding an interim Government for France after the invasion. Britain wants to put in a government under de Gaulle but the Americans would prefer to have Eisenhower. I would have expected it to go to a Frenchman. Certainly not an American. But why can't they stop this squabbling and get on with the job. We are half way through the year now!

Saturday 3rd June
According to last night's news there is still friction between Britain and America regarding a leader for the French Government. It is time they stopped this nonsense and got on with the job. Yesterday's newspaper quoted the American magazine *Time* as saying that Churchill has asked Roosevelt and Stalin to agree to hold up the invasion until 1945. Personally I can't imagine Churchill suggesting any such thing. Anyway, I hope it isn't true.

Sunday 4th June
Of all the blasted cheek! The German Officer Commanding had us do a 'march-past'. Eleven thousand of us were obliged to 'march-past' him and give him an 'Eyes-right'. Why it was demanded of us is a mystery. He's got his own army to play with if he wants to play soldiers. Anyway, we showed how it's done. We are the smartest army he is likely to see. But I'm depressed – no joking! Last year when the Germans brought us from Italy we thought the war was almost over. We consoled ourselves: just a matter of months, we told ourselves. But it's now nine months since Italy capitulated and though we know the Germans are beaten they are not showing it very clearly. The German leaders are hiding behind their people. Every one of them seems prepared to fight to the 2nd last German!

Tuesday 6th June
Allied troops are occupying Rome. Although this was announced to us last night it may have happened some days ago. I'm inclined to believe that our wireless buffs keep back the news from us until after it has been made known to the German people. Other than this activity in Italy the war seems to be free-wheeling again. According to camp reports the Germans are not taking the Italian situation very well. And they must have worse to follow.

   Rumour! The Allies have invaded France again. That's several times this year but it is said to be true this time. But I'm afraid to believe it.

   IT HAS HAPPENED! ! ! the Invasion is on! But we are all taking it quietly. As yet the Germans don't know that we know. And of course a lot of Germans won't know yet but they soon will. I've just seen and heard a Frenchman running round in circles, shouting his head off, "La guerre est fini. Vive la France", and he's a bit premature: the cheeky plonker! I must go and try to find my Dutch friend. Yesterday when I was talking to him and the invasion was mentioned, he sighed and said, "It is just a beautiful dream!" I must go and find him and tell him dream has come true. If he doesn't already know. According to the excitement in the Russian compound I think they must know.

Wednesday 7th June
I found the Dutchman. He was bubbling over with excitement. He took my hand and pranced around me like a fairy. He's no fairy. He's over six feet tall

and about a yard across the shoulders. He was as delighted as a child who's been promised a trip to the seaside. "I will go to England," he told me, "and I will marry a beautiful English lady with two childs and I will be happy for ever!" Perhaps this dream also will come true for him.

Thursday 8th June

I've received a parcel of books – five *Everymans* volumes – from Doris. I haven't got them yet. They're being censored so it may be a week before I get them.

The invasion is going well. The Cherbourg Peninsula is about to be cut off, I think. This will be rather good as Cherbourg is an important port. According to the news last night our tanks were operating almost as soon as our troops had landed. Will the war end this year?

Friday 9th June

I have just written postcards to Doris and Pam. I wonder why it is that I feel so awkward when I write to Doris?

Our forces in France and Italy are doing well but nothing much seems to be happening in Russia. In France we seem to have a consistent depth of fifteen kilos for a good length of the coast. There are several rumours which have it that our convoys are now sailing in the Mediterranean and also in the English Channel. This information is said to have come from the Swiss Radio. We'll see later!

Sunday 11th June

The 50th Division is in action in France. There must be many new faces in it since I was captured. It was mentioned in the news last night. Montgomery in an Order of the Day congratulated the division on the good work done in the landing in France. The 50th does it again! France 1940, Tmimi, Gazala, and Marath 1942, Sicily 1943, and now France again! The war is as good as over!

Tuesday 13th June

The war in France seems to be progressing satisfactorily but the Germans don't seem to have suffered any big losses yet. But they have in Italy. Since the fall of Rome they admit having lost 70,000 men. And now their 14th Army in Italy is cut off and scattered. In their prison camp newspaper they say it would be superfluous to explain to us why they will win! We, too, think so!

Saturday 17th June

Lettercards were issued today and I've written to Evelyn. I got my books today and I've put brown paper covers on them. The war is going nicely but not all that fast. However, according to our generals, we're in a position to make a big offensive in France. We here believed it had already been started! Perhaps they are waiting for the next big Russian offensive. Now *they* DO make big offensives! Big things are expected.

The Germans are sending pilotless aircraft across to England but so far they don't appear to have done much damage. But we would say that, wouldn't we? Our Camp Government has issued instructions regarding what we must do in the event of an armistice. Are these instructions their own idea or have the Germans suggested it?

Wednesday 21st June
A man has just been shot and killed. He was reaching through a fence to pick some wild strawberries and a German soldier drew his pistol and shot him. Deliberately! From just a few feet. It is an inside fence which wires off a Russian workshop. The murdering bastard: shooting to kill for such a trivial reason. But their day is coming! Our bombers are over today. I hope their bombs are not being wasted. Finland is nearly finished and Cherbourg is surrounded. 'Der Tag' cannot be far distant.

Monday 26 June
Postcards to Evelyn and Sheilah. I have not received any letters from Evelyn since 10th of this month but the mail isn't coming in very well this month. The news is good. Cherbourg is very nearly ours if it isn't already. We are expecting a big offensive in France soon and the Russian push started some days ago.

I went to the French Theatre this evening. Ron Briton got tickets for Eric Buckley, Jerry, and myself. It was an orchestral concert but it wasn't very good. The atmosphere was stifling: perhaps that put off the musicians, although the 1st violin and the viola were very good but I think they were both Dutchmen.

Tuesday 27th June
Cherbourg is ours!

Wednesday 28th June
The news is very good tonight. On the Russian front 5 German divisions have surrendered and there are five cut off. The Russian thrusts are converging on Minsk. In France the British and American forces are doing well. We have been warned that some men will leave this camp in a few days. The names of the unfortunates were drawn out of a hat. Seventy two will be leaving this hut. Jerry and I are lucky and are staying here. Exactly two years ago tonight I was making good Germans, ie, I sprayed them, with noticeable effect, with my 'tommy-gun'. Tonight, on three fronts thousands of good Germans are being made. A stupid, brutal nation: who

can sympathize with them? But this is awful and I should not have written it. They are just as much victims as the people on either side.

Sunday 2nd July

When I started this 2nd book (note book) of this prison camp diary I fully expected the war to end before I had filled it. I was wrong. Although the war is moving faster now the end still seems to be some time away. When is it going to end. I have asked that so many times. Sometimes we are optimistic and set a few weeks during which it might happen. Other times, in gloomy mood, we think of a year or more. Yesterday morning a batch of Dutchmen were brought in. One of them boasted of having heard the BBC only a few days ago. But we have the BBC news every night! It helps to keep us cheerful. Last night's news had it that the Russians were effectively carving up the Germans. Keep up the good work, Joe! There are still too many Germans.

And now I must start on my third – and, possibly, last – notebook.

Start of 3rd notebook

Tuesday 4th July
I've just written a lettercard to Evelyn. I wonder how many of these letters and cards will reach their addressees? Not many, I'd be willing to bet. In the recent issue of *The Camp*, the Germans have informed us that owing to the Portuguese ships not being allowed to call at the southern ports of France the transporting of parcels for prisoners of war has ceased. However, in Switzerland, a supply of food parcels is available. These should be sufficient for six months. Perhaps the war will end before these have been consumed.

Last night's news was good. The Russians are said to be only 350 kilos from East Prussia. In a very short time we ought to be seeing them sweep across Poland and into Germany. Our western offensive seems to be about to start in France. It has been said that our combined bomber forces (British/American) will be used for this offensive alone and not used in the smallest degree for reprisal raids on the 'flying bomb' sites. It looks as though we intend to blast our way through the Germans and follow with a steel wall of tanks and guns. We've been told that Germany has lost about 150,000 men as prisoners during the last couple of weeks. The steel ring is tightening: Germany is being strangled.

My nerves are becoming worse. I can hardly write legibly now. What is causing it, I wonder? However, I shall have to put up with it until the war has ended. Perhaps I ought to do some work of some sort. In Italy I studied English and wrote essays. The latter may not have been of any literary value but at least they gave me something to think about. I am sure the mental effort must have been good for me. I wonder if I could do something like that now? Not writing: I've nothing to write about. Rather an ungratifying state. What can I do about it – instead of this pointless rambling. Classes are difficult because of the dearth of text books. Those enrolling must be prepared to write down word for word everything said by the lecturer: I discovered that in a photography class which was supposed to be for beginners but when I joined I found myself surrounded by professionals and very experienced amateurs. But I'm moaning too much.

Tuesday, same evening We have just had the news: Minsk is in Russian hands! The Germans are said to be surrendering to the Russians by whole battalions but no other details were given. Their morale must be completely broken. Of course the awfulness of their situation can't be exaggerated. There are so many millions of Russians that they can simply swamp the Germans, so the Germans, where possible, are simply retreating before they become engulfed. And our armies in Italy are doing well and our offensive in

France is smashing the Germans there also. This year could be the last year of the war.

Thursday 6 th July

The speed of the war seems to have slowed down rather but of course it is still going in our favour. Today Churchill made a statement concerning the 'flying bomb'. Up to date 2,600 have been projected but many of these failed to reach England. The casualties caused by those which reached their objectives amounted to about 2,700 killed and 8,000 injured. These figures may seem high but are small when compared with the casualties inflicted on the Germans by the Anglo-American bombing on their cities. The German newspapers are claiming that these flying bombs are inflicting death and destruction all over the south of England.

Hitler is making a speech almost every day. Today he tells the Germans they will win the war: their technicians are making this possible. But I doubt if the people are impressed. Our camp Germans seem as happy as we are when our side has had a major victory. At the same time they seem to have a very virile hate for us. Not so long ago one of our fellows was shot as he went through an open window of his barrack in daylight! He was merely taking a shortcut. And they are really brutal with the Russians. They are kicked and punched and bashed over the head with pistols and rifles for merely begging from us scraps of bread, potato peelings, etc. We British and Allied prisoners are receiving Red Cross parcels and can afford to give a little away. The Germans insist that if we have spare food this must be distributed through the organized channel. This is done, of course, through the British padres who give it to the senior Russian medical officer. The Italians as well as the Russians benefit this way.

We are still awaiting the details of the fall of Minsk. It would be interesting to know how many men Germany has lost there, and with no reserve replacements. Hitler and his mates must be absolutely mad to continue when they are losing so uselessly.

Friday 7th July

Swarms of our bombers have just passed overhead. There must have been at least a thousand. They were flying from the direction of Berlin but, overhead they changed direction to the southwest indicating Leipzig to be one of their targets.

Evening, same day We have just heard the news: Hitler has sacked his western front commander when he, the commander, said Germany could not possibly win the war now and that further resistance would be futile. So Hitler sacked him. Germany's situation now is likened to that of 1918's situation. Even worse! Today's bomber objective WAS Leipzig!

A couple of days ago an escape tunnel from the recreation hut was discovered by the Germans. It was worked from the recreation hut to a field just beyond the wire. Unfortunately when the wheat was being cut the tractor went through the tunnel roof. Apparently it was such a good tunnel: properly timbered by the use of bedboards which the Germans had assumed had been burnt as firewood. It had electric lighting and also a ventilation fan. But the camp commandant has been very decent about it. Initially several of the lads concerned were put in close arrest but were then let out. One of them was a Green Howard. As he slept in the hut the Germans assumed that he knew about the tunnel. Of course he knew nothing at all about any escape plan! There was no punishment: apparently the commandant was rather intrigued by their effort and workmanship. Also, he himself, had been a prisoner during the 1st World War. He's not a bad sort of bloke, really. It's the shower of bastards under his command who are the trouble. But one or two of them are not so bad. An older one, about sixty, was in here this morning drinking tea with us. We wish there were more like him.

Sunday 9th July
The news is good tonight. The Russians are fighting in the streets of Wilna and it is thought that the fall of the city is imminent. Also, Pinsk is surrounded and is expected to fall soon. Three more German generals have surrendered to the Russians. One of these was commanding the 41st Panzer Division. A whole panzer division will be an awful loss to the eastern front German army. Junior generals don't matter much on a front as extensive as the Russian front.

Our offensive in France is progressing satisfactorily and the Germans have moved their HQ from Paris to Nancy. Won't be long now – we hope!

Monday 10th July
Wilna has fallen and the Russians are now only 145 kilos from Eastern Prussia. The Russians now believe the war to be in its final stage. It has already taken a long time but it seems the end is approaching. It can't last much longer without the German nation being completely wiped out. And really, they deserve this no more than we do. Both sides have believed lies about the other. In France our armies are smashing them. It must be horrible for the German troops. They have nothing to back them up. Their air force is practically non-existent now. They are being slaughtered vainly protecting the Austrian rat who ought to be burned. Good lives are being thrown away in what is really a delaying tactic to save their mad leader who holds the lever of power. But this lever is shortening: he is losing the advantage of its fulcrum. His advantage of power is decreasing rapidly.

Postcards have been issued but I won't write mine until tomorrow. Writing! Mine is becoming worse. It will soon be illegible. But trying to write neatly is so much trouble and encourages insincerity. We write, they say, as we live. I'm nervous so I suppose it shows in my writing. This, of course shouldn't matter: nobody will ever read this nonsense.

Tuesday 11th July

Have just written my postcards to Dad and Evelyn. I ought to have written to Jenny but I felt that I must write to Evelyn to let her know I'd received a letter from her some days ago. Actually it's a week! I've received another letter from Pam: a surface letter, ie, not airmail. It's an affectionate letter. Much more so than it ought to be but then I suppose she must be affectionate to somebody. There is an urge to love and protect in all of us. But, in all, she knew me only a matter of weeks and our association amounted to no more than talking – and we were never alone!

The Russians have captured another German general. They are now a long way beyond Wilna and are rapidly getting closer to Germany proper. Soon!

Have just received a letter from Dad, dated 21st April. Apparently Emma was not married at Christmas. I believe she was too young anyway. She's not twenty yet. Apparently Fred is working now but Dad doesn't say what he's doing. It can't be much: he's only fourteen. I hope he doesn't go into mining. It's a rotten job with no future.

We have had no news tonight. The Germans had a search today which unfortunately coincided with the news reception. We can, of course, survive without news but it does cheer us to have our own news.

Thursday 13th July

A letter from Evelyn this morning dated 20th April. Almost three months to get here. Why do they take so long, I wonder? Evelyn's Dad is ill. That is, he was at the time of her writing. Pneumonia. But Evelyn says he is on the mend. Pneumonia in the Italian prison camps was nearly 100% fatal.

Saturday 15th July

There was no news last night. Some German SS men came on the 8pm check parade. Every British prisoner was asked a question. I was asked merely my name and number. Some were asked their civil occupation, when did they leave home, and how long had they been in the army. Apparently they merely wanted to hear us speak so that they could check up on our nationality.

There is a rumour going around that our Army in France have had to withdraw some distance owing to the Germans having flooded a certain area. We are all hoping that this can't be true.

LATER The rumour is partially true! The Germans have flooded a marshy area but there is no mention of any withdrawals. The Russians are pounding a town situated a few kilos east of the East Prussia border. They will soon be there! In the far east our forces are successfully carving up the Japs. Apparently there are 18,000 of them cut off without supplies or outside support. I was talking to a RAF bloke tonight. He was shot down over Berlin a few months ago.

Sunday 16th July

A sea-mail letter from Pam dated 30th April. She tells me that she detects sadness in my cards to her. Here I am, unselfishly trying to convince my friends that I am bubbling over with happiness and all they observe from my efforts is my sadness. But, apparently, only Pam notices this.

Our armies in France are still doing well but the Americans seem to be getting all of the publicity, as usual. The Russians are nearly, if not already, in East Prussia. The Germans say they are going to fight to the last in the Balkans. Their nation is being annihilated all to no purpose. Also it is rumoured that the Russians have started another offensive in the lower sector.

Thursday 20th July

It was my intention to make an entry last night but I was intercepted by Harry Beale and obliged to listen to him until 'lights-out'. Last night's news cheered us considerably. Our combined armies in France have started to push hard and are utilizing all of our available aircraft to do so. They are blasting their way through. The latest report has it that they crossed the River Orne.

In Italy our forces have taken Ancona and are advancing satisfactorily. The Russians have reached Brest-Litowsk and are fighting in the suburbs of that city. Next in line is Warsaw, a great blow to the Germans when they lose it. Monday's news told us of an MP who asked, 'What would happen in the event of a revolution in Germany?' Churchill's answer was that 'That possibility was being catered for.'

Yesterday morning an RAF bloke was slung into the camp pond by his comrades. It appears he predicted that the war would end on the 18th of this month. It didn't! So he was tried by Prisoner of War court martial and sentenced to be thrown into the pond. The sentence was carried out at 8am. He was strapped to a table-top and carried to the pond where his clothes were removed. Our band played the funeral march. His sentence was read out, and: one–two–three! was carried out. He swam to the edge and emerged. But the Germans didn't approve. They said it was a demonstration which was not allowed. They drew their pistols and made arrests – they have no sense of humour, these Germans – but eventually somebody managed to convince them that it was all fun and nothing political. But in their orders last night they said, 'duckings, in future, must NOT be accompanied by music!' So there! Suspicious people, aren't they?

Saturday 22nd July

Yesterday morning there was a rumour that somebody had tried to kill Hitler. We learned this morning that it is true. Fancy! Somebody doesn't like him! A general, it is said, was the culprit. Although some were killed or wounded, Hitler apparently was only slightly injured. And so the war must continue. The would-be assassin has been shot. Poor man, he meant well!

On Thursday morning we were 'blitzed' by the Gestapo. They took diaries, maps, anything they considered suspicious. It is believed they were looking for our wireless.

A captured German general (by the Russians) has made a speech to the German people[5]. He has advised them to end their struggle. Who is to blame him?

The Nazi High Command has stated that the generals must obey orders only if they are issued by Hitler, Göring, or Himmler. Put simply, it means that those three are fighting for their own lives and are hiding behind helpless women and children and old people huddled together in their demolished cities: And they're hiding behind the gallant fools who are being slaughtered in their thousands. Confucius said, 'He who rides a tiger cannot dismount.' I'll bet they're pondering this.

Have received letters from Evelyn and Pam. Pam tells me that my old battalion is, or was, on the south coast. Of course they'll be in France now. Evelyn is very sweet in her letter. I mentioned to her how I liked South Africa when I was there and asked her would she be prepared to go there with me after the war. She would agree, she says. Oh well, a possibility.

Sunday 23rd July

I've written post cards to Evelyn and Jenny. It is four months since I wrote to Jenny but I mustn't write to her too frequently because it makes Dad jealous.

The news isn't bad. The Russians are still doing exceptionally well and are – latest report – 110 miles from Warsaw. Nothing much however seems to be happening in France.

The German Army has now been banned from using the recognised military salute. Only the Nazi salute may be used.

Wednesday 26th July

We hear that the Russians are moving fast and are now only 80 kilos from Warsaw. The situation in Italy seems to be satisfactory and in France we started our new offensive yesterday morning. The RAF dropped 3,000 tons of bombs on Kiel and eleven more German generals have been captured by the Russians. Churchill has said that the present unrest in Germany might well end the war sooner than some people think!

I have been told that some June mail has arrived in camp.

Saturday 29th July

I have received no letters this week. Some airmail stuff has been received but there was none for me. I wonder when shall I receive my next?

---

[5] Russian Radio broadcast.

The Russians are still moving fast: the last report had them within 30 miles of Warsaw. Unfortunately our forces in France are not doing particularly well. The Americans have gained some ground in the St. Lo area but the British Army had to give back a little in the Caen sector. But when are we going to make a big advance, I wonder? Several times I've thought it had started but I've been wrong. Naturally of course the Allied intention will be to minimise our own casualties while doing our utmost to inflict the maximum of casualties on the enemy and wear him out. War is cruel! Left to it, of course, the Russians would beat the Germans alone now at this stage of the war but it would be nice to see the British and the American forces take a large part in the defeat of the enemy.

Monday 31st July

I have received a letter from Pam, dated 7th May. She doesn't say much about anything. 'Salute the Soldier Week', and her five weeks old kitten are all she mentions.

A rumour tells us that Riga has fallen and that Warsaw is about to fall. And the Russians have reached Cracow. This rumour may be 'just a rumour' but in any case it will soon be fact.

Tuesday 1st August

I have written a lettercard to Evelyn. Roll on the time when I shall be able to write anything I like to her and not have prying censors reading it all before she sees it. But when will that be? The silliest rumour came into our billet today: 'Armistice is going to be signed at 5pm today!' The time now is about 3.30. Only an hour and a half to go! But this rumour has come from the Dutch prisoners. All of the good rumours come from the Dutch, the French, or the Swiss radio, purportedly. None of them having been correct so far, I'm not holding my breath for this one. But, regardless, the war must end soon anyway. The Russians will soon have reached Germany and, so far, nothing has stopped them. At their present rate of advance the Russians will be here in a couple of weeks.

Here at IVb Stalag, we are all worried lest the Russians reach this camp before the British or the American forces get here. Although the Russians are war-time allies of the West there is an obvious antagonism and distrust between them and the west and we prisoners are rather afraid that they, the Russians, will use us as bargaining counters. Churchill would not agree to Russia taking over Germany in which case Britain and America could go to war against Russia to prevent this happening which would be unfortunate for us prisoners, were we on the wrong side of the line.

But about the last rumour: the armistice! It is now six o clock in the evening and the war would still appear to be in progress. The poor Dutchman has lost his bet and will now have to be thrown into the pond. All authors of rumours, when identified, are thrown into the pond.

3rd August

The Russians still appear to be scrapping around Warsaw but will soon have the city, I think. In France the Americans are going for Rennes. When they take that they will not have much further to go before they will have cut off all of the Germans in the Finisterre peninsula. Apparently Germany has two new weapons: a long-range rocket, and an ME 109 which will carry an explosive packed JU-88 fuselage. I can't see this latter contraption doing much! While its power of destruction may be terrific, to reach its target it must avoid our fighter aircraft. Still, it's a menace! But the war will last several months yet, I think. My optimism fluctuates with the news.

Last night I attended a lecture on Immigration and Life in Canada. It seems to be a wonderful country for those who are willing to work there – but not for me: I'm sure I wouldn't like their near arctic climate.

Friday 4th August

Rennes has fallen to the Americans.
Yesterday I received a letter from dad, dated 10th May. He doesn't tell me much. Fred, he says, is now working in the local cinema operating box. This is a good clean job and I hope he can keep it.

The latest report has it that our forces in France are now 20 miles south and east (or west?) of Rennes. The Brest peninsula is rapidly being cut off.

Sunday 6th August

A batch of British and Amercan prisoners were brought in yesterday. They were captured in the early days of the Normandy invasion. My own battalion has been cut up a number of times since I was captured and, I've been told, there are not a score of its original members left.

I am depressed this morning. I have a cold coming on. And the end of the war seems to be as far away as ever. It seems such a long time since I received my last letter from Evelyn and I want one so much.

Monday 7th August

I am still waiting for letters but the news is good. We now have the whole of the Brest Peninsula and we have two thrusts heading for Paris. Warsaw is still in German hands but the Russian force is now 130 kilos west of the city.

My cold is rather bad and I've been between my blankets all day – now 5.30pm – but I'm going for a walk around the recreation ground. It might clear my head. At present it feels as though it's full of cotton wool.

Tuesday 8th August

I've written postcards to Evelyn and Margaret. It's fifteen months since I received my last letter from the latter and I don't know why she has stopped writing to me. I have told her that I will write to her periodically until I can go to Castle Cary. That is, of course, unless she writes to tell me not to do so.

I'm still waiting for a letter from Evelyn. I have checked up and find that I received my last letter from her on 22nd of last month.

Thursday 10th August

I am still waiting for a letter from Evelyn. It's about three weeks since I received my last letter from her – and that was written in April. It is weak of me, I know but I can't help it: she is all I have.

Friday 11th August

I received four letters last night: one from Evelyn dated 15th July, and three from Pam, dated 31st May, 4th June, and 2nd July. Evelyn's letter bucked me wonderfully. I wonder is it possible for anyone to want anything as much as I want Evelyn! Oh, how I want her! In her letter she says she is going to Weston-Super-Mare for a holiday. She says she wishes we were going on OUR holiday – our honeymoon. She wants to marry me as soon as possible. That suits me: I'd marry her on the dock where I am disembarked if that were practicable. But I shall marry her one day if she doesn't change her mind when she sees me. Time has not been kind to me since she last saw me. Rapidly I am going bald and there are many lines on my face which were not there when she last saw me. Taken at face-value, I'm in debt. But I must wait and see. Today I learned that Vic Grey, a fellow prisoner, was in the same artillery unit as my cousin, Tommy Beadling. He told me Tommy was awarded the MM in Italy.

The news is very good. There is little information from the Russian front but we know they are rapidly approaching Germany. In France the British and American forces have almost completed a pincer movement which is expected to entrap 350,000 Germans. If it succeeds it will surely be a death-blow to Germany. Surely at this stage of the war Germany couldn't lose so many men and still carry on. It is estimated that the climax will be reached by the weekend. Should Germany lose so many men and our armies cross the Seine – there being nothing to stop them – our armies will have a straight unopposed run into Germany. And the Nazis, afraid for their own lives, are demanding of their people, to fight harder and apply more effort to their tasks. But a whip can't make a dead horse run!

I have just received letters from Jenny, 15th May, and Sheilah, 22nd May. Sheilah doesn't tell me much but it was thoughtful of her to write to me. Jenny is, as usual, my affectionate cousin. She talks of the many weddings she hopes to attend after the war. I suppose Evelyn and I ought to invite her to our wedding. My cousin Tommy – her cousin too – was on leave when she wrote. Lucky Tommy! But I suppose he'll be in France now and not a lot better off than I am. Jenny has promised to send me a photo. I wonder, is she very fat yet?

RUMOUR! A landing in the south of France somewhere near Cannes and Marseilles. Said to have taken place this morning! Hope it's true. Every little helps!

Wednesday 16th August
The rumour of yesterday is correct! Our troops have landed in the south of France making the situation more and more perplexing for the Germans. But I'd like to see a landing nearer Germany: Belgium, Holland, or even Germany itself because, internally, the Germans seem to have nothing. Hordes of our aircraft have just passed over. We believe their targets to be Leipzig or Berlin. And there wasn't a German aircraft in sight!

Thursday 17th August
I've just written a lettercard to Evelyn. I'd received two letters from her since my last letter to her. There must still be many letters to come as I've received none between 22nd April and 15th July. They would be sea-mail letters of course and must necessarily take longer in transit. I've just received three sea-mail letters from her, dated 10th, 22nd, and 31st May. One of them contained a snap of her and seeing it made me tremble so much that I was barely able to read her letter. She has developed into a most beautiful young woman since I last saw her. But, for the moment at least, receiving this photo hasn't done me much good – I am unbalanced, restless and can't eat. All I want to do is to dream that I'm holding that lovely girl in my arms.

Friday 18th August
The Americans are fighting in the outskirts of Paris! The other news is good too. Our pincer encircling the German 7th Army is now closed. Unfortunately, a lot of their armoured stuff managed to get away. But, apparently about 200,000 of their men are trapped. And those who managed to break through have still got the Seine to cross. Also our push from the south of France is doing well and is 40 kilos inland. When this force links up with those in the north many thousands of Germans will be cut off from the remainder of the German Army. They will have lost about half a million men in France since the Allied invasion of Normandy on June 6th. But this must be said for the Germans: they are good soldiers who don't give up easily.

Saturday 19th August
I went to our camp theatre last night and saw *The Barretts of Wimpole Street*. It is a good play and it was well put over but the theatre – an army type hut – was much too warm. Several hundred sweating, near naked bodies, are rather a distracting influence. After the show I was delighted and surprised to find a letter from Evelyn waiting for me. She had, she said, gone out that afternoon to do some shopping for a parcel for me. But before this shopping could take place she espied a 'half' tea service, whatever that is. I visualise

only cups and saucers. Anyway, she bought it. This is just as well because she has already spent a lot on parcels for me – which I seldom receive – and, anyway, I already have sufficient kit to last me until the end of the war. And another thing: whatever she buys in the household line will be mine as well as hers. Ours! China, she tells me, is almost unprocurable these days and is usually a plain white. The outfit she has bought is hand-painted, and therefore, was irresistible. So there!

Wednesday 23rd August
It seems ages since I last got a letter from Evelyn yet is only four days. And yesterday I received a letter from Pam. She doesn't tell me much. She has been decorating her room, she says, and requires only a pair of curtains to complete the job. What an interesting subject for a prisoner of war! Really thrilling! I don't think. Now my Evelyn's bedroom would be a different matter entirely – but I mustn't dwell on that.

The news is good: the Seine has been crossed and the object of our troops in France is to cut off Calais with the next objective being Belgium. But how much longer are the Germans going to take the thrashing that they have been taking so long. At present, in France, there are many German divisions cut off and without hope but they won't surrender. Wonderful spirit: but what foolishness! But how much longer?

Thursday 24th August
There are literally thousands of our bombers going over. They would appear to be dropping rather a lot, too, because we can feel the ground trembling and that started a couple of hours ago. Thousands of people are dying while I'm writing this merely because the bastards who are ruling this country are afraid for themselves knowing that their lives will end when the war ends.

Harry Beale has given me some lettercards and postcards. I've given some of these to Jerry but I've kept most of them as I have more people awaiting replies from me than he has.

The Allies are now occupying Paris!

Friday 25th August
Rumania has capitulated to the Allies and has become an Allie (is that the correct spelling?). Bordeaux has fallen to our forces and, also, a town on the Swiss frontier. Every day brings our forces closer to us. And the Germans appear to be getting awkward with us as a reprisal. They are keeping us on check- parade much longer than would seem necessary and they are getting stricter all round. Today they have been searching in the RAF compound. I wonder if they'll come here tomorrow? I'd better hide my diaries in case they do come.

I've written postcards to Dad and to Sheilah. I've just received a June 12th letter from Evelyn.

Sunday 27th August

The Germans are still 'blitzing' us so our News service is temporarily suspended but I hope it will be restarted soon because we get too many silly rumours without it. The RAF compound has been put out of bounds to us army prisoners and the Germans have threatened to shoot any of us who venture near the separating wire. There is a dividing area between us and the RAF lads and this is swarming with Germans. Forty seven prisoners escaped last week and the Germans are annoyed, hence their current nastiness.

Current rumour has it that Bulgaria has capitulated and that the Russians have taken over the Rumanian oil wells.

Thursday 31st August

Five years ago today all classes of reservists were recalled to their respective services. It has since seemed an eternity.

I have received no letters at all this week but I suppose this is due to our troops invading southern France but now that our troops have reached the Swiss frontier our mail ought to start coming through again. Hope they won't take too long about it!

Our advance in France seems to have slowed up again. Our recent gains seem to be Reims and Rouen but I'm inclined to suspect our 'News Agency' of holding back our news for a couple of days so that it will synchronize with the German announcements. If our armies don't enter Germany soon we will be here for Christmas. Apparently, there is a bit of squabbling between the western allies and Russia about some arms which we have dropped for the Poles. The Russians are claiming that the Poles are using these weapons to shoot at the Russians. A fair complaint if this is the case. Hope they settle this difference soon. We can't afford any ill-feeling at this stage of the war. Bulgaria is asking for peace terms but, in the meantime, has ceased hostilities. There will soon be only Germany left!

'Sailor' Haynes has told me that an old squad mate of mine is in the camp: Wilkinson! I haven't seen him since I talked with him on the train as we were going on leave Christmas 1933. 'Wilko' borrowed a shilling from me. And he didn't pay me back! I'm going to see him now.

Friday 1st Sep

I went to see Wilkinson yesterday. He is a sergeant. And he remembered the shilling he borrowed from me on the train twelve years ago. He's a sergeant now. I was surprised when he told me that he had been posted to our 7th Bn. after I'd become a prisoner. And he got my job. But he had it only a week when he was transferred to the job of provost sergeant, a job requiring strong character and no mental effort. It is said that while a signals sergeant can do any other sergeant's job, it seldom happens that any sergeant can do the signals sergeant's job. Signalling (communications) takes years to learn. I was a signaller six years before I became a signals sergeant. But Wilko!

He told me lots of things I wanted to know. All of the lads of my platoon who were not taken prisoner when I was are still alive and well. None of them has been promoted.

Saturday 2nd Sep

I have written to Evelyn. In her last letter she said it won't be long before we are together again. How I hope she is right! It is now more than three years since I last held her. How shall I meet her? I don't want to meet her at her home in the presence of her family. Fate will arrange.

The latest news tells us that this will be the last September of the war. How I hope that it will be! They are saying that the war in France will end in a matter of hours. If so, it must have ended before I started to write this entry. But has the war in Germany started that's what I want to know. It must start soon because our armies were last reported to be only 80 kilos from the German Frontier. Roll on our armies! Roll on peace and the end of the Nazis.

Sunday 3rd Sep

Five years ago today I sat on the barrack room steps at our depot in Richmond and I told myself that war wouldn't really come. But war did come and so started my perambulations over Europe, Asia, and Africa. Before it all started I thought my travels and adventures were over. I was, I thought, settled down as a civilian with nothing to do but to make good my job and to find myself a wife. But war came: my travels and adventures started again. And sad as it has all been, selfishly, I'm glad because it brought me to Evelyn. Had there been no war we would never have met. I've just received a letter from her, dated June 29th, in which she chides me for doubting that she would wait for me. But she would have to be in the situation in which I am at present to appreciate fully my fear that I may lose her. Losing her would devastate me. In a short time I may be able to show my appreciation.

Monday 4th Sep

I went to our theatre to hear Alan Bolt's[6] symphony orchestra. In the queue I saw a fellow who was so like Edith Jones that he could have passed as brother. Am I never to be allowed to forget that girl? She has haunted me ever since I met her nearly four years ago. And why she haunts me I don't know. She wasn't attractive. All she had in her favour were her youthful exuberance and her openness. But I was fond of her, perhaps still fond of her though I have not seen her during the last three and a half years. It certainly wasn't sexual attraction. She didn't excite me that way. If it is love it is the sexless love that a man has for a child: the urge to protect. Perhaps, away beneath the surface, I am grateful to her. I met her when my morale was very

---

[6] A professional musician in civilian life.

low shortly after I had ended my devastating acquaintance with Helen Cary. Perhaps meeting Edith soothed me. I became her protégé and she was my link with Evelyn. And since then she has of her own accord slipped out of my life. Perhaps my transferring my attention from her to Evelyn hurt her. I am sorry: I didn't want to hurt Edith.

Wednesday 6th Sep

Events are moving fast. Our troops have passed through Belgium and have entered Holland. It is thought that they may be now on German soil but we have had no confirmation of this. We, in this camp, expect a rapid advance into this country when once we have the whole of Belgium and Holland and have smashed the Siegfried Line. There will be very little opposition. The whole of the Germans force in Germany is said to be about 750,000 and this number includes many of those who were invalided back from their front lines. And, of course, included are those guarding prison camps. According to one report the German High Command has issued an order that all troops outside the Reich must return to within its borders. It would now seem to be 'it's every man for himself'! The Germans have evacuated Crete and this camp has received information from Geneva that the issue of Red Cross food must be cut by 50%. And if the war doesn't end before Saturday, Harry Beale has vowed that he will, voluntarily, jump into the camp pond!!! I've advised him to postpone his jump for a few days. But do we hear again the tinkle of jingle bells and Bing Crosbie's everlasting *White Christmas*.

A year ago tonight we learned of Italy's capitulation to the allies and I thought, as so many of us did, that we would all be home for Christmas – that so overworked milestone! – but soon our hopes were shattered when we found ourselves bound for Germany. But we cheered ourselves in the belief that the war could last only a few months more. But another year has passed and we are still waiting although we believe it can only be weeks now. Our troops appear to have halted temporarily but in a short time, we hope, they will be smashing their way through Germany. But are we allowing our exuberant hopes to allow us to forget that we have been at this hoped for point of deliverance so many times only to find ourselves again frustrated and in despair. It is awful! Here we are, prisoners, fervently hoping that our combined force of bombers will blast the country – and destroy it and leave it like a devastated hell. But, eventually, it will all end and it will be vowed, as it was vowed at the end of the last war, 'Never Again!'

We have learned that in Britain the 'black-out' restrictions have been lifted. From this, we gather that the Germans are soon to have so much on their hands inside Germany that the bombing of England by their bombers will be a thing of the past.

I've written postcards to Evelyn, her Mum, and to Jenny. There is very little mail coming in now and I wonder will there be much more.

Monday 11th Sep

According to instructions issued by Geneva only one Red Cross parcel
between two men was issued today. Jerry and I will survive on this of course
as neither of us eats much even though the colder weather has boosted our
appetites a little.

Tuesday 12th Sep

There was nothing much in the news today. Our troops in France are still
bringing up supplies. Naturally we expect this to be for the final drive at
any moment. A pipe-line is being laid from Cherbourg to our front line.
This diary served a useful purpose last night when it won 'Spike' Otterburn
some cigarettes. 'Spike' had made a 'bet' with Norman Reid that a certain
incident hapnened before the Allies invaded France. Norman said that it had
happened after the invasion. It is in my diary: 2nd June. Spike won!

Swarms of our bombers have just passed over. We know they are ours
because there is such a lot of them. I wonder, do the Germans still think they
are winning?

Have just received a letter from Evelyn, dated 3rd August. She was sitting
on the sand on Bournemouth beach when she wrote it – lucky girl! – and she
tells me that she is looking forward to my sitting there with her soon. So am
I – but not this year now. It's too cold. Next summer, perhaps? I had hoped
before Christmas but I think it's already a bit late for that now.

Wednesday 13th Sep

It has started again! Our troops in the west have started their invasion of
Germany. I learnt this yesterday but it may have taken place on Monday.
We don't know how far our troops have advanced but we are expecting
big things from them now. Ever hopeful, we believe the war could end this
month. If it doesn't end soon we are going to be in a very bad way here. We
are expecting several thousands more prisoners to be brought into this camp.
This is not a rumour! Extra bunks are being erected in all of the huts. With
these extra men to feed there can't be sufficient Red Cross food to last more
than a couple of weeks. Happy days are here again! !

But, hopefully, with our troops already fighting in Germany, perhaps it
won't last much longer. The shell may be hard to break but the inside is
already rotten. Their heavy losses combined with the terrific bombing they
are receiving must be breaking their morale. Their special newspaper which
is printed for prisoners doesn't fool us. We know that their much advertised
'V' weapons are dropping on England and are causing a lot of damage and
casualties but they are merely weapons of spite. They claim that they are
fighting for their freedom and their culture but all they are doing is protecting
their Nazi leaders who brought about all of the devastation and the cruelty.
Poor disillusioned people!

I've received a letter from Evelyn, dated, July 10th. She says she had been to see Ruth and had slept with her. Lucky Ruth!

Our aircraft are overhead again. This heavy bombing seems to be an every day occurrence now. Germany is being battered well and properly.

Friday 15th Sep

We are still winning. Victory is imminent – we are told.

I have been to the camp library but the books I want are not on loan. It's a dead loss this library: I queued up for half an hour to learn that what I wanted is not available.

According to latest reports Aachen was occupied by our troops on Tuesday. Our News service is slipping. We are told that there seems to be very little opposition in the west. But our troops don't appear to be moving very fast! The occupation of Germany – when it takes place – is to be as follows: Northwest Germany, British. Southwest Germany, American. Eastern Germany, Russia. Berlin is to be regarded as an International Administrative Centre. The plans have been made and the hopes are high. All that is required now is an armistice.

Sunday 17th Sep

I've just dashed off a lettercard to Evelyn. I don t like to hurry when I write to her but this morning the lettercards were called for sooner than expected. I'm already remembering items I had intended to include. When I'm in a hurry I forget things I've been planning for days.

Monday 18th Sep

Our troops have broken through the Siegfried east of Aachen. This news may be some days old so our forces may be well into Germany by now. The report says they are fanning out on a 17 kilo front and are advancing on Cologne. Everything seems to be going exceptionally well now. Churchill has returned from Canada where it appears he and Roosevelt agreed on all points discussed. We know nothing of the results of this conference except that it concerns Japan. Japan, apparently, is due for a severe bashing when we have finished with Germany.

I was with Jimmy Brown when we met a Frenchman known to Jimmy. The 'Froggy' can speak English fairly well but, as usual, Jimmy wanted to impress those about us. Noticing that all eyes were on him, Jimmy beamed at the 'Froggy', and his audience, and said in his Filey accented French, 'Comment allez vous, Jack (Jacque)' the Frenchman, returning his beaming smile, answered, 'Très bien, Jimmy, et vous?' The centre of attention, Jimmy answered, 'Yes, isn't it!' Several observers smiled but Jimmy, quite happily, believed he had impressed us all.

Tuesday 19th Sep

Another Allied airborne invasion has taken place behind enemy lines in Holland. It is said that this is the largest airborne force yet used in the war. The report received says they are meeting very little opposition and four towns have been taken. Another report – not yet authenticated – says that Cologne has been taken and our troops have reached the Rhine in three places. If this is so, what will the poor Nazis do now, poor things?! Must break-off for soup now – have had it. It was pea-soup – so they reckon – and about as thick!

A few letters have come in and I've got one from Pam, dated 10th August. Rather good going for surface mail. According to information received, the Germans are going to 'blitz' us again. It may happen tomorrow or some days hence so I shall have to hide my diaries very carefully. Also it means there will be a dearth of news: these 'blitzes' always put our news service out of step. But they can't have many more. The dying donkey is kicking its last.

Wednesday 20th Sep

We are still waiting for the threatened 'blitz'. It looks as though it may have been a false alarm. Perhaps they are hoping to catch us unawares. There was no news this morning but according to the news received last night by the RAF[7], our airborne force in Holland has linked up with the British 2nd Army. This would indicate that we have bridged the Rhine in Holland. The problem with these 'good' news reports is that quite frequently our jubilation swamps commonsense and we then have prognostications which, euphorically, we accept as having happened. But then comes reality and we are in the dumps again.

Another letter from Pam, dated 25th June. Affectionate, witty, and catty. The first for me and the latter for Olive (Olive Coleman). Poor Pam!

Still no 'blitz' but no news either. I am beginning to think that this whole thing about the threatened 'blitz' was just a hoax. If the war were at an end, or about to end, our camp authorities (British) wouldn't want us to know until the Germans announce it. This being so they wouldn't dare allow us to have any wireless news because of incidents which might occur between our knowing it and the Germans being informed. But if they just refuse to let us have some news some of the hot-heads amongst us (most of the RAF lads) might start acting independently. So our camp government – I believe – would invent an excuse for not providing us with any news. That looks a bit involved but I know what I mean. A threatened 'blitz' would provide a sound excuse for hiding the wireless. Is that why we are not getting any news? I am wondering. We are all wondering. But, anyway, we should soon know.

---

[7] The RAF prisoners were in a different compound and had their own secret radio.

Friday 22nd Sep

Eight days of this month to go and the war not yet ended. I wonder what is happening? We are still awaiting wireless news while the German newspapers merely give us news we know to be several days old and suitably distorted for the German public. But the war has not yet ended – at least, not entirely, because we can hear the guns on the local artillery range and the local troops are firing rifles and machine guns on a firing range a mere distance of a hundred yards away. But the end must be near (but how often have we thought this?). Despite this fear of a Gestapo 'blitz' no one is going to convince me that the blokes with the wireless are going without news during this critical period. I am sure the news is coming in and equally sure that it is being kept from us by that blasted Scotch 'Vet' who is our alleged British Medical Officer. Why can't he mind his own business and content himself with his pills and temperature charts? Holding back the news isn't doing us any good: the morale of the camp is now minus. Letters and news are our spiritual food but I suppose we will just have to wait and carry on waiting.

From a source which I think is reliable I've been told that Germany is prepared to accept our terms for peace less the occupation of any part of Germany by Russia. This sounds feasible and may actually be the case. It would also fit in with Churchill's going to a secret destination. Has he gone to Moscow to talk it over with his pal, Joe (Stalin)? Anyway, the tale goes that our War Cabinet is split over the question. But when are we going to learn the truth? But I'm back to the old wireless question again.

Saturday 23rd Sep

Still waiting. There was the sound of what I believed to be aircraft overhead. However it didn't last long so perhaps it wasn't. I almost hope they weren't our aircraft because there is a rumour that none of our aircraft has been over on account of 'Peace-Talks' taking place. This is a silly rumour; how would we know if there were none of our planes over Germany? There is too little news and too much wishful thinking and too much stupid rumouring in this camp.

It has just been announced that 4,000 WOs and NCOs will leave this camp on Monday. They are going to Stalag IIb which, we are told, is near Hanover. It strikes us as queer that British prisoners would be sent to a camp near the Allied front line and I'm wondering is there a catch in it? The list of those who will have to go has not yet been made known so I don't know yet if I'll be on it. It strikes me as very funny.

Have the Germans reached the 'drowning man and the straw' stage? If the Germans have prisoners to move into this camp when we move out why don't they send these prisoners to Staling IIb instead of us. I'm assuming I'll be one of them.

LATER Have been ordered to move and my kit is packed. We are to move out of this hut at 0645 tomorrow (Sunday).

Sunday 24th Sep
Reveille was at 0500hrs this morning. Those of us who are moving were paraded at 0645hrs, had red triangles (POW markings) painted on our trousers, jackets and greatcoats, had our kit checked, had a shower and our clothing fumigated, were searched and then marched a couple of miles out of the main camp to where we are now, a subsidiary stalag near a railway station. We are due to be moved tomorrow. We have had no news for about a week now. There are some wonderful rumours but these are too fantastic to mention. We are all wondering what the new camp will be like. I still can't understand why we are being sent to a place near Hanover. It ought to be soon in British or American hands.

Wednesday 27th Sep
Settled again – we hope! It isn't IIb as we were told but a subsidiary of that stalag in the same area. There would seem to be no catch in our move at the moment but I still don't understand why the Germans have sent us here. As a camp it isn't as good as IVb at Mulberg but there may be some improvements we could make. These barracks have been reconditioned and are very cold. Of course we are nearer the north coast here. All around us is churned up mud. We arrived here yesterday and were disinfested, searched, and registered before being allowed into our huts. There are 72 men per hut. Each hut has a commander appointed by the others. We are in three sections of 24 men and I am the leader of one section. Last night we were given only one blanket per man so most of us spent a very uncomfortable night. We have been promised another blanket and a palliasse per man today. I hope this materializes because the temperature here is very wintry.

We have not had any news yet but according to the fellows who were already here everything is OK. Apparently there was already a secret wireless here.

I met Jack Rolls last night. He looks fit. He has just come from a camp in Poland. He tells me that I am nowhere near the fellow I was when he last saw me. I am aware of this: I must have lost a couple of stones in weight since he last saw me in the prison camp at Tobruk.

Thursday 28th Sep
On Wednesday we were each given the other promised blanket but no palliasse yet. We shall have them in the course of the next few days, we have been promised. This is a very cold place and the fuel issue is very small but the soup is good and always hot. Also there is an issue of hot German coffee at seven a.m. every morning. This latter item proves that we are near the front line because only front line troops get it. We didn't

have it at Mulberg. The German troops here are better too. Here, there is no drawing of pistols and hysterical screaming at us as there was at IVb. A large number understand English and they seem friendly and considerate. Are they anticipating judgment day? Churchill has made another speech. This one curbs our exuberance somewhat. One item was that although some people believe the war will end this year he thought it possible that it may drag on into the early months of next year. This is a little disheartening but it is something to have Churchill give a time early in 1945. But we have a quarter of the year yet so there may be hope! Perhaps it can be done.

One postcard per man was issued yesterday so I have written to Evelyn.

Saturday 30th Sep

The end of another month and still this hell on earth. How much longer? Wilf Taylor came to see me last night. I hadn't seen him since the night we were captured. He told me something I hadn't known about that night. On that last night, as acting company sergeant major, he had been ordered by Major Girling to go round and warn everyone to stand by ready to pull out at eleven thirty. When I told him that I'd received no such warning he told me that I, and the men I commanded, were to be left to hold the enemy while the others of our unit evacuated the position. We were not to be told lest it demoralize us!

Cold blooded desertion. But commonsense really. The few for the many. The little number I commanded – voluntarily since I was just passing them when the emergency arose – was the part of our unit which was engaging the enemy and checking their advance. And while we were doing this our comrades intended to slide away into the darkness of the night without so much as waving us 'goodbye'.

But this plan didn't come off. Since I, and my little band of reluctant heroes were obstructing them the Germans decided to try another way – the point at which our colonel had decided to move out. There was no conflict really. The Germans were on there way in to do battle. Our lads were snugly in their vehicles believing they were on their way to Cairo. Our colonel knew when he was beaten and there, their conflict ended: they were prisoners.

But I and my heroes didn't know and carried on until the conflict petered out. Realizing that we were up a well-known creek with no means of propulsion I went over and informed the Germans that we desired to take no further part in the conflict. They were quite friendly now and agreed with this. My little bunch suffered no casualties. While it would be nice to think that our colonel believed that I, and my bunch, would continue to hold the enemy while he got away with the remainder, any other sergeant and bunch of unfortunates would have been expected to serve the same purpose. But that was over two years ago. Water under the bridge.

Monday 2nd Oct

This area seems to be getting more than a fair share of air raids. There was another good one last night. We have had one every night we've been here plus daylight raids now and then. Fortunately our bombers seem to know where the prison camps are because they seem to be able to drop their bombs all around us. I had hoped the war would end in September but we are now in October and it is still raging. Our forces seem to be still bashing away at the hard shell of the enemy's defence. We in this camp are hoping that our blokes will make a lightning breakthrough in the area of Cologne and Bonn, and then come around to the north and cut off this area before the Germans can move us.

The Germans are funny people: they know perfectly well that they have lost the war but still they fight! The nation is ruined: it has lost the cream of its youth and a large portion of its middle aged. Perhaps they are fighting for terms – terms which will allow them to replenish themselves and to build up another war-machine as they did last time and again tear the peaceful world to pieces. The German has a bee in his bonnet: he doesn't want to be equal with other humans, he must be superior. Anyway, that was Hitler's belief.

Tuesday 3rd Oct

My watch spring has broken but it works if I give it only a few winds several times a day. I'm sure there must be a watch maker in the camp. I must enquire. I'd feel lost without my watch. I've had it such a long time. The news is good but nothing to get excited about.

Thursday 5th Oct

We have to be inoculated, vaccinated, and X-rayed again. Parties of 50 have been going to the hospital since our check-parade this morning but I don't think I shall have to go until tomorrow. A few letters, redirected from IVb came in yesterday but there were none for me. Jimmy Brown got one dated 5th September.

Although the news is good the allies have suffered some setbacks between our last bulletin in IVb and the first one we heard here. Our airborne troops who were dropped in Holland were almost wiped out! And we seem to have suffered in the Aachen area. I wonder are we going to be here for Christmas after all?

I've just been inoculated and X-rayed.

Friday 6th Oct

Many hundreds of our bombers have flown over and are still flying over. Their target must be quite close because we can feel the ground shaking. Allied forces have invaded Greece and in a short time the Germans will be out of that country. The Greeks, of all people ought to be liberated. They had faith in us. They were always sure that we would return to help them. In the west our armies are slowly but surely pushing eastward. At present there is a truce in the Dunkirk area. This is to allow the evacuation of the civilians. I wonder will Dunkirk hold out longer than Calais did?

Sunday 8th Oct

Today's news – yesterday's really – is very good. Our combined airforces have made a special effort and have churned up the German landscape considerably. Whole residential areas have been blotted out. This seems inhuman but all war is inhuman so what does it matter! And at this stage of the war – and the year – the bombing of residential areas is almost as important as bombing industrial areas. The German people must be struck very forcibly with the fact that a cold and homeless winter awaits them unless the hostilities cease. With their enemies closed around in an ever diminishing circle men cannot be spared for their home front and all of their materials are going into their war effort which is rapidly becoming no more than active resistance.

But still they fight! In the words of the cockney 'Pore bastards!' But our tactical air force has been busy, too: strafing, bombing, and rocket-firing aircraft are being used on the western front to some effect. The Americans have effected a breakthrough at Aachen and are pouring through. In Holland, too, our troops are doing well. At the present rate of progress the Allies may force the Germans to surrender before Christmas. What a Christmas it would be! I am sure I shall cry when the cease fire sounds.

Tuesday 10th Oct

I sent a postcard to Dad this morning. I wonder am I being fair in always sending him a postcard and never a lettercard. But there is so little I could tell him if I used a lettercard. And, really, I doubt if he'd appreciate the difference. Evelyn deserves the lettercards more than anyone does. When I was a child Dad neglected me, he was a bully, and he lacked sympathy. But there is little object in regurgitating the past. I have left the slums and the unhappiness that went with that environment. I shall never be clever but I'm no longer illiterate. I can afford to forget my dad's neglect of me. Sentiment is out, however and Dad must know this.

I've written a postcard to the Electrical & Mechanical Engineer at Corsham asking for re-employment after the war. I have explained that I was employed there before the start of the war. Of course as the establishment is a munitions depot it may then be superfluous to requirement. There are to be no more wars, we have been told!

Friday 13th Oct

There appears to be no mail coming in. I received my last letters from Evelyn on 11th and 13th of last month. There may, of course, be letters for us which are still at IVb. We may have to wait some time now before we start getting letters direct from England. And, it seems, we will still be here to collect them!

Our troops appear to have been checked for the moment. Unreasonably, perhaps, we prisoners regard this as a mystery: we have a couple of million men in France, more armour than the Germans have ever possessed, and the largest combined air force in the world, and still the Germans are saying, 'NO ENTRY!' Are our generals incompetent? Or are they playing some deep game, a game destined to make Germany a desert before she is ultimately destroyed man, beast, and structures?! !

There are only a couple of months of this year still to go so obviously our Christmas will be here. But it is going to be a thinner Christmas than the previous two. Apparently, we have almost run out of Red Cross food – only one parcel between four men – and there are no more in transit as far as we know. Of course we won't starve on the food issued by the Germans but we certainly won't grow fat on it, ie, as we are receiving at present.

Churchill is in Moscow – has been for some days – I wonder what diabolical schemes he and Stalin are hatching? We are told that the Russians are still doing well but they don't appear to have covered much ground despite the good reports. They have still not taken Riga in the Baltic and they are still fighting on the eastern side of East Prussia. We console ourselves with the fact that the war can't last forever. But we'd like to know: how much short of ever?

Sunday 15th Oct
I've just written a lettercard to Evelyn. It isn't much of a letter. I just seem to have rambled on about nothing, The lights in our hut were installed a few days ago but are not yet working. I have been asked by my barrack mates to get them going if I can.

Later On tackling it I found the wiring to be a bit of a mystery but I've sorted it out – in a fashion – and now there are three rooms with lights working. The Germans will do the others tomorrow.

Monday 16th Oct
I have written to Margaret Hebden. I wonder what she thinks when she receives my cards and letters? Does she think I'm impudent? Perhaps she does as I have not had a letter from her during the last seventeen months. But she and her sisters were so kind to me when I was in Castle Cary that I must give them the benefit of the doubt and send them the occasional card or letter.

Wednesday 18th Oct
The news is good but not very exciting, the most important item being that Hungary is asking for Peace terms. Horthy, their president, has turned against the Nazis and told his people to oppose the Germans.

Our bread ration has been cut and there is no sign of any Red Cross parcels coming our way. And there are still no letters.

Thursday 19th Oct

I've grumbled too soon about the mail: some letters were brought in this evening but there was none for me. It is a month since I received my last letter from Evelyn but I don't mind so much if she is receiving mine.

Our troops in the west seem to be static now and we are wondering what is holding them. Surely it is strategy and not the Germans. That's what we hope anyway. In today's news the far east wasn't mentioned. We regard this as bad as the German news say that Japan claims a big naval engagement in which they destroyed a large part of the American fleet. Our news quotes Goebbels as saying the Germans will fight until they are given 'a safe peace'. This is the first time Peace without victory has been mentioned by the Germans. They are weakening but how long before they snap? This waiting is awful.

And we have run out of Red Cross food. Tomorrow will be our last issue. We are beginning to feel the pinch now that the cold weather is with us again. All we can do is read. Read and dream. And the latter isn't good for us. This eternal wanting and not having access to it is sending us all bonkers.

Saturday 21st Oct

Some more mail was brought in this evening – but none for me. It is wonderful what a letter can do. And it is awful what NO letter does. I am depressed and the end of the war seems to be as far off as ever. The news is generally good but nothing would seem to happening in the west. Why? Aachen has eventually fallen to the allies but nothing else of importance was mentioned. The German newspaper tells us that in Leipzig a man of 62 was executed for talking defeatism when he was merely voicing the opinion of all Germany. He was hanged! The murdering shower of pigs' bastards.

Sunday 22nd Oct

Postcards have been issued but only one per man. I've written to Evelyn. I've read and reread what I've written to her this morning and somehow my effort seems to be bald and uncommunicative. Perhaps it's because I have no letters to answer. I have a spare card which Jock Taylor gave to me. I think I'll send that to Jenny. I haven't written to her for some time now and, after all, she is my cousin. What an age it is since I last talked with a woman. Sister Keogh in Sarafand hospital was the last woman I talked with. Her Irish accent was very attractive. She chided me as though I were a little boy. 'Now, sergeant, you know you shouldn't have a pillow! Now give it to me, there's a good boy. My Sergeant David mustn't make his poor head ache.' She was my age – twenty eight! I find myself smiling rather wistfully when I think of her.

The last two girls I spoke to in Castle Cary were Pam, and Olive Coleman. When I left and shook hands with them they cried. Perhaps I ought to have kissed them. I'd kissed Edith Jones several times before I met Evelyn but she was as passive as a block of marble. But I'm being vindictive now and all because the girl changed her good opinion of me into one of indifference. And it was all Ruth's fault:

It was New Year's Eve 1940. Evelyn, still a nurse at that time, was on duty at the hospital although I had seen her in the church club earlier in the evening. Later I left the club with a number of teenage girls including Edith and Ruth. I was escorting them all home. The last of the bunch to be delivered were Edith and Ruth. Having left Edith at her door there was now only Ruth who lived rather further away but I'm sure she selected the most devious route home. On our way to her home she became clinging and tearful. She said that she loved me and that she knew that I loved her (she was only sixteen). By this time I was engaged to Evelyn and Ruth already knew this – she had viewed and had admired the ring on Evelyn's finger. It was past midnight and absolutely black dark as she sobbed on my shoulder. I'd never seen a near adult so distressed. We were just outside her home and I was worried lest some one might think I was molesting her. I kissed her and told her I was sorry. Finally she cried herself into silence broken by an occasional sob. I left her, returning to my battalion the following morning.

Some time later I received a letter from Edith. Ruth had turned to her for sympathy and understanding. Edith made no bones about it: in her eyes I was the lowest of the low. She had, she wrote, previously regarded me as on a metaphorical pedestal but, no longer, and was now seriously considering ending her friendship with me. Reading this I was shocked and worried. I'd done nothing wrong.

Looking back to that short period four years ago I realise that I'd been the victim of two immature teenagers. But, on reading Edith's denunciation of my character I was immediately worried lest Evelyn think that I'd been two-timing her. It was all sorted out: Edith even relented sufficiently to continue writing to me 'although I would no longer be on a pedestal!' I was vulnerable and dismayed. Since enlisting I'd been denied any friendship or even conversation with girls until I was twenty six and, there I was, as innocent and vulnerable as a three-year-old. And Edith has not written to me since I've been a prisoner of war. But what am I nattering about: I'm just talking to myself. It's this prison camp life!

But I'm virtually talking to myself here. It's late and I'm tired. Too tired for long winded soliloquies. Tired of being a prisoner. Tired of this bloody awful war. Christ, I'm... but there's no Christ, is there?

Monday 23rd Oct
I have written to Jenny. I haven't told her much – there's not much can be written on a card but sufficient, I hope, to hold her interest.

Our troops have started another push and appear to be doing reasonably well. And the Russians, too, are doing well and have entered Norway from Finland. If we, and the Russians, can only keep up this pushing! But we no longer hope to be home by Christmas. It's all vain, hopeless. The war goes on. But it must stop one day, we all know that. But when? when? when? An air raid is in progress and some poor unhappy and hopeless Germans are being blasted to hell while I'm writing this. And we selfish, cynical bastards are delighted. And it is such a beautiful night!

Wednesday 25th Oct

A letter from the Red Cross at Geneva tells us about the medal, the Africa Star. It seems I am eligible for it but not for the 'clasp'. The latter is awarded only to those who have served in Africa after 23rd October 1943. But what do medals and clasps matter ? We are out of Red Cross food and are now living entirely on German rations.

There wasn't much in the news today. It seems to me that it is only yesterday's news re-hashed. This is likely because there is a search taking place in the RAF compound. It is funny but the Germans seem to be afraid to leave us alone. They are becoming as bad as the Italians were.

Saturday 28th Oct

We have just got rid of the Gestapo. For some days they have been searching the camp. They confiscated diaries, fountain pens, ink, coloured pencils, written material, and writing material. They even took army paybooks when they found them. My stuff, including £5 in Egyptian money, has been hidden in the German office. They wouldn't look there, I hoped. They didn't, apparently!

Some personal parcels arrived yesterday but there was nothing for me. Jerry got two clothing parcels, one posted June last year and the other July this year. It's a wonderful postal service! But at least he received them. But what's happened to mine?

The news is good. The Allied navies have engaged and have destroyed quite a lot of three Japanese fleets. If they should have another such bashing before they have time to re-build Japan will be negligible as a sea-power.

Our troops have cleared and are occupying two thirds of Greece. The Russians are doing well in East Prussia and are also making progress in Norway. In Western Europe our troops have made a landing on the island whose guns were covering Antwerp. We should now have the use of that port. This will be of importance in our in our final drive. We prisoner of war strategists have got it all mapped out! But in the meantime our troops are still clearing out the enemy from the back areas. But when is the final drive going to take place?

I have written to the Regimental Paymaster and asked him to send Dad £10. I've asked him, also, to send me a statement of my account. We ought to have had lettercards issued today but we got postcards instead. Jock Taylor gave me two. I shall write to Evelyn and to her Mum and also to Sheilah.

I have felt very depressed all day. It has been a very depressing day, raining unceasingly since early this morning. And to make matters worse our Red Cross representative brought in an old gramophone this afternoon since when we – at least I – have been tortured by Bing Crosby and Judy Garland: one moaning and screeching with the gramophone adding its tinny rattle. What an unearthly row! And I am depressed and likely to remain so for some time.

Churchill has returned from Moscow and is now talking about himself and Roosevelt having a meeting with Stalin before the end of the year. At least another half year of this hellish existence. No letters, no Red Cross food, nothing of anything worth having, and I'd rather have Evelyn's letters than anything. A letter from a loved one feeds the spirit as nothing else can. And I'm sorely in need of spiritual food. Will I ever see and hold my Evelyn again? And I am so miserable.

Sunday 29th Oct

There has been a heavy frost overnight and this morning is cold. But the sun is shining brightly and the sky has no clouds in it. What a wonderful day for our bombers! I have just looked at the German news bulletin but there is no communiqué on it. They quote Bernard Shaw as saying that England cannot look after herself far less than look after Germany. Naturally the Germans would make a lot out of this. Shaw, the old rat-bag, ought to go back to Ireland if he's not happy in England. And that blasted gramophone is still churning out awful noises. Nigger jazz or something. What an awful row! And my music loving comrades are listening, open mouthed and ecstatic. But it's only organized noise.

We are expecting a truck load of Red Cross parcels. A truck load is about 3,000. There are about 7,000 men in this camp. We have been asked would we prefer to wait until sufficient parcels are here to make an issue of one per man. The majority have voted for an issue – when the truck arrives – of one parcel between three men. This isn't just impatience. It's a vacuum where food should be. A bird in the hand! We are not yet starving but we are permanently hungry. I don't feel it so much as most of the blokes here because my appetite is normally small but what I do feel inclines me to feel sorry for my heftier comrades. The gramophone is at present giving us a cooperative effort of Bing Crosby and Judy Garland doing *Jingle Bells*. And they were paid for doing this. And I once used a pick and shovel with my dad and we were paid £1 for every 8 tons of coal we produced. I wonder what Bing and Judy got for their *Jingle Bells*?

Today's news is good. Although little activity is reported on the western front, elsewhere the Germans are being hit pretty hard. The Russians are pouring into Czecho Slovakia and are also breaking the German defences in East Prussia where Hitler has ordered into action his reserve troops. Conditions are very bad in this country. More train services have been discontinued and there is little or no amusement. Although it is now winter their soldiers have only two blankets per man. That is all we have but I thought the Germans would have three or more. The winter complement of blankets for troops in Britain is five. And there is no coal here. We've been told that we can have no more hot showers until November 25th. In our hut we have a stove in which we have a wood fire three times a day for cooking purposes. We have nothing to cook other than the spuds issued to us by the Germans but a fire occasionally warms the hut – so I'm told!

Peace terms have been signed with Bulgaria and the Russians are doing well in Norway. I've written to Evelyn and to her mum.

Monday 30th Oct

Evelyn's birthday and I'm not wishing her many happy returns as I promised I would. She is twenty two and it is now almost four years since we met. I remember, it was a Friday or a Saturday evening, 9th or 10th November 1940. A long time ago. And she still waits for me – I hope, since I have had no letters now for such a long time. Although I wrote to the paymaster I learned today that it was unnecessary: when I took the postcard to the office to be countersigned by our Camp-leader I was informed that special forms are available for the purpose. I was given one. I filled it in and then left them to deal with it. The important thing was to get some money to Dad for Christmas. Of course I believe a lot of it will go on beer but, as they say: 'Well, it's Christmas, isn't it?'

There wasn't much in the news today. The RAF bombed a German battleship but didn't sink it but as one direct hit was claimed I suppose this will have put it out of action for a time. For some reason or other the Russians have stopped pushing on the East Prussian front but they have started to push in Estonia.

Today's weather has been terrible: heavy rain driven by an icy wind. But we have been cheered up this morning by the sound of our bombers overhead. We know they were ours because we could hear the steady drone as they passed over for half an hour or more. The Germans haven't the aircraft for such a performance. They can't put more than a dozen in the air in any area. With such a dearth of men and material at their disposal it is a mystery to us how they are managing to hold back our troops who are out-numbering them many to one and have the backing of terrific armour and aircraft. And yet they are doing it. Talk of Horatio on the bridge!

It sometimes seems the war will never end. Our troops are only about a hundred miles away. So near and yet so far! The Germans must be the easiest people in the world to discipline. They are suffering the most awful hardship and death. Archimedes said he could move the world if he had a lever big enough. Himmler operates almost such a lever: his Gestapo! But your lever is weakening, Himmler, and they are coming for you! Roll on that day of reckoning!

Reading this in the future, should there be such a time, perhaps I'll derive some pleasure from it, but at the time of writing it life is not really a lot of fun. But life in retrospect is always 'the good old days'. Filtered through the mist of time the picture of the past loses its harshness. But I don't think I'll ever look back to this time of my life with any enjoyment. I remember an incident in February, 1938: we were somewhere near Razmak Narai in Waziristan, altitude about 8,000ft. There was snow on the ground and there was a very heavy sleet brought down to us by a howling north wind. The sleet soaked us and the freezing cold made our clothing stiff as cardboard. We were dressed in shirt and shorts. And sun helmets.

'Yan' Hardey and I were laying a telephone line up to pickets about a mile away and above us. It was still early afternoon but we could see nothing because of the blinding sleet. Our rifles, slung over our shoulders, kept catching our bare knees and we kept falling during that rough climb. I don't know about 'Yan' but I ached with the cold and my fingers were numb and useless. Occasionally a bullet would whine past us but we didn't care. Obviously the belligerent tribesmen couldn't see any better than we could but they knew where the troops were and were sending down the odd bullet in the belief that it might hit an unfortunate soldier. We staggered onward and upward.

Oh, what an endless mile that was. There was ice on our eyebrows and eye lashes. 'Yan' lost his sun helmet and his hair froze. But we got there. Suddenly, through the driving sleet and snows we saw our objective, the sangar, a little square fort built of boulders earlier in the day. A tent had been erected over it to protect its inmates from the elements. Inside was dry and comparatively warm. We crawled in and collapsed, wailing and moaning like a couple of distressed children. The fellows in the sangar took off our frozen clothing and dried us with their towels. They wrapped us in blankets. Our own blankets were there having been taken up on the mules with the picket's equipment earlier. They gave us tea and filled water bottles with boiling water and shoved them inside our blankets. One of them connected the telephone and reported our arrival. Pneumonia, I suppose, could have been expected but, next morning, we were both fit with not even a sneeze between us as evidence of our ordeal.

Good old days! Well, everybody said so: Even 'Yan'! The last I heard of him he was signals storeman with our 1st Battalion. And he's had a whale of a time in this war: France, Norway, Burma, Africa, Italy... Good old days? I wonder does he still say so?

Wednesday 1st November

Another fine day for bombing. It is bitterly cold but there's not a cloud in the sky. I've just done my washing – in cold water – and my hands are almost too cold to hold my pen. What a life!

Goebbels has made another speech. They must all pull together and they will win! Well, Goebbels says so! But as he's been saying so since 1939 his promises are not now being received so happily. Admitting that they have been pushed back all over Europe, he says all of this will be explained later. He is telling them now that new tanks, aircraft, and ships and sub-marines are in the process of being built. When these have been completed the invaders will be thrown back and victory again will be on the side of the German Nation. What a hope! He is trying to convince the German people that the Allies are fighting for time. Imagine it: The world fighting for time against a shower of misled squareheads. Was ever anything so ridiculous?

The writing – in big block capitals – is on the wall and the miserable German people can see it. And are seeing it. It is a pity that a race, intelligent and capable of working hard as the Germans, should waste such qualities on so despicable an aim as to wish to put the remainder of mankind under their subjection. They claim that the British are imperialistic. But we haven't yet gone to war against the world! But I'm waxing all too psychological now and getting out of my depth.

But here is the news bloke! Churchill has made another speech cautioning the too-optimistic. He forecasts the war's lasting until spring or early summer owing to the apathy of the German people to their present living conditions and the horrors of war. But, he adds, some military strategists, more competent that he, think it could end much earlier. This is the first time Churchill has made such a statement. Our spirit hovers between optimism and pessimism as we consider the pros and cons. But all of this soliloquising is depressing me.

Danger! The air-raid sirens are warbling merrily. Men at work. The RAF and/or the Amercan Air Force are on the job! But I'd better close down: I'm rambling too much.

Thursday 2nd November

I wrote a card to Sheilah last night. I have not heard from her since my previous letter to her. Lost or binned by the censor?

We've just been issued with miles of toilet paper. It must be from the Red Cross. The Germans don't issue it. Just the stuff for starving men! But we have heard that a truck-load of parcels has arrived at the station. We are in doubt as to whether these will be issued one per three men or one to four men.

Some personal parcels have arrived but I've given up hope of receiving any more. Evelyn is sending them but who is getting them? Swiss yodellers[8] or thieving railway staff. Certainly not yours truly. I have received only two next-of-kin parcels while I've been a prisoner and Evelyn has been sending one every three months. But these parcels are containing clothing and other items which can't even be bought in war-time Europe. No wonder they are swiped. But surely no one would steal books. But where are they?

The news was rather scanty today. Apparently wireless reception is bad owing to the weather. A lot of bombing has been done – we know, we've heard it, and Salonika is now in British hands. Greek, really. Also we are doing well in Holland.

I've just spent a whole morning doing repairs. My socks were in such a bad way that I've had to patch them. They are so rotten that darning them is out of the question. My sweaty feet and all of the walking I did around the recreation ground at IVb has been too much for war-time wool. Aren't they feeding the sheep properly? Poor joke. Also my trousers needed some attention. Too well ventilated for our prevailing arctic wind. But I had to darn here as I have no cloth for patching.

We had a lovely air-raid last night and the Germans put out our lights. I'm sure this was just spite as we have quite efficiently blacked-out windows. It was just the right sort of night for an air-raid: raining cats and dogs and freezing cold. And the Germans are saying nasty things about our RAF lads. I think they prefer the Yanks who come in daylight and usually they come mainly on fine days such as today. And they are overhead now. Perhaps they are looking for the bits the RAF lads missed last night. But it's started to rain again – stair rods – and bombs. They, the Germans, will think we don't like them. Don't we? In their newspapers they say the Allied nations want to occupy Germany and treat the people as criminals. As though we would. Criminals indeed!

Friday 3rd November

Red Cross parcels have been issued, one between three men. We hope there's another two truck loads at the station. Hope this is true! The German issue of food is not sufficient. They've cut the meat and the bread and they are no longer issuing cooking fat. And we've heard that the bread ration is to be cut! The Red Cross is something we must be thankful for.

Nearby is a camp of Polish women prisoners who, according to our Man of Confidence (official title recognized by Geneva), are in a pitiful plight. They are short of clothing and have absolutely no toilet requisites. We have been asked – not by the Germans – to contribute anything we can in the way of clothing. Winter is almost with us. Apparently all they have is the clothing they are wearing. Squalor and degradation. Just like cattle. All we can give

---

[8] All Red Cross Parcels etc. come to us via Switzerland.

them is our spare clothing, rough and already worn out. And we're sending all of the soap we can spare. Man's inhumanity to man!...

Saturday 4th November

Today's news was good. The Germans have been pushed out of Belgium and Greece. The Russians are advancing in the east and our forces are doing well in the west. Air raid sirens are sounding at all times of the day and night. Germany is being churned up well and properly but the people are suffering so dreadfully. But are we merely playing with them: dragging it out to their absolute exhaustion. Sterilization to the last Nazi! Needs must...!

We are still awaiting letters. What a time it seems since I received my last letter. And we miss letters more than anything else as prisoners. Food, comfort nor amusement can allay our worry if there are no letters. I can't imagine what it must be like for the few of us who are illiterate or nearly illiterate. Their existence in these circumstances must be little better than that of beasts. I spend a lot of my time reading, or in writing down my whines and moans. But according to the BBC the passage of letters to and from prisoners is going without a hitch. Some one ought to ask the people at this end about that!

Sunday 5th November

I've just written to Evelyn. At first it was rather hard going. I could think of nothing to say which has not already been said by me. I wonder does she save all of my letters. Perhaps she does. Girls are said to tie up their received love letters in silk ribbon. I still keep all of hers. That is, all of those I've received as a prisoner. But if she's saved all of mine she must have hundreds. Perhaps one day we will sit together on the rug in front of our fire and burn them all. When she's in possession of the writer she won't need the letters. I think I shall write to Pam with my last lettercard. Does *she* keep all of my letters I wonder?

Monday 6th November

There was some mail came in last night but as usual there was none for me. We've had some fine weather today and tonight the sky is clear and the RAF are taking advantage of it. The sirens sounded a short while ago so I expect the lights to go out soon. They ... (*diary illegible*)

Tuesday 7th November

The lights beat me last night. They went out while I was writing. I've just written to Pam. I wonder how many of my letters reach her. The few I write to her leave no margin for any not to reach her. Not that it matters all that much but as she writes to me so frequently – almost as many as Evelyn – I wouldn't want her to feel that she doesn't matter.

The news isn't bad but there were no big events mentioned.

A rumour is circulating that there is to be a move from this camp. But why dump us here if their intention is to move us again? But as the square-heads think differently from us there is no knowing what they intend to do with us. But a move in this weather during the present spree of our bombers doesn't bear thinking about.

Wednesday 8th November

There is something wrong with my pen. The spring and the sac don't seem to be cooperating. But I can't get another pen here. I've had this pen such a long time that I'd hate to swop over to another. It's become an old friend, being one of the few items remaining of the articles I brought out from England. I valued it with my camera which was stolen from me when I was taken, unconscious, into hospital. Thieving bastards.

There is still little in the way of war news but I don't think we have had any set-backs recently.

A telegram has been received from Geneva advising us that 4,000 parcels have been dispatched to us. They ought to be here within the next few days. We hope!

I saw Jimmy Brown today and he showed me a book of photographs of India's North West Frontier. Seeing them made me almost homesick. It is the wildest country in the world and populated, I think, by the wildest people in the world, but it provides a wonderful life for a soldier. The air is always clean and sharp and the country is beautiful despite its ruggedness, and it's these two qualities combined with the danger provided by the fearsome tribesmen make it the young adventurer's playground. With a clear sky, the sun, and a heliograph, the signaller was king. All in the past now and read about only in such authors as Rudyard Kipling. But I'm romancing again. Those were the days! '...though we cursed you and we flayed you, by the living God that made you, you're a better man than I am, Gunga Din.' Those were the days!

Thursday 9th November

A special visit by the Protecting Power's representative was paid us today. He came as a result of our repeated complaints of bad conditions. As his visit was short only the major points of our discontent were presented to him. These were: no Red Cross food in the camp; no fuel; bad living conditions in our huts. Of course we don't know if he obtained any results. The Germans will give him the usual excuses and promises. But, as they say, 'You can't get blood out of a stone'. And the Germans appear to be suffering from metaphorical anaemia.

Nothing of importance was mentioned in the news but we are hoping for a big push in the west soon. Roosevelt has been voted in as President again. The Presidency seems to be a Roosevelt monopoly. But I rather think this period will be his last.

Today is the anniversary of the breaking out of the Hitler disease so long ago (soon to be cured, we hope). It is a national holiday for the Germans. Our reveille was at 8 o'clock this morning. We expect to hear tomorrow what he said in his speech. The usual stuff: promises, pleas, threats. All so repetitive, boring and sickening.

I have repaired my pen again but appear to have made it worse. However, if I treat it with care and don't use it too much it may outlast my sojourn as a prisoner. Of course if the worse comes to the worst I shall have to use a pencil.

Saturday 11th November

The lights went out last night so I was unable to make an entry. This morning I got a parcel of 200 cigarettes from my regiment. It is time they remembered me. Others, some only war time members of the regiment, have received clothing and book parcels and cigarettes.

I've been in the regiment thirteen years and I've just received my first regimental parcel. Of course, *my* regimental parcels must have gone where all of my other non-delivered parcels have gone: to the aforementioned Swiss yodellers and the thieving railway staff. So I mustn't be too hard on my regimental associates at Richmond. Obviously all they are responsible for is the making up of the parcels and addressing them. It is unlikely that they know the prisoners to whom the parcels are addressed.

Apparently Hitler didn't make his expected speech. Perhaps he thought his 'old, old, story' was getting a little threadbare and that the people were beginning to doubt him.

We have just been told of another 'cut': light and water this time. On Saturdays the lights will be turned off until 9pm. Daily, the water will be turned off from 2pm until 5pm and from 7pm until 5am the following morning. Conditions are becoming worse and worse.

In the news today the German 'V2' weapon was mentioned. This is an explosive packed rocket which is projected into the stratosphere 60 or 70 miles before dropping on the selected target (the Germans hope!). Here nearly everybody says it would be impossible to send a rocket so high but I think perhaps it is feasible. The lads here reckon I'm mad. But that's been their belief for some time. But even the artillery men amongst us say that a rocket couldn't reach that height. But Churchill mentioned it in the House of Commons. About the war in general nothing of importance seems to be claimed.

Monday 13th November

The lights beat me again on Saturday night. We could very nearly be as well without them considering the illumination they give us. There is still no news worth mentioning. We are told that Hitler gave the reason for not addressing the people as pressure of work at his headquarters. He allowed Goebbels to do it in his place.

On our side, our troops appear to have made no headway at all. There is still fighting at Aachen, or Aix la Chapelle, as it is again now called. And the Americans are trying to cut off Metz. But I think that Metz will turn out to be another Aachen: they'll spend a couple of months on it. But every little helps, as the old lady said as she relaxed in the sea. And every yard eastward brings the war nearer to its close. The trouble is, these yards are adding up so slowly.

Cards have been issued and I've written to Evelyn.

Tuesday 14th November

Checking up on the cards and letters I've sent I see that I have not written to Dad for some time so I have now written to him. It is now more than three months since I last heard from him and I'm beginning to wonder why. And I haven't had any letters at all for two months and I'm finding writing rather difficult without having any to answer. I suppose if Evelyn asks me questions which I don't answer she may not appreciate that I am not receiving her letters.

Wednesday 15th November

What a lousy day! There is a slushy sort of snow dropping by the ton driven by a howling wind. I am freezing to death. My fingers and feet are covered with chilblains and my boots are soaked. I walk as though I am on hot coals. And I'm shivering like a jelly.

I have written to the Hebdens – Edith, this time. I wonder, will she write back? I am just wasting precious cards. What have I done to annoy them? Has Pam spoken out of turn? I can think of nothing else that would have got the old cats' backs up. But why should I worry because a couple of silly old cows won't answer my letters. But I do worry because they were very kind to me when I was in Castle Cary and I'm afraid I may have hurt them unintentionally. While in Castle Cary I know they didn't like my being friendly with Pam: she nineteen and they hovering on forty. But they, and she, had been told of Evelyn and had met her and knew that she and I were engaged. But I am cold and hungry, and my patience is rather worn.

A bloke has lost two pet rabbits and is offering a reward of 600 cigarettes for information which will lead to their recovery. Poor rabbits! But surely, he's been guilty of hoarding. Live rabbits, and we haven't had any Red Cross supplement for weeks! In prison camp in Italy once, someone had a cat – till some one else put it into a pie. Poor old Tabbie! But it was quite tender, I was told. And another couple of the lads caught the Commandant's dog. That went into a stew.

But all of those who shared it claimed that it was tough and stringy. And it had always been considered to be such a nice dog! A pair of gloves was made from its skin and presented, anonymously, to the Commandant with the explanation that the prisoner who had received them in a parcel from home had no need of them in Italy's warmer climate. But I wonder: has anybody else got any rabbits?

The German battleship Von Tirpitz has been bombed by the RAF and has sustained several 12,000 lb. bomb hits. This ought to have put it out of action for the remainder of the war.

Friday 17th November
Another consignment of Red Cross food parcels has left Geneva according to a telegram received today. This makes a total of about 29,000 in transit. But when are they going to arrive here.

A lot of letters came in last night but few blokes received them. Those who received them had them in bundles of a dozen or so.

I had a cold bath today and I'm sure it nearly killed me (water from a stand-pipe). It was necessary. It was weeks after my previous all-over wash. But I notice, nobody else is chancing it!

Saturday 18th November
I've written to Evelyn. It's too dark to write.

Sunday 19th November
The lights were not switched on last night. There was an air raid instead, plus the latest economy measure. There is a very disconcerting rumour afloat today which has it that all prisoners are to be moved from this camp. Although I would rather it be a rumour there are a couple of things which incline me to think it may be true: no Red Cross parcels have arrived at this camp despite our having been informed that almost 30,000 have been dispatched from Geneva; the other thing is that our library has closed down and the books are to be issued to huts. This would happen in the latter case because the Germans could hardly be expected to provide us with packing cases and the transport for the thousands of books which are at present available to us. Of course, should we be moved, the books would have to be abandoned. We will be devastated if we have to move again, particularly as winter is almost upon us. I'm fed up. More heartbreaking marches, searches, and the degradation of travelling in cattle trucks.

Monday 20th November
We have all been allowed to have a hot shower and I had mine despite the cold wash-over I had the other day. For some reason or other the bath-house fire is going today and, we are told, will be going again tomorrow.

My ink seems to be getting rather weak – rather like the writer – I wonder if putting water in it causes this? Roll on the end of the war!

And it *is* rolling! Everything is going well on all fronts. The Germans have evacuated Greece because it is of no further importance, they say. But that is what they say of all of the places they evacuate. Why go there in the first place if they don't want it? Now our forces are rumbling towards the Rhine.

I wonder will there be a big offensive on the western side or will the Germans withdraw and merely defend the eastern bank? Prestige rather than strategy seems to be the big concern of the Germans so I think it's likely they'll fight for every inch of the western side. They are misers as far as territory is concerned. They hoard it and defend it trying to make their State shop-window appear great to the people who are obliged to shout: 'Heil Hitler!' But their State shop-window display is looking tatty. Their shop is rapidly running out of stock and will soon have to go out of business. While I'm not so optimistic as some of my comrades I am ready to believe that the war could end in the early spring. I shouldn't have said that. Cross my fingers and hope to die, whatever the antidote is. Really!

But I must, if I can, forget about the war. It's rather like the kettle which won't boil while it is being watched. But what a kettle. And what a long time it has taken already. I'm whimsicle (spelling?) rather than mad, I think.

Tuesday 21st November

I have received a tin of tobacco from the Chester le Street branch of the regimental association. It was dispatched last year and was addressed to PG70 in Italy. Some Red Cross food parcels have arrived but only sufficient for an issue of one between three men. However some more may arrive soon. I'd like us to have a good stock in because our forces seem to be about to start pressing much harder and nothing is more important to us at present than food. We are now looking forward to the passing of Christmas.

I am looking forward to having had it pass by. It's merely a milestone of time. 'How far is it to Bethlehem?' asks the rhyme. Three score miles and ten! But how far is that in Christmases? I am going again! It must be this pure German air making me light headed. My spine is oscillating like a banjo string and I'm quivering as though suffering from malaria. Leave out the malaria, I *am* suffering. Gosh it's cold. And my chilblains are killing me. My brave front is starting to crack. Well, something is.

Wednesday 22nd November

Happy days are here again! More Red Cross parcels came today so we are having an issue of one between two, to last us a fortnight.

I got two letters today from Dad dated August and September. But when am I going to get letters from Evelyn again.

Thursday 23rd November

My chilblains are getting worse. Some of the nails of my left foot have dropped off and my feet are painful and heavy as lead. If they get any worse I shall be unable to walk. But we are all in the same boat. We are all suffering and we are hungry and cold. And our spud ration has been cut again. I didn't think it possible! What a diet! Our bread has a large saw-dust content (good quality wood, the Germans assure us) and we have vegetables, margarine, and jam. But vegetables are the only items which is not ersatz, ie, artificial.

I have written to Dad and told him of my instruction to my paymaster. That should put his mind at rest: beer money for Christmas!

Friday 24th November

I got my watch back from the camp watchmaker today. He has replaced the broken spring and fixed the celluloid front (no glass). The news is good these days. On the western front our armies are advancing. That also included the French Army; they have reached the Rhine east of Belfort and they have turned left and are heading north. If they make a successful advance they will either cut off the Germans who are still on the west side of the river or compel them to withdraw to the eastern bank. The Germans are quoting the Manchester Guardian as saying that it is the Allies' intention to finish the war this year. But it is a vain hope. There are too few weeks left. Still the Nazis are doing all they can to hold together the German people. But I suppose there is a chance they might crack.

Saturday 25th November

I've written a lettercard to Evelyn. But when am I going to get a letter from her? This waiting is terrible. All I have to keep me going is my faith in her. I know of no one whose fiancée has remained so long. No wonder I worry. She is all I have. To my family I am merely the man who pays Santa Claus. But would she marry anyone else now having waited so long? But I do, so much, want a letter from her.

The news is still good and the Germans are about to lose Strasburg. Now, it seems, they are unable to hold us anywhere. There is a report, so far unconfirmed, that the French Army has crossed the Rhine but I don't believe this. Should this be true, they, the French, will endeavour to establish themselves northward on the eastern bank of the river and the Germans on the west bank will then have had it! The Germans are still claiming to be holding Aachen!

Sunday 26th November

We have had beautiful weather today, The first day we have had no rain for weeks. The sky was cloudless and ideal for bombing. Our bombers were over in strength. About midday they were over in their thousands their vapour trails in the sky being made into pretty patterns by the wind. The bombers are shooting across the sky like shoals of tadpoles while their escorting fighters loop and criss-cross, and gambol like lambs in the spring. What an inspiring sight for us prisoners. It must be a hateful and terrifying sight for the Germans in the areas being bombed. But surely it can't last much longer. Optimism reigns in the camp just now. It is thought that with a clear sky and a good frost our forces will cut their way through the German defences and soon put an end to it all.

Tuesday 28th November

We had no lights at all yesterday but we've put that down to the excessive bombing that's been taking place during the past few days. The current weather is ideal for our bombers and they appear to be taking full advantage of it – day and night! All last night the sirens warbled merrily while we listened joyfully in the darkness. But, really, I'm sure some of us felt uneasy about our jubilance. It is winter and cold and where once stood homes and ordered living there is now dereliction and virtual desert and dead and maimed people. And terrified screaming children. During the periods of silence we could hear the low rumbling of the devastation taking place in the distance – Germany crumbling. But it was dark only in our barrack huts because a beautiful moon was lighting up the landscape until – if we looked out of our windows – we forgot that it was night. Away in the distance there was an almost continuous display of anti-aircraft shells bursting in the sky in a seemingly panicky effort to drive away our bombers. Obviously they succeeded in shooting down some of our aircraft but this number is trivial when set against the numbers taking part in the raid. Germany's might is tumbling down! The other day I read a poem: *Egypt's Might is Tumbling Down*.[9]

> But the dreams their children dreamed,
> Fleeting, unsubstantial, vain,
> Shadowy as the shadows seemed,
> Airy nothing as they dreamed,
> These remain.

The Germans, delusioned people, bullied, regimented, underfed: being battered into submission or destruction by the allied forces or being executed as traitors if they suggest surrender. In the meantime the German news says that they are just waiting for good weather before they take the offensive against the allies. My personal belief is that this statement must have been made during the recent bad weather which seemed to indicate that it was

---

[9] This is the second verse of a poem by Mary Coleridge. The first verse reads:

> Egypt's might is tumbled down
> Down a-down the deeps of thought
> Greece is fallen and Troy town
> Glorious Rome has lost her crown
> Venice is nought.

going to remain so throughout the winter. What do they suppose our forces were waiting for? Up to date we have had three days of glorious weather, with a heavy frost each night. Our tactical air forces have had three full days to blast the German defences, and last night's frost will have rendered the ground ideal for our tanks. Surely we ought to be hearing very cheering news during the next few days. To me, it will be compensation for having to sit here in my frozen state. My hands are blue, my nose is purple, and pus is oozing out of my burst chilblains. And I'm hungry. The fact that so many thousands of Germans are suffering more acutely doesn't console me at all.

I have written postcards to the Jameses and to Jenny.

Wednesday 29th November

Our short spell of dry weather broke during the night when the rain again came and poured for hours. And so goes my hope for a hard frost and good advances by our tanks in the west. Our troops are still advancing but slowly. According the French GHQ the French Army has not crossed the Rhine. I'd regard this as strategy and not their inability to cross because, while I'm sure the French are no match for an equal number of Germans equally armed, it is to be assumed that the French will be superior in arms and numbers and are able to call on countless aircraft to support their troops. So I'm sure the Froggies could cross the river if it were deemed advantageous that they do. Since the start of the war the UK has lost 500,000 men killed, wounded, and missing. Most of these, of course, I believe will be prisoners.

Thursday 30th November

A depressing day. Churchill has been agitating about the complacency of everybody regarding the terminating of the war. He says the time has not yet come when people can sit back and take things easy because there is still some time for the war to run. He says that in an earlier speech he voiced the hope that it would end by late spring or early summer but he now thinks he was being too optimistic. His hope, up to date, is that the European issue may be settled by late summer, perhaps! This has shifted the balance of our mental comfort considerably. I am as depressed as I have ever been. We have in view what we believe to be the top of the hill after a long, tiresome climb, only to find when we reach it that we have not reached the top but merely a false crest which has been concealing a further ascent. And I think of Evelyn waiting for me, and when not receiving a hoped for letter, wondering if is she still waiting for me. Am I being disloyal in worrying as I do ? But I haven't received a letter which wasn't written months ago. The last letter I received from her was written four months ago when we all thought the war was almost at an end. But the end has not yet arrived and, seemingly, won't for months. Is she still waiting? But I've already said that! Has her real fiancé, in her mind, been insidiously usurped by her ideal? Is she ignoring the good Tom, Dick, or Harry in her preference for the ideal which she is hoping I will turn out to be. What a horribly unsettling thought! But, as I see her, she is a good sensible girl and I hope she has too clear a remembrance of my faults to allow herself to be 'conned' by a self-made fairy-tale prince-like bloke in a battledress. But whatever she has done, or thought, will not be known to me for some months yet – if ever! And I wonder: is she still waiting?

Friday 1st December

According to a Red Cross notice, there are 10,000 food parcels on their way here. There are, also, according to our camp newspaper, some Canadian Christmas parcels being rushed to us. I am intrigued by the term 'rushed'. I can see the alert wireless operator with his hand trembling on the morse key, transmitting this urgent order. The warehouse men falling over each other in their eagerness to load the trucks. And the German railway staff egging each other to further effort to speed this Red Cross food to their starving prisoners. And I know what our own railway workers in Britain in similar circumstances would say: 'Bollocks to the bloody prisoners; get the lid off that bloody crate, mate!' But the news report merely states that they have left Canada. They certainly won't have been dispatched from Geneva because we have not received an advice note telling us so. But if the 16,000 ordinary Red Cross food parcels arrive within a week from now we shall not be absolutely on the rocks. Not quite. But there is still no news of any mail. Surely our air forces have not disrupted the communication system that they can't even get letters through. Of course censorship may be the problem. But we know the country is in a bad way. According to a German NCO there are some civilians who are actually living in holes which are merely covered by ground sheets. What an awful state of affairs! And we are grumbling because they have given us no jam this week! We have been told they have none to give to us. And grumble though we do, we believe them.

Sunday 3rd December

We had no lights yesterday but this was just the result of their latest electricity saving scheme. We are in almost total darkness from about 5pm but the evening passed not unpleasantly: a South African came into our hut with a violin and played to us during a couple of hours. I like the violin and believe it to be an instrument into which the player can put his whole feeling. During the evening I talked with Pat Corrigan, a Rhodesian. He went out there when he was seventeen. We talked until ten o'clock when I went to bed only to be alerted by the drone of an aeroplane. As no sirens had sounded I believed at first that it must be a German aircraft. As it passed over the camp I listened to its fading away in the distance but it continued to drone for a while and then it got louder. It's coming back, I thought. Louder! Louder! Louder! Suddenly our camp was shaken by two violent detonations – two bombs! All of the quiet conversations stopped. Condensed vapour and chips of wood dropped from our roof. There was sudden panic as the fellows jumped off their bunks and grabbed their great-coats and boots. 'It's one of ours! It's the RAF! He's bombing the camp!' All of the lads were shouting. I stayed where I was between my blankets, hoping the pilot would realize he was over a prison camp. I listened to its droning away again. But again he came back: closer! closer! Everything in our hut was quiet. I could feel my heart thumping like a ship's engine. The drone got louder. He's over us! He must have let his bombs go! I could feel my face twitching and I started to count, all the while listening to the now screaming aircraft. With relief, I stopped my counting. There were no more bombs. He must have flown over again merely to survey the damage he'd inflicted. Tonight we have been told that it must have been the headlights of a car which had caught the pilot's attention. Four men were killed and some were injured (German soldiers). Also there was damage to some buildings.

I have written to Evelyn but what a job it is when I am not receiving any letters. But I must continue to write. I must show faith.

Monday 4th December

I have just received two letters from Evelyn! ! ! What a relief! I have worried myself sick during the past few weeks. One of the letters was dated August and the other one September. How wonderful it is to receive letters which are so affectionate and sweet. How nice to feel that I am loved and wanted by at least one person. In one of her letters she says that I must meet one of her friends, a young woman named Ethel. Ethel is thirty one, ten years older than Evelyn. I suppose that when the letter was written in September Evelyn had visions of my being in England for Christmas, that good old benchmark! I hoped so too, but it was just wishful thinking. All of us have been doing that throughout the war. But not this Christmas now. Next Christmas? Perhaps!

Thursday 7th December

I wrote to Pam on Tuesday. It is now some time since I received my last letter from her. I wonder when I shall get the next one? During the last couple of weeks the lights have been switched off at nine pm every night, with the exception of Saturdays when there was no lighting at all. This we considered bad enough but now they are not switched on until six pm. So we enjoy three hours of lighting each evening, less Saturday, unless we have an air raid. What a country! But I mustn't be unfair: yesterday we got two weeks' issue of jam – last week's and this week's.

Saturday 9th December

3,000 food parcels – many of them pilfered – arrived yesterday so today we got an issue of one parcel between two men. But the Germans have started to puncture the tins as the Italians used to do.

This is explained as a security measure but, personally, I fail to see the necessity. We are hardly receiving sufficient food to live on far less hoard any.

Sunday 10th December

The Russians are now only 120 miles from Vienna! That may seem to be a long way but at the rate the Russians move – when they move – it will not be so far. They said they would start their advance when they had changed over to their winter equipment. Apparently they have changed over: Joe now has his snow shoes on! But the Greeks are letting us down. There is a small civil war taking place in the country with our army backing up one side.

There was snow on the ground this morning but it has all been dispelled by the sun and the rain. But it is very cold again tonight so perhaps we shall have some more snow tomorrow.

Wednesday 13th December

There was some Red Cross clothing issued yesterday. I got a pair of socks and a pair of gloves. There are a few battle-dresses but those of us who require them must parade tomorrow to have the worn-out items condemned. I've had my present suit nearly two years but I doubt if I'll get a new one.

Friday 15th December

It is a freezing cold day and our hut is like a refrigerator! I have tried to read a text book on photography; I have tried to read poetry; I have tried to read a book on somebody's travels in South America. But I am asking too much of me! I am too cold to do anything. Ice-cold, and the war is going to last forever.

I've just had something to cheer me up. Some mail came in and I got five letters: three from Evelyn, dated 12th, 20th, and 30th; one from Sheilah, 8th October, and one from Margaret Hebden, 19th September. Margaret's letter surprised me: I'd given up all hope of receiving any more letters from that source. But there was no apology: merely a mention of how busy they are in their post office. Too busy! For 18 months! But here I am, rambling on about a middle-aged woman when I have three letters from my Evelyn. She has been ill and has been in hospital to have an abscess lanced but at the time of her writing was almost fit again. Bella, who had spent a few days in Poole, had visited her but she has not enlarged on this. As Evelyn was incapacitated, Iris looked after Bella. I'd like to know what sort of impression Bella made on my future in-laws. I hope her rough edges were not too obvious but, perhaps, the RAF 'sand-papered' these a bit. Evelyn has said so little about the visit and I wonder what the general verdict was.

The war news is still good as far as we are concerned but our advances seem to be painfully slow compared with that of the Russians. At the present rate of progress in the west it doesn't look as though it will all end by next summer. This is so depressing on top of the prevailing prison-camp conditions. Condensed vapour is continuously dripping down on us from the roof and our huts are freezing cold. The issued food is poor and insufficient and the Red Cross food has diminished considerably in quantity and regularity. We used to have an issue of one parcel per man per week. Now we are lucky if we have a parcel for two men per two weeks. And to make matters worse we spend a half hour twice a day on check parade. This would be tolerable were we sufficiently fed for the climate but, underfed as we are, it is little short of torture. But I am going to carry on and go back to Evelyn to live 'happy ever after'.

Some mail has been brought in and there was one for me from Pam, dated 3rd November. This is very quick considering that it has been re-directed from IVb. She tells me she has met the brother of a friend who has been repatriated from India. And Pam tells me he is madder than I am. Madder than I am! ! !

Some days ago I asked Jerry – he speaks French fairly well – to approach a certain French-speaking unter-offizier to get us some ink. I suggested we give him some cigarettes in exchange. We got the ink but the German would not accept our offer of cigarettes. This was extremely kind of the German as British cigarettes are priceless outside a prison camp.

Sunday 17th December
Received an old letter from Dad dated 11th July. It is just a note and not very informative. At the time of his writing he had not heard from Evelyn for three months. All that concerns me is that she continue to write to me. We had another hot bath yesterday, our third since coming to this camp, our last this year. The commandant ordered that any man who was without a coat and cap to wear later was not to have a bath. Perhaps he believes we would catch our death of cold! Very thoughtful, some of these Germans! My chilblains are sheer torture. I've got them all over my fingers and my feet are covered with them to such an extent that I can barely walk. I used to have slender fingers but at the moment they are swollen and shapeless. Roll on the warm weather if we can't have an armistice.

Postcards have been issued. I've written to Evelyn and Margaret.

Monday 18th December
Received another letter from Dad this morning, dated 24th September. Emma, he tells me is stationed only two miles from home but he never sees her. Well, home life was never very cheerful so we can't blame her. As a child she was never the favourite. Dad is losing us one by one and all because he didn't give us a home worth living in. First he lost me. Then Bella. Then Emma, both of them now with the air force. Dad, I suppose, believes they will both return home after the war. What a hope! Like other young women they will marry.

Friday 19th December

Four years ago today I went on leave to Poole. Although I wasn't aware of it at the time I believe it was the finest time in my life. Everyone was so kind to me. A couple of the church club girls, unaware that my accommodation was arranged, and supposedly with their parents' agreement, offered me accommodation at their homes. I was amazed and touched by all of the magnanimity. At that time I little thought of the hardship which may be ahead of me. Four years! And two and a half of those as a prisoner of war. What a life!

Last night I received a letter from Bella. It is the longest letter she's written to me. She didn't mention her visit to Evelyn – she didn't mention Evelyn at all – but as this letter was written in November perhaps she's told me everything in a previous letter which I have not yet received.

It seems the Germans made a big push yesterday but we don't how big or how serious. We'll learn during the next few days.

Wednesday 20th December

The German push is apparently serious although our news doesn't tell us much. The Allied High Command has blanketed the news but it seems the Germans have penetrated twenty miles back into Belgium. 'I'm dreaming of a white Christmas' ! – but the real one is as black as could be. We have no Red Cross food and there is little German food. There are hardly any cigarettes in the camp – doesn't affect me – and our troops are falling back faster than they advanced! Here, we are all saying the German High Command has committed a terrible blunder: that they have fallen into a trap. But is it stating the obvious to mention perhaps the German High Command can see as much as a prisoner of war! Churchill has promised to make a statement after the Christmas holiday. Come hell or high water, or war, our statesmen must observe the Christmas holiday! Fiddling while Rome burns!

Friday 22nd December

The situation in the west still looks bleak: the Germans are still advancing and our troops seem to be unable to stop them. And the war is going to last forever at this rate. I am hoping that our forces in the west are merely waiting for the Germans to wear themselves out when our armies will close in and liquidate them. Well, that's my hope. But what a Christmas! Could any Christmas be bleaker?

Tonight we have a quantity of turnip tops and peelings, the refuse from several days' soup. I've just finished cleaning the share Jerry and I have received. Pig food! But it's very welcome. I think we've all forgotten what it's like to have a satisfied stomach. This is where the good old British sense of humour takes over! Some of the lads have just been down on their hands and knees, amongst the refuse, grunting like pigs, to the tune of 'Oh Come All Ye Faithful' ! And I laughed with them because it all looked so funny.

Our side is most certainly winning and the Germans who are prisoners are being treated almost as unfortunate guests while we, soldiers from the winning side, are starving and not even receiving the food which our country is sending to us because the Germans are stealing the food which has not been destroyed by our bombers. At the same time we acknowledge that similarly placed as they, we would behave as we believe they are behaving.

Saturday 23rd December

Four years ago today I went shopping with Evelyn. We bought an engagement ring for Evelyn and a silver propelling pencil for Edith Jones. The ring didn't fit so we left it to be collected the following day. It was Edith's birthday, hence the silver pencil. Happy days: When will they return?

The German advance is coming to a halt it would seem. Now, we need some good news to cheer us up.

Sunday 24th December

A beautiful day – in fact we have had several beautiful days in a row – but it has been so cold. In our hut the comparatively warm air is condensing as beads of water on the roof where they are released periodically when they drop where least wanted like needles of ice – quite frequently down my neck. I have a 'top' bunk so consequently my blankets catch a lot of this home-made water – what a life! What a Christmas Eve!

But the German news seems to indicate a change-over of initiative on the western front. They are claiming that they have repulsed thirteen of our attacks. This would indicate, I think, that they are expecting a thorough bashing in the near future and are preparing their people for the bad news. Roll on! But we don't expect anything big to happen until after Christmas.

Christmas Eve! But my Christmas Eve is living at Poole, and: *I wonder who's kissing her now?*[10] But that's disloyal of me. Is it, though? Four years is a long time! I haven't kissed any girls since I last saw her, but then, I haven't had the opportunity. But what matters at the moment is: is she thinking of me now?! ! I am thinking of her.

Christmas Day 1944

Glorious weather and only the lack of food to spoil the festivities. However we have done the best possible with the little we had. It's all gone now but another Christmas day is in store for us in the uncertain future. A telegram has been received advising us that 8,000 Christmas food parcels were dispatched to us on the 18th of this month. But parcels which were dispatched to us a month earlier have not been received. Where are they? They will arrive one day, perhaps, if our air forces have not already blasted them to hell with the train in which they were being conveyed. But in the

---

[10] A song of the 1930s resurrected for the occasion.

meantime we are happy although this happiness is a temporary state in a prison camp. It fluctuates with the season and the association of ideas. But it's nice to be happy if only for a short time. It's like the re-charging of a battery.

I wonder if Evelyn will be at a party tonight and I wonder… But I've put that sort of thinking 'out of bounds'! I've written to her today but I wonder when she'll receive it – if she receives it. This is my fourth Christmas away from her. Will there be any more, I wonder? I am doing an awful lot of wondering.

We are all cynical now. We used to say: 'Happy Christmas! We'll be home next year!' 'Be home next year!' I heard no one say that today. It was mostly something like, 'All the best, mate.' We have no idea of how long the war will go on. Our time slips by imperceptibly: seconds, minutes, hours, days, years. Yes: years! Some of the fellows here have been prisoners since Dunkirk. But I started this entry by saying I was happy and now I find that I've unconsciously worked my way into an awful state of depression. But it's Christmas and I have a nasty cold – there's always something the matter with me – so I'd better close down.

I've written to Bella. Eight o'clock on a Christmas night and I'm going to bed! And Evelyn may be dancing... Damn and blast Hitler and Himmler and all of the other pox-bound Nazi bastards!

Wednesday 27th December
The lighting is bad tonight. I can barely see the paper I'm writing on. At last some parcels have arrived. One truckload yesterday and ten this morning. Also there was a truckload of clothing arrived. I hope there's a good supply of battledresses as my trousers are in shreds. They are so bad that I must wear a pair of khaki drill shorts underneath. There are some rumours of mail but so far these are only rumours.

The news isn't bad although the situation in the west is still rather vague but we are hoping for some good news from that front. The Russians are doing well and are reported to be only 60 miles from the Austrian border. Budapest is surrounded. The weather is still consistently good and the sky has been cloudless for days although the cold has been intense. Our aircraft have not been much in evidence at all in this area but I suppose they'll be doing overtime in the west. This of course would indicate that the situation in the west is much more serious than is mentioned by the BBC.

Friday 29th December
Because of the large consignment of parcels received on Wednesday we received an issue of one parcel per man yesterday. They are Canadian parcels. Wonderful parcels for starving men, containing among other items, a pound of butter, a pound of powdered milk, and a large packet of unsweetened biscuits. Just the parcel for a hungry man! But that isn't

all! Some more arrived yesterday and some more today. Today's lot are
Christmas food parcels. Happy days are here again! The aspect is much more
cheerful now that we have something to supplement the issued German food.
The latter is less than half of that which we were receiving until the late
summer.

Churchill and Eden have left Greece. Their ship, a cruiser, was shelled by
the so-called partisans but the nearest one dropped 200 yards from the ship.
Also, on leaving the embassy they were sniped. Are the partisans hinting that
they don't want oil to be poured over their troubled waters?

In the west it is said that Von Rönsted has lost the initiative. Big things ought
to be happening there soon and I am expecting the Germans to be hurrying
back to the Rhine soon. They have come up against the 51st Highland
division and they seem to be regarding it as a foul blow when they were
doing so well against the Americans.

Saturday 30th December

We have had – and are still getting – our first really heavy fall of snow
today. It has been an unpleasant change to see the sky all black and clouded
over after the cloudless days we have been having. Last night, the full
moon shining was light as day, I hope our bombers took advantage of it as
we won't have such fine weather again for some time to come. It is a pity
the adverse weather has come just as the initiative in the west has changed
over to the allies. Our superior air forces are almost useless in this weather
and they always seemed so necessary. The number of aircraft the Germans
have is so small that the disadvantage to them caused by the bad weather is
negligible. But whether our troops in the west beat their way east or remain
static the advance of the Russians goes on. The latest report has it that they
are now fighting in the streets of Budapest. There, the weather must be
simply awful and the Germans will get no quarter from the Russians. This
morning, because of the weather, we had no check parade. The Germans
actually counted us in bed! I got up at about half past seven, washed and had
breakfast, and then had to get back into bed to be counted!

Sunday 31st December

A lovely day and our bombers have been over in force. Hamburg, Bremen,
and Hanover, seemed to be their targets. The bombing lasted a couple of
hours and seemed to be fairly heavy.

I've written postcards to Evelyn and to Pam. I am so fed up of writing to
people as a prisoner of war. It seems so endless and summer seems to be the
earliest we can hope for an end to it all. Here we are: a bargaining counter for
the Germans and a liability to our own government. We lounge year in and
year out, sweltering in summer – freezing in winter – waiting for the end and
making silly prognostications which don't happen as we had hoped while all

of the time we are getting older. And the people at home think of us as we were when they last saw us. Roll on!

1945

It is now midnight. 1944 is dead. 1945 is born. Will it bring peace? Or will it be another year of slaughter and hardship? Advance 1945 and let us see what you have in store for us! The Germans have promised to leave our lights on until a half hour after midnight. It is now a quarter of an hour past midnight. 1945 is a quarter of an hour old. The lads are jolly. There is singing, and also recitations. And I am being watched! Some fellows are looking at me and are obviously talking about me. I suppose they are wondering why I sit here writing while everyone else appears to be so actively happy. But it is getting late and our lights will soon be out. I wonder where is Evelyn? Will 1945 take me to her? Or sever her from me forever. 1945! It doesn't seem true – but I'm tired.

Monday 1st January

Another lovely day and the RAF are overhead. For the past hour there has been an almost continuous rumbling. They have been bombing almost incessantly during the past three days and their targets seem to have been Hanover, Bremen, and Hamburg.

Recently Jerry and I have been much more friendly with each other. We haven't ever fallen out over anything but we spoke with each other only during meals. Which one of us has changed? Or have we both changed? Anyway it's nice to have an intelligent conversation which isn't being merely polite to one another.

I am having trouble with my pen again. It is tending to flow much too freely. When I return to England I shall send it to the makers and ask them to repair it.

Tuesday 2nd January

It is eleven a.m. and the sky is as heavy as lead but the RAF lads are over again. The sirens have just sounded. The other day somebody worked out that the sirens sound an average of four times a day. It is very cold today and the ground is covered with several inches of sharp, uneven ice. With chilblains walking is extremely painful. I am sorry for the South Africans. Some of them had not seen snow before this winter and they are not particularly inspired by it. And I sympathise with them. I've experienced cold winters – in Waziristan and in Iraq where the temperatures drop below zero – but I still find cold weather unpleasant. Perhaps I'm soft. I need a bed-warmer – but that sort of thought is out of bounds for the duration! But what an idiot I am: I sit here writing any nonsense that comes into my head. Dreaming. Always dreaming! But we all dream but most of us keep our dreams secret.

Thursday 4th January

There has been a thaw during the last two days and I feel a little warmer, but not much. This morning we were kept on check parade for about an hour. This was on account of the RAF lads. They refused to turn out and the commandant wouldn't dismiss the army prisoners until the RAF blokes turned out to be counted. The RAF blokes are just being stupid. They know that the Germans won't let them get away with this childish behaviour but to them it is just a joke. But it was a very bad show. The army prisoners were kept there standing in driving sleet from 8a.m. till 9.15a.m.

The snow has all gone now and if we could have a dry spell with a drying wind the ground would soon be in a fit state to walk on.

The Christmas food parcels are not to be issued yet because we are still short of 1,000. Instead, we are to have an issue of an ordinary food parcel between two men. This is to last us a week and if, in the meantime, the missing 1,000 arrive we shall get them, the Christmas parcels, at the rate of one per man on the next day of issue. But the RAF has bombed this area so much that the missing 1,000 parcels are likely to be non-existent. Hanover is the main railway junction, I think! Still it's in a good cause. Carry on, RAF!

Friday 5th January

We had a frost last night and the ground is still hard although the temperature seems to be above freezing now. The sky was very clear last night and a very strong force of our bombers flew over in the early hours of this morning. There were also some yesterday evening. But they always seem to be flying over! The RAF dropped over half a million tons of bombs on Germany in 1944. So far this is their record for a year but perhaps they may improve on this in 1945. But let's hope the war will end before another record can be achieved.

The Germans are still holding out in Budapest. How much longer? We have an offensive going in the west now and we appear to be doing well.

Saturday 6th January

The RAF is over again tonight. And they were over here last night, too. There can't be much of Hamburg, Bremen, and Hanover remaining. Those thousands of tons of bombs every day must be creating havoc. But it all brings the end nearer!

Lettercards were issued today and I've written to Evelyn. It is – or at least it seems – a long time since we had any letters. I wonder when the next batch will arrive. The lights are likely to go any moment now so I'd better close down.

Sunday 7th January

A very dull day and cold, too. The war news is cheerful but nothing outstanding. I suppose they are waiting for the good weather again as they have in the past! The good old spring offensive which takes place in the summer but which is never quite successful owing to unforeseen circumstances. (What! in war?) It then drags on into autumn when bad weather puts off further action until the following spring: a new spring offensive which will succeed. As in the past, I expect an offensive in the spring but this time I won't expect success: success, victory – is a fairy tale: England is a fairyland! No such place exists. I was conceived in a prison camp by prisoner of war parents; born in a POW camp; nurtured on turnip soup and wooden bread; educated. But I'm going round the bend! Anyway, hopes of/for this spring are out of bounds during the indefinite future. But all of the current favourable news is making us blasé: we've got to satisfy ourselves with the belief that we're winning.

Tuesday 9th January

We are spring-cleaning today! That is, we are going to spring-clean today. The big event is due to start after we've had our soup which will have been disposed of by about two minutes past mid-day. It is due to arrive at mid-day. This spring cleaning is the Germans' idea. A German who couldn't mind his own business went nosing about the RAF huts and unearthed dead dogs, rats, and empty bully-beef tins, etc under the beds of the RAF lads. Now the RAF lads were hurt – very hurt – about this. Apparently they are not to blame. No, the people responsible, apparently, are those who occupied the huts before the RAF lads moved in – Russians, Jews, etc – who didn't sweep out before they left the premises. And the poor RAF lads are being blamed for the unclaimed dead dogs etc. So, just in case the huts occupied by army prisoners were not swept out by the previous occupants, the Germans have intimated that we move out everything on to the cold, cold snow lest there be unwarranted dead dogs, etc in our huts.

Actually, the army huts are swept out every day and we scrub our tables. The people at home would be surprised if they saw how clean and well mannered we are. But our soup is coming so I'd better get my spoon ready.

Our spring-cleaning has been completed but the impetus has carried me further: I've done some repairs to my clothes and I've sewn some buttons on my greatcoat where they were needed. I wish I could receive a next of kin parcel as I now have only one set of underclothing and I can't wash these as I've nothing to wear while they're being washed and dried. And my socks are going fast. Roll on the end.

There has been no mail for some time and we are all looking forward to its coming. In a prison camp we always seem to be waiting for something: letters, personal parcels, food parcels, clothing, the end of the war.

But it just goes on and on. Just like Tennyson's *Brook:* 'Men may come and men may go ...' but this blasted war goes on forever!

Thursday 11th January

I've written a lettercard to Jenny. Yesterday I bought three in exchange for cigarettes. There was no jam issued yesterday and we, Jerry and I, have none at all. This morning I mixed some powdered milk with sugar and water to spread on our bread for breakfast – three thin slices of bread. Hard times indeed. There is still no sign of any mail and consequently we are all down in the dumps.

Saturday 13th January

Postcards have been issued – two per man — and I've written to Dad and Sheilah. I have two cards which I got from Jock Taylor so I'll hold these in reserve. And I've got a lettercard which I've put aside which I'll write to Evelyn tomorrow. Writing to Evelyn when I'm not receiving letters from her is a probem. I've told her so repeatedly that I love her and want her that it must be starting to jar on the poor girl. There's too little space on a lettercard to expand on anything.

It is only four weeks since I received three letters from her but I'm back to the state when the sight of her writing makes my heart skip a beat. I'm terrified that I might lose her. All I do is wait and worry. And I try to write to her every week, lettercard being available, trying to seem cheerful. But this waiting and wanting in a prison camp, a spiritual darkness, is simply awful.

Monday 15th January

I didn't make an entry yesterday because we were busy all day trying to make our hut comfortable after the Germans took our mattresses and furniture. They left only one table and two benches (seats) in each hut. This, they claim, is a reprisal because they say a camp of German prisoners in Egypt has not had mattresses during the past two years. This is a stupid claim because British troops in Egypt don't have mattresses. Their bedding is laid on groundsheets on the sand which is softer than any mattresses they have ever issued to us. But we don't believe this reprisal. We believe they've taken from us to give to their own bombed out civilians. We had little comfort before but now there is none at all in the present temperature with only two, small and very thin, blankets. Without a mattress, it's like sleeping on a horizontal ladder. The Germans obviously anticipated that their taking our mattresses from us would be a shock so they took them while we were on check parade. We were covered by machine-guns and there were wolf-dogs. Perhaps they were afraid of our demonstrating. What a chance: half starved men against machine guns and wolf dogs! Not likely. We'll wait until the end of the war.

I wrote a lettercard to Evelyn yesterday. It was a rambling effort and will make the poor girl think that I'm quite mad. I am sure my comrades here would corroborate!

Wednesday 17th January

A cold, biting wind is blowing this morning, driving a dry, powdery snow before it. This must certainly be the coldest morning we've experienced this winter. There is still no jam in the camp but we've been promised honey in lieu this afternoon. This honey, of course, is artificial. Made from coal apparently! In fairness to the Germans it must be said that they themselves are suffering the most awful hardship of hunger and cold, and a lack of all civilized comforts.

And our bombers give them little respite. There were hordes of them over last night and for nearly an hour I listened to the throbbing drone. I could hear the awful rumbling of their bombs in the distance and I felt the ground and the building shaking. The ordinary German people must be so miserable. Being bombed is awful but in this weather it must be beyond description. It is disturbing when borne in mind that their horror is being caused by our side. And it must go on before it can end.

As far as our war effort is concerned, big things seem to be taking place all over. The Russians are moving again and are only fifty miles from Germany proper. If they could keep up their present rate of advance they'd be in Germany by the weekend. They won't, of course, they must stop to consolidate their gain and to replace their casualties.

And it shouldn't be long before our forces in the west start another move eastward. They've been static for some time now so perhaps a big attack has been prepared. Let's have it quickly before we all starve to death here!

Six years ago today I sailed from Karachi fondly believing my soldiering days were over. How wrong I was!

Thursday 18th January

Another wild day but a thaw seems to be threatening. This morning there was a layer of snow on the ground but it has gone and left in its place a semi-frozen slush. However there's a good wind blowing so perhaps it will dry or freeze up properly. We got the promised 'honey' yesterday but it is really a sort of syrup and not at all sweet. Still, even German artificial syrup is better than nothing.

We have had several air raids since yesterday morning and now nobody seems to know when our bombers are coming or going. 'All clears' suddenly turn to 'Overhead!' They now come at all times and in all weathers. Nothing stops them. The communications in this part of Germany are in a terrible state. A German soldier has said that three or four days for inland post is not at all unusual.

Friday 19th January

Another horrible day with a blizzard which seems to be blowing from all directions but we were counted outside as though the weather were agreeable. Conditions are so bad it would seem that we are in a punishment camp. There is no brutality but the neglect and bad conditions are simply awful. Last night our lights were put out for no apparent reason. There was certainly no air-raid as the search lights were on all around the camp. Perhaps the military bashing they are receiving is making them vindictive. The last report had the Russians just 17 miles outside Germany. Good old Joe: keep it up! We had another hot shower today, the first this year. And then we were medically examined to see if we have TB. Some fellows had their names taken and are to be examined again.

Some mail has come in and there were three for me: Evelyn, Sheilah, and, of all people, Edith Jones. They are all August letters. Evelyn's is very sweet. She loves me she says and would like a wedding with no frills. So would I, in fact, any sort of a wedding would do for me so long as I marry Evelyn. But her parents and her sisters want the frills. Oh well, it will be in a good cause! Sheilah said she expected me home for Christmas. So did I but I was unavoidably detained! Edith's letter indicates a great change in her. I can't explain but her letter indicates a different girl from the one I knew. Perhaps her work and changed life-style has matured her. Rather pompously, I thought, she says, 'Now Evelyn has given me your address and permission to write I need have no qualms about writing to you.' But if she had qualms before why didn't she say so instead of just cutting me off when I was captured? Surely she could have told me her conscience was urging her to stop writing to me as I was engaged to Evelyn. She mentions a possible romance. I wish him luck. He's taking on a handful. Two handfuls if my memory serves me correctly. She must be about fourteen stone now and, perhaps, no longer the pious schoolgirl, but the best of luck to both of them.

Saturday 20th January
I've written to Edith and told her off for not writing sooner.

Joe Stalin is still going 'full speed ahead' towards Germany and is sixty miles from Breslau. Warsaw and Cracow fell some days ago and Lodz and some other places are now in Russian hands. The Russians are doing very well indeed but our own troops in the west are not yet doing much. I wonder why? We are hoping this is strategy and not inability.

We have had an unofficial warning that we are to have another search. So far, we don't know what they will be looking for. Is it for food which they believe we shouldn't have? Watches, rings, etc? You can't tell with the Gestapo.

Two more men have died in the camp hospital. We don't know why but it is believed they have died of malnutrition. It happened so frequently in Italy but the Italians simply stated it was pneumonia. These chaps are to be buried tomorrow.

Sunday 21st January
The expected search didn't take place. Apparently it was all a mistake by the German office.

Monday 22nd January
I got some more mail tonight. One was from Pam, dated 25th August, and two from Bella, dated 11th July and 15th August. Bella's letter tells me she is going to do – will have done now – some crooning. I wonder, can she sing? It hasn't been mentioned before! Pam's letter has a rather wistful tone to it!

Joe (Russians) is still moving and is now twenty miles over the border on a 65 kilo front. We weren't expecting anything half so good. But he must stop soon, his lines of communication must be getting rather long. Oh well, we can't expect him to end the war in one push! He will stop for a breather, consolidate his forces, stabilize his positions, and then bash forward again! His breathing spells are usually of some weeks but his lengthy advances justify these. The activity in the west seems, to us, slight but the Germans are being driven steadily eastward. Surely it must end soon now that the Russians are actually in Germany. And the Russians want revenge so much they're not going to be content to sit on the fence and wait for the western forces to occupy Germany! Roll on our blokes from the west – roll on Joe from the east. Just take me back to England!

Tuesday 23rd January
The Germans are being awkward again. The Red Cross Christmas parcels were to be issued this week at the rate of twelve parcels per day for six days for each room of 72 men. This was started yesterday but this morning the Commandant and his security officer would not allow any more parcels out. No reason was given. All we have been told is that the Commandant and the security officer require today to consider the matter. According to the Geneva Convention, the detaining power (Germany, in our case) has no jurisdiction over the issuing of Red Cross food other than the censoring of the contents. But what is the good of such an agreement when dealing with bombastic Germans. Perhaps there will be an issue tomorrow.

But the situation isn't entirely black. The Russians are only thirty miles from Posen which means they are only 160 miles from Berlin! They, the Russians, are cutting up north through East Prussia and are only thirty miles from the sea at one point. Also, they are only thirty miles from Breslau. Their army in the south has reached a river so perhaps they will stop for a while now but the army in the north have not yet met any solid opposition so perhaps they will continue their advance for some days yet.

There is still not much activity reported in the west but our tactical air forces had a field day when they pounced on three German columns. It is claimed that the extent of the damage is such that a whole enemy reserve army is temporarily out of action. But when are our armies going to start pushing? The Russians will not like our comparative inaction while they are devastating the Germans in the east. Or is there some dark game being played?

Perhaps! And I wonder will Jerry and I get our Christmas parcel tomorrow. Apparently our store of ordinary Red Cross parcels is almost empty and it is doubted if there are sufficient for an issue of one parcel between two men next week. We are not expecting any more to come in. The railway is so strained the Germans are not going to be concerned about getting Red Cross food to mere prisoners. I doubt even if we'll get any more mail. It seems the German people are not being allowed to send letters. I've been told that no mail from us has left this camp since December.

What a state the country is in! A lot of the German soldiers seem to think it will be all over in a few weeks and have civilian clothes stowed away in readiness for the end. I hope they'll be able to make use of them soon!

Wednesday 24th January
The parcel situation has been cleared up and the Germans are allowing them to be issued again. I've written a lettercard to Bella but I doubt if she'll get it. It seems to be true that no outgoing mail has left the camp during the past five weeks. Things are rapidly getting worse.

The Russians are now 25 miles north of Breslau and about the same distance south-east. Perhaps they intend to surround it? A very important point is that they are fighting for German Silesia. This is a great mining area and losing it will be a great blow to the Germans. I hope the Russians make it before they stop for a break. Losing Silesia will be a devastating blow to the Germans as they are getting most of their steel, coal, and oil from this area. But the Russians must halt soon. Their recent advances have been too fast and long to be kept up.

Thursday 25th January
Jerry and I drew our Christmas parcel today. We've just had our pudding for supper. On Saturday there will be another issue of composite parcels that will leave us on rock bottom. We'll be in the midst of hard times again when we've eaten this lot as we aren't expecting any more.

But some mail came in today – recent stuff – addressed direct to this camp and dated early December.

The Russians haven't stopped yet. They are only four miles south east of Breslau and only 45 miles from Danzig. And 150 miles from Berlin. Roll on the Russian steam-roller. Surely they'll keep going until they've sealed off East-Prussia and have swiped the whole of Silesia. But there is little happening in the west! What are they waiting for?

Friday 26th January

Some more mail came in today but none for me. They're fairly recent letters so naturally I'd very much like to receive one from Evelyn. Letters from others are not so important to me. I've written to Pam again. It's only a couple of weeks since I last wrote to her but as she writes to me almost as frequently as Evelyn she deserves answers when possible.

The Russian advance is slowing down. However, it has not stopped entirely and they now have two thirds of East Prussia. They are only five miles from Posen but they are outside Breslau although 300,000 of the latter town's population have been evacuated. This evacuation would indicate that the Germans don't believe they can hold it. But may, as, with the exception of a couple of bridge heads, the Russians are still on the eastern side of the River Oder. In the west it is thought the Germans may start another push but they can't really expect any success: the most they can hope for is a bit of pointless propaganda value. Of course it means also that they are not yet prepared to surrender. So it will go on until our forces in the west, and the Russians, deliver the coup de gras.

Spring! Perhaps? Roll on spring!

Sunday 28th January

I went to bed early last night. My chilblains were throbbing and pains were shooting up my right leg. Chilblains have to be treated with care here! Sometimes they have been the reason for amputations. Still, the health of the camp isn't as bad as it might be. Our senior medical officer has telegraphed Geneva and asked that sufficient Red Cross food parcels be sent to make an issue of one per man per week. The justification he gives is that we are living in very cold barracks with only two blankets per man and no mattresses. Two days ago a barrack-room temperature was -15°F (perhaps 15° of frost, but we are all confused about Centigrade and Fahrenheit). The Russians are 120miles from Berlin!

Monday 29th January

Another fellow died yesterday. He is to be buried tomorrow. The deaths are mounting. It is all so unnatural, too. The average age of the prisoners here must be under thirty and yet these deaths occur with disconcerting frequency. Obviously they are caused by the very cold weather (today, inside temp. -7°C), and malnutrition. The surge of optimism which I've been enjoying has left me and I'm depressed again. And yet, on taking stock of our situation, there is reason to be optimistic. The war situation is good. True, the Russian advance appears to have lost its speed but they are still moving steadily westward. And in the west the British and American forces are moving rather more slowly, eastward. Our troops are said to have reached the Siegfried Line again. Are they lining up for a big break-through? We hope! Is this the case? and if so, when will it happen? Although there is a whining tone to the

German newspapers they still talk of Germany's fight to save Europe from the 'RED PEST' and the Anglo-Americans. Also, they talk of their ultimate victory. Hitler has been with Quisling and has promised to give Norway her independence when Germany has won the war. What a hope!

But in the meantime we prisoners are not in a very envious position. If the war would end in the next few weeks there would be no reason for us to worry but the weather is so cold and the food so insufficient that our future doesn't bear thinking about. Geneva has answered our telegram re the German reprisals (German prisoners in Egypt). They are appealing to the German Government and have informed the British Government. But we are still without our mattresses in the coldest of barracks with only two threadbare blankets per man. I don't see what Geneva can do – or the British Government for that matter. It is more a 'sheep or a lamb' for the Germans now. They have gone too far to concern themselves with what they'll regard as trivialities. The best we can hope for is that some Red Cross stuff will filter through to us. But if only a little could reach us it might tide us over till the warmer weather is with us again. But, of course, we are hoping for victory before then.

Now the Russians are only ninety miles from Berlin and our western forces are on the Siegfried surely a combined effort could do the trick. We think we ought to know within a weeks We suppose the Russians will stop to consolidate but when they are ready to move again will ours in the west be ready to move too? Gosh, I'm cold!

Tuesday 30th January

Another terribly cold day and my foot is throbbing and sending spasms of agony up my leg. I'd never have thought that little chilblains could cause so much discomfort. I received an old letter from Pam today, it was dated 30th July. Six months to reach me. But it proves that there must be a lot of mail due to me – and others – but will we ever receive it?

The Russians are ninety miles from Berlin, sixty miles from Stettin, and tightening on Breslau. Evacuees are said to be pouring into Berlin. The newspaper admits that a lot of civilians are actually sleeping in open shelters on mattresses. And still they fight! They have no stabilized line in the east on their own admissions and, also, in the Posen area, the Russians have broken the frontier defences and are pouring into the country. In the west, although they have the Siegfried Line and the Rhine to assist them they can't have much hope of holding our armies there when these armies make a concerted effort. The German defences in the west have been considerably weakened to reinforce their battered, beaten, and routed troops in the east. Their only hope would seem to be that the British and American Armies don't push. Our only hope is that they will.

There is optimism in the camp again. But prisoner of war optimism is illusory, uncertain. It rises like a soap bubble – and then it bursts. Where is it? Where's it gone? Did it ever exist? Like children contemplating a burst bubble we contemplate our dispelled optimism and then feel foolish and depressed. But now, I'm keeping my hopes on a tight rein: I'm not going believe any rumours and I'm not suggesting any future date for an end to the hostilities. I am just hoping. Hoping! England can be so lovely in the spring!

Thursday 1st February

A thaw came yesterday and it is still with us. Unfortunately it has brought wind and rain but we are much warmer. All of the snow has now gone but we are almost knee-deep in mud – we're never satisfied! But I hope the change in the weather doesn't check the Russian advance. Tuesday's report had them 67 miles from Berlin and still going strong. It looks as though they intend to make it with this push. And they will unless the River Oder holds them up. The Germans are not at all optimistic.

Those in this district are disgusted and, so we are told, won't even read the newspaper. The local soldiery think: 'another two weeks?' More of the camp staff troops have gone. We suppose they've gone away to fight. Poor sods! In the west our troops seem to be pressing harder. A big push would seem to be indicated. May it come soon!

Tomorrow we are to have a food parcel between four and then it's rock bottom. How often have we been on rock bottom? The last cigarette issue was made today: five cigarettes per man or two ounces of tobacco between ten men. I got tobacco for Jerry. I'm glad I don't smoke. These conditions are very trying: portioning of food has to be done with hair-splitting exactness under the eagle eyes of hungry men. Everyone is irritable and bad tempers are the normal state. It is all very unpleasant. Fellows lose their temper over silly little things which, normally, they would laugh at.

And we are worried, too! Worried lest the Russians be so successful that they reach us before we can be rescued by the British or the American armies. If the Germans suddenly stop fighting we aren't so sure the Russians won't keep up their advance and swipe us as hostages. Nobody trusts Joe Stalin! It could happen. We know all about their being our Allies but we also know that the diplomatic 'good-feeling' between them and the west exists only because we have a common enemy. Our own troops in the west are much closer to us than the Russians are but the latter are moving this way with, virtually, no opposition while our troops in the west are still being held at the Siegfried and the Rhine. We are all worried. The country is in a chaotic state and the Germans are in a panic. They are being told by their so called leaders to stay calm: that the situation is well in hand, but their fears aren't allayed. The Russians are coming, demanding an eye for an eye – and, apparently, taking it. We, in this camp, will feel much more comfortable when our troops are this side of the Rhine and Siegfried. But our aircraft must be overhead. The sirens are warbling like a thousand cats out whoring.

What a hellish night to be bombed out! What do the Germans believe they are fighting for?

Friday 2nd February
I've written cards to Pam and Sheilah. Am I wasting my time – but I have plenty. It's all we have in abundance. We were given a small issue – a spoonful of syrup per man today and we've been... (*diary illegible*)

Saturday morning The lights went out last night because of our bombers. There are so many raids these days that we can never be sure when there is, or when there isn't, a raid in progress. The Russians are claiming to be only 60 miles from Berlin.

Saturday 3rd February
More of our bombers – thousands it would seem from their roaring – are passing overhead and flying eastward. Berlin must be in a chaotic state with the outside refugees pouring in, the siege preparations, and the three allied air forces bombing almost continuously. It seems the Russians have reached the Oder and the Germans have hopes (!) of holding them. In the west Eisenhower has had a conference which lasted twenty four hours. Surely it isn't coming at last! Are our forces really going to make a push? The Germans have been pushed out of the last town they held in France, that is, other than those they are still occupying on the Atlantic coast. But they are now isolated and are of no further consequence in the war. Goebbels has left Berlin and has, apparently, gone to prepare another HQ for the Nazi rats. It is obvious that it is the intention of each one of them to fight to the 2nd last German!

I had a spare card so I have written it to Edith Jones. Lettercards were issued today but I'll wait until tomorrow before I write to Evelyn. We've been warned that another 1,000 men are coming to this camp and to accommodate them an entire block is to be vacated and the occupants are to distributed over the remainder of the camp. It will soon be 'standing-room only'! As there are no additional beds available we are going to be provided with tables which will be used as beds. Roll on the end! There is no more Red Cross food left. Already tempers are flaring up. I lost my temper this morning when I misunderstood a bloke about a silly little item I'd normally have laughed at.

At the moment there is a lull in the air raids but I suppose we shall have our bombers over before the night is over.

Sunday 4th February
I was right! Our bombers did come over again last night. As usual, our lights were put out but we're quite happy about this as our side is causing it. What is a couple of hours of darkness – in the dry – when we think of the poor unfortunate civilians in their panic-stricken dash from the Russians: bombed

out of their shelters when they can find any, and into the most awful weather. Our conditions are poor and uncomfortable but we are dry and unlikely to be bombed out every night as is the German population! Our bombers did come over again last night.

I've written a lettercard to Evelyn.

Tuesday 6th February

I couldn't make an entry last night because the lights were out most of the time. The reason, I think, was technical rather than tactical: there were no air raids. But there were several raids after 9pm until after mid-day today. There have been so many air-raids of late that the 'all clear' doesn't sound. We just hear the warbling siren when our aircraft are overhead. If ever a nation was fed up with war the Germans must be.

Last night I went to a recital of chamber music. It was performed in the church hut, the only building other than our barrack huts the Germans allow us since they started their reprisals. We had a performance by a string quartet, including one of New Zealand's leading violinists. There was also a performance by a French pianist. He was good, too. What a pity such talent is risked in the army but, as he is a member of the Free French, he must have volunteered to fight.

Just now my nerves are in an awful state. I jump at the slightest sound and my writing is becoming very wobbly What's causing it, I wonder? I am not really worried about anything other than the war, of course. But this life is so unnatural that the nerves are strained all the time. The end of the war will cure it. We've been prisoners too long.

Wednesday 7th February

The weather is simply awful. It has rained almost incessantly since early this morning and we are up to our eyes in mud. A south African has translated Hitler's latest speech. It is pathetic! Pleads, threats, promises! The people must have faith in their leaders, he tells them. And Leipzig has had another mayor executed. And the chief of police in Breslau has been shot. Not so long ago they hanged an old man because he was heard to say that he didn't really think the Germans were winning. The Russians have crossed the Oder south east of Breslau and they've advanced 12 miles on a 50 mile front. Who says the Germans are not winning? I wonder, will the River Elbe be the Russians' next obstacle?

The big Churchill, Roosevelt, Stalin meeting is taking place now.

Thursday 8th February

A very mild day – almost like spring although I'm feeling a bit 'off colour' tonight. I have a throbbing ache in the back of my head and I've a pain in my right groin caused, I suppose, by the chilblain on my right foot. It has burst. This life is depressing. It is a good thing we have cheering news most of the time. According to the Germans' own report the Russians have crossed the River Oder at a point approx. 35 miles from Berlin. When this bridgehead is properly established there would seem to be nothing to prevent their reaching Berlin!

We have not yet had any report of the big conference. It is said they have been making final plans for the defeat of the common (very!) enemy. What we want to know, of course, is: when? I was talking to Jimmy Brown and he was very optimistic – but when is he not optimistic? He is pretty certain, he says, that he'll be home for his birthday which is in March. Did I say he's optimistic?!! The war will end this month, he thinks. With our troops still on the west of the Rhine I can't see it happening. Hard luck, Jimmy! And my head is throbbing – life isn't much fun.

A representative of the protecting power is due to visit us on Sunday. We are all wondering what he'll think. We are in a bad way and there's a lot of blokes in the hospital with suspected TB. There's not much chance for a chap with that complaint in this camp. If we don't have peace soon! ! !

Friday 9th February

Another dilemma! On Sunday we've got to take our blankets on check parade with us. The Germans want to inspect them, they say. But we've grown rather cynical. We think, perhaps, they want to take the personal blankets from those who have them. It is very awkward. If those of us who have them conceal our personal blankets and the Germans record only those issued to us they may blitz us later and confiscate the blankets we've concealed. And if we don't conceal them they may take them from us on Sunday. They are a shower of bastards. Why can't they allow us to wallow in our misery in peace.

What a state we are in! This morning Jerry lost his temper with me over something so stupid. As we were going out on our check parade he remarked to me that he had been awake for some time before he got up. I replied, yes, I'd heard him whistling. Bad tempered, he snapped that he'd not whistled a note! We got separated in the crowd and I didn't see him again until we were having breakfast when he accused me of having called him a liar. I said it was a trivial little thing of no consequence. But he persisted, claiming that, in effect, I had called him a liar. Then I became as bad as he. I found myself literally speechless with rage. For over two years I've pandered to his childish sensitivity and moods and superiority and now all I wanted to do was to smash that smug self-righteous face into the wall. I was rising to my feet when I felt a restraining hand on shoulder. It was Paddy, our sergeant major (ex-guards).

He addressed Jerry: "you're behaving like a silly little school boy," he said. "I was here and I didn't hear any bugger call you a liar. Somebody was whistling. It's not a crime to whistle. Now for Christ's sake pull your socks up or I'll have you transferred to another hut!" Jerry just sat sulking and didn't utter another word. I just sat until my trembling had stopped. Water under the bridge. Later, Paddy sympathised with me.

"I don't know how you can tolerate that supercilious twat!" he said.

Saturday 10th February

The blanket inspection took place this morning. We didn't parade for it. The Germans said they just wanted to see all bad blankets. They have promised to replace unserviceable blankets. And we were counted inside today as the weather was inclement. But we have been counted outside when the weather has been much worse. Perhaps they are bearing in mind the visit of the Geneva bloke tomorrow.

But I've been in trouble again. There was a squabble about the way I've been cutting up the rations. I wasn't cutting up the sausage the right way. I wasn't careful enough about sharing the potatoes. And the bread... ! So I decided that somebody else do the job. Sergeant Major Middleton said he would do it so I handed over to him the duty rolls and the spud-boxes. But George Cartlidge agitated and said he wanted me to carry on. I got all of the votes so I am to carry on – and I feel so childish about the whole affair. But this squabbling over the division of food is so irritating. We sit dreaming and romancing about food.

Just now the war is still jogging along but there's no sign of the end yet. Joe Stalin is quiet on the eastern front and there seems to be little activity in the west. When is the next big move coming? Are they waiting for better weather? And I wonder what are the results of the recent big conference? But everyone is wondering. It would seem that the intention is to finish the European issue in the near future. But in the meantime we are in a sad plight, wondering and worrying about what is in store for us in the meantime. Hungry. Cold. Irritable. Utterly miserable. And no mail which is really worst of all. And here I am moaning – forever moaning.

Sunday 11th February

I've written a lettercard to Evelyn. I wonder what she thinks of my letters? Do they bore her? Are they all monotonous replicas of one another? In these conditions it is hard to write a spontaneous letter. The last letter I received from her was dated late in October, nearly four months ago! When am I going to get another one?

I am so depressed and, despite our hopes, the war seems as though it will never end. And Jerry is depressed too. Yesterday morning he told me why: his parents moved to Australia from New Zealand. His mother wants to return to England but his father wants to stay where he is, suggesting that Jerry go out there after the war. But Jerry doesn't want to go out there as he is intent on literature as a career which he believes will only be achievable in London. But if he doesn't go out to Australia he won't see his mother again and he is very much a mother's boy. I think his mother must have been disappointed that he wasn't a girl and compromised by making him effeminate. Poor Jerry! He's not cut out for anything hard. And he's got the temperament of a prima donna. He's querulous as an old invalid and babyish as a little boy when he can't have his own way. Presently he's accusing his father of being selfish. His mother would like to stay in Australia if Jerry will go there. His fiancée (English) would like to go out there. But he wants them to come to him although it was he who left them out there. He is being so blindly selfish. Poor Jerry! He's such a selfish pig – even though he's the best friend I have here.

Monday 12th February

We don't know yet what the Geneva bloke said when he came yesterday other than there is a central Red Cross food dump which is only 80 miles from here. Perhaps we shall get some more parcels? We had another search today. Somebody stole a case of German sausages. It has been found and we are wondering who did the stealing and do they know? There has been a lot of stealing of communal food recently so it is expected that the punishment will be severe.

The news has improved again. The British are only four miles from the Rhine and Joe Stalin has crossed the Oder north of Breslau on a hundred mile front. He has advanced 30 miles and is only 80 miles from Dresden. Keep going, Joe!

Wednesday 14th February

This morning I sent my trousers to the camp tailor to be repaired but he merely condemned them and sent them back to me. I shall have to repair them myself as best I can. I shall get a new suit when the next clothing arrives. The news is good but our armies have a long way to go yet. But East Prussia has almost been wiped up and the Russians are across the Oder in full force. But there is still little happening in the west. Our armies there seem to be stuck in the mud. It is said they are massing up men and materials for the spring Another spring offensive! But they have not, they say, forgotten the possibility of an earlier collapse of the Germans – but this cannot be banked on! How we wish it could!

The big conference is over. It lasted eight days. We don't know much about it. Apparently they have completed all of the plans for the complete destruction of Germany as a military nation, but what we want to know is when are we going to put it into operation. Oh, if it doesn't happen soon!

I feel that I should write cards to various people but it is so much of an effort. It is so hard to write when there are no letters being received.

We missed our jam ration this week. The Germans say they haven't got any.

Thursday 15th February

I've repaired my trousers as best I can. It isn't a neat job but I feel much warmer now. An American 'mouthpiece' has stated that big things are laid on for March. The 'spring offensive'?

Friday 16th February

I made a great effort today and have written to Margaret and Jenny. I am certainly slipping when I find it an effort to write a couple of cards. I remember when I could write letter on a sheet of foolscap without effort. But that was in the good old pre-war days.

We have had glorious weather during the past few days. After the rain of course we were knee-deep in mud for a while but now the ground is dry underfoot. It will soon be possible to do a bit of walking about the camp. Soon, I suppose, the physical training classes will be started but I'm having nothing to do with them. Our diet over the past half year has not prepared us for physical effort.

But these activities usually start with spring. Spring, with the hope of imminent victory and summer in England, gives the fellows a new hold on life. Keep fit is the slogan. What is really meant is: 'Get fit!' So we go about in a half naked state, glorying in the sunshine and trying to acquire a sun-tan. We breathe deeply and feel fit and happy. Yes! Even when we're starving which was our near normal state in Italy.

Last year, of course, we were reasonably well off. In fact, we were well off with a food parcel per man per week. I lived off half the German bread ration plus the Red Cross parcel. All the remainder I gave away. Now when I am permanently hungry even the German rations are insufficient. It maddens me when I think of those glorious few months in IVb when food was so plentiful and could eat no more than a spoilt Pekinese.

But now we have a hint of spring and with the warmer weather. We are reasonably certain of these coming with the time of the year. But how many weary war months have we yet in front of us? I've depressed myself now.

I've just had another battle of words with Jack Grant. He is claiming that for weeks I've been robbing him of potatoes, bread, and German sausage. He's being ridiculous. I've robbed him of nothing but I've spoilt him by always giving him the benefit of the doubt. It is all so silly. I don't believe he thinks I've robbed him of food. His problem is the lack of cigarettes. But while I understand this I can't very well carry on as platoon commander with one of them accusing me of dishonesty. So I've appealed to Paddy Ferguson, our hut commander, that Jack and his mate must be transferred to another platoon. They've been transferred but I still feel rattled.

Saturday 17th February

We've just had another bath and it has left me feeling incredibly weak and my foot has started to throb again. I am going to bed. And it's only four thirty in the afternoon. What a life! – but I've said this before.

Sunday 18th February

A dry but bitterly cold day. I had nightmares all last night and I'm feeling rather wobbly. Everyone is rapidly losing weight and the excessive cold is accentuating our hunger. There is a gnawing vacuum under my belt. I can actually tie a handkerchief around my waist. And my arms and legs are as spindly as those of an eleven years old girl. Gosh I'm hungry! And cold! But I'm one of so many.

I have written to Evelyn and have virtually told her to wait for me no longer if she meets someone else. I feel that I'm bidding for something I really can't pay for. And I wonder what she thinks? Oh how I wonder what she thinks! And this I may never learn.

Monday 19th February

Some bulk Red Cross food arrived yesterday with sufficient cigarettes for an issue of 20 per man. The latter have been issued but the Germans are being awkward about the food. They are going to let us have the dry articles – sugar, cheese, butter, jam – tomorrow, but they haven't yet decided when to allow us to have the other stuff. Oh well, it's something to look forward to. Jerry and I are pooling our cigarettes and are going to try to buy a loaf. A loaf is six days' bread for one man.

There is nothing much in the news. The lull before the storm. We are all wondering – and hoping!

Tuesday 20th February

As was promised yesterday some of the Red Cross food was issued today. It was wonderful to see real food again. We got jam, butter, cheese, soup-powder and chocolate. I can understand the German resentment. These are items some of them barely remember. They sneer and say it is just propaganda and that, because of their German sub-marines, the British people are starving as they are. Once more my stomach feels satisfied, or as nearly so as it is likely to be while I am a prisoner.

Thursday 22nd February

My birthday. Thirty one years ago today I ceased to be a physical part of my mother when I was launched, a screaming independent fragment of humanity into this cruel world. The poet said: 'I am the master of my fate; I am the captain of my soul!' or it may have been the other way around, but he was never under the jurisdiction of a sergeant major or the inmate of a prison-camp! Personally, at an early age, I dug myself a morale refuge hole and have ever since been afraid to come out of it. And, like so many thousands of others, I have blundered stupidly on and on like a piece of driftwood on the ocean: a victim of unkind circumstances too helpless, or too craven, to offer resistance. So we, prisoners and the others too, wait here for our Red Cross parcels and, finally, our knight in shining armour – or a bloody big tank – to come and rescue us. Surely the Germans can't oppose the Allies much longer!

I went to collect my new battle-dress today. The trousers fit reasonably well but the jacket is much too large so it will have to be changed tomorrow.

There seems to be no change in the war situation. March perhaps?

Our rations have been cut again! Our potato ration has been halved. This is a blow as potatoes are 2/3rds of our food. We have been promised barley and turnip to the extent of half the weight of the potato we are losing but that's a poor swop! We have eaten all of the Red Cross food which was issued the other day. The remainder which ought to have been given to us today is being withheld because the Germans say they are too busy to witness the issuing of it.

More prisoners are coming to this camp. More unfortunates. More unfortunate than we because we are housed in buildings. They must go into improvised tents. The latter are being erected now on the parade ground. And so we ask ourselves: how much longer? The usual answer to that question is: about three months ahead, with the reasoning, 'they can't last much longer than that!' But they always have in the past. And only they know how!

All of my eggs in one basket. At Poole in Dorset!

Saturday 24th February
Another bomb-shell has hit us! From 5th March the present issue of rations, for 28 days, will be issued for 35 days. This is really dreadful. It would be bad even supplemented by Red Cross food but we have no Red Cross food! We are all really down in the dumps. Some blokes are talking of suicide or escape. But they both amount to the same thing really. Even good news fails to cheer us.

Turkey has entered the war against Germany and Japan. A couple of the smaller nations have decided likewise but they'll have little bearing on the war. Three of the American armies have started pushing and one of them is only twenty miles from Cologne. I doubt if this is the real offensive. We expect that to happen in a couple of weeks.

Sunday 25th February
And still they take from us. Anyone with more than two blankets must hand over the others. And the weather is freezing. The explanation is that more prisoners are coming in and the Germans say they have insufficient blankets for them. How much worse can our situation become? We are not going to receive the barley and turnip in lieu of the potato we're being deprived of.

Worse and worse! No letters either. I've just written to Evelyn but I think I'm just wasting my time. We are all sure that there are no letters leaving the camp. Telegrams have been sent to Geneva and Berlin advising them of our plight – but a lot of good they'll do!

Our offensive in the west has started but it is moving only very slowly. Will it never end. Egypt has entered the war against Germany and Japan. That'll set them trembling! Apparently it was on Churchill's suggestion. Has Germany no friends? Well, not many in this camp!

Tuesday 27th February

They haven't taken our personal blankets yet but say they will confiscate them if we don't hand them over voluntarily. I am certainly not going to hand over one of my blankets to a German soldier. They may be in a bad way but they are still fighting. We have hardship in front of us and we are on rock bottom. And we're not receiving any letters. My last letter from Evelyn was dated August. Am I still engaged? I wonder!

Thursday 1st March

Another month starts. But things are very much as they've been during the past few weeks. Ours is a monotonous existence and most of us seem to have lost interest in everything. Personally, I can't read, write, or take an interest in anything. I can't walk because my foot is still troubling me and just waiting for an excuse to turn septic, and when there is any wood to saw for our stove I weaken after a few moments' work. The shortage of food is having a devastating effect on us. Three letters came into the hut today but I wasn't one of the lucky recipients. Tonight I've written cards to Dad and to Pam and I wonder will they receive them. The war is still jogging along but nothing big seems to be happening. Perhaps our forces in the west intend to line the west of the Rhine before they make a big scale offensive. We are hoping it will take place this month. We are doing a lot of hoping!

Saturday 3rd March

Yesterday was a horrible day. After an almost sleepless night I got up with my limbs aching with cold – we are all suffering. It was an icy cold morning with a cold wind. From about nine a.m. we had intermittent spells of sunshine, sleet, rain, and snow, and there was sufficient snow to leave a fair ground cover. I soon decided that the cold was too much for me so I went back to my bunk until noon which is our soup time. In the afternoon I walked to and fro in the hut trying to keep myself warm. I went to bed finally at 5pm. and last night was as cold as the previous night. I arose this morning feeling as tired and having as many aches and pains as I had yesterday morning. Today started with a gentle wind and a clear sky but now, eleven a.m., the sky is overcast and there is an arctic wind howling.

Hundreds of our bombers passed over about an hour ago. Fellows who watched them say that they have not seen a greater number. We ought to feel sorry for the thousands of people being made homeless but, at best, I think we're indifferent. 'Man's inhumanity to man!' But it's reciprocal. We're trying to exist on a diet, per day, of a little bread, a couple of potatoes, a mugful of thin soup, and a little margarine (ersatz). Also, there should be some jam but we've had none of this during the last two weeks.

But I wonder what our armies in the west are doing? We are hoping that by the end of the month they will have cleared the west bank of the Rhine and by May they ought to be churning up this blasted hypocritical country. But, in the meantime, the square-headed bastards are trying their utmost to create trouble between the West and the Russians. They have put up propaganda posters warning us (western prisoners) what will happen should Germany lose the war and advise us to choose before it is too late. They are actually asking us prisoners to join the German Army and fight the Russians. And at the same time they are recruiting Russian prisoners to join the German Army to fight the British and the Americans. We have seen some of the Russians, now in German uniform, passing through the bath and disinfester before leaving our camp. And I suppose some, but not many, I hope, British and American prisoners have gone to fight the Russians. These latter will deserve what I think the Russians will mete out to them.

Sunday 4th March
We've been given a ½ issue of jam. They owe us only 1½ issues now. Tomorrow a new system of food issuing starts. We are to have soup at noon and at 4pm but no potatoes will be issued – these are to go into the soup – so they tell us! Oh how I'd like to feel my stomach pressing against my belt! But there are to be no more good meals as prisoners.

I've written a lettercard to Evelyn. I feel more ashamed each time I write to that unfortunate girl. She's waited so very long already and still the war keeps dragging on and keeping so many of us apart. I think I'd feel almost relieved were I to get a letter from her breaking off our engagement. This continuous worrying that I shall lose her and that I've wasted so much of her life isn't good for me – or her. I'm irritable and so nervous. But were I to lose her I'd quite likely be worse. Here, I think we'd all go under if the news wasn't good most of the time.

The Russians are still battling for Breslau and are gradually gaining it. But there are a lot of Germans in Breslau. It's a German city!

Tuesday 6th March
Last night I got a letter from Dad, dated 8th November, and one from Bella dated 23rd November. Bella mentioned her visit to Evelyn's home but said nothing of Evelyn's being in hospital. Perhaps she thought the information would worry me. She says Evelyn is much prettier than her photo depicts

her. I know that! But I know also that Bella would have said the same were Evelyn the most horse-faced hag she'd ever met. She likes Evelyn's mother and quotes everyone as being 'pleased to meet David's sister'! But she was surprised when they said they saw no resemblance between us. Perhaps she didn't tell them that she and I had different mothers – and an age gap of almost ten years. She has told me of what she thought of all those she met but I'm still in the dark regarding what everyone thought of Bella! And Evelyn hasn't told me. Of course, Evelyn saw her only on one fleeting hospital visit. Dad didn't tell me much. 'Ethel and Fred are getting very tall' and Bella is 5ft 8inches tall and weighs 10 stones. Quite a handful for someone – lucky or unlucky! But I'm still awaiting a letter from Evelyn and wondering am I still engaged?

The news is still consistently good. In the west our troops are gaining more and more of the western bank of the Rhine and are entering the suburbs of Dusseldorf and Cologne. The Germans will fight hard for these two cities but it is inevitable that they will be lost. But our troops may first of all cross the Rhine and cut them off. The Russians are fond of this method. Our side is already in possession of several large towns in the Ruhr.

Hopes are again high in the camp. Most of the fellows here believe that our troops ought to have reached us by one to six weeks. I don't doubt that they will reach and pass this area but will we prisoners be here to greet them? My pessimism is now in gear and I'm sure the Germans will move us if they can. We are a 'counter' in the game and the Germans don't have many counters. I refuse to allow my hopes to soar only to have them crash and leave me devastated again.

Wednesday 7th March

Cologne has been taken by the Allies. Nothing is said about our troops having crossed the Rhine so I assume that part of the city which is on the east side must still be in German hands. The Americans have made some good headway in the Bonn area. Churchill has been to Germany and has spoken to the 51st Highland Division. It looks as though they are going to get another 'death or glory job'. The same happened to our division, the 50th Northumbrian Division, until now, they are no longer a division. Smashed up so badly, it was disbanded. And now, our partner, 51st Jocks Div, must carry on by itself. Good luck to the 51st, the finest division left in our Army!

Churchill chalked a message on a shell for Hitler and fired it from a gun already laid for him. The old battle-axe ought to stay at home lest he get himself hurt. In my entry for yesterday I said the hopes of the camp were high. Well, they've gone up since then. They're in the stratosphere today. Jimmy Brown (our camp Nostradamus) reckons our troops ought to reach us by the end of the month. No one thinks we will be here by the middle of next month. Some even think they'll be here in a week. I don't expect this. I

believe the German Army discipline is still too rigid to allow a 'buckle-up'
yet. But we'll soon know!

But I'm getting myself too excited writing about this so I'd better close
down for today.

Friday 9th March

Stratosphere yesterday: in the dumps today! We are to have a 20% ration
cut by the 5th April. This news is devastating. Jerry really believes that
three months of this will kill us. While I don't really think we will all die of
starvation I agree it will be an extremely thin time for us. The best we can
hope for, other than our troops reaching us, is that the weather will be good.
Today is cloudless and we are quite warm when in the sun and sheltered from
the wind. Yesterday we had snow, a really heavy fall , but it has all gone
now. We shouldn't see any more this year. We all hope we don't because we
aren't in a fit state to bear the cold.

Our bombers are creating hell in this vicinity at the moment. The night
before last we heard the biggest raid we have ever heard. It lasted for hours
and I think, according to the sound of the explosions, an ammunition place
must have been the target. They were over here again last night but on a
smaller scale it seemed. We are awaiting the news that our troops have
crossed the Rhine.

Later Troops of the American 1st Army have crossed the Rhine south of
Bonn. Opposition is said to be slight. Armour and equipment is said to be
pouring over. How much longer now? They may reach us in a few weeks!
But will they? And will the Germans leave *us* here to be collected? Or will
they try to move us before the Yanks arrive? These are very exciting times
indeed!

Saturday 10th March

We've been told that on Monday a German officer and an NCO are to go to
Luebec, the nearest Red Cross depot, to see if they can get some food here
for us. We really need it badly – every one of us is pale and sickly-looking
and the hospital is full. It isn't unusual to have five burials in a day. There is
to be no sugar in the week 16th - 23rd April but that's some time off. Sugar
may seem a trivial item but it is calories – heat! Our rumours include also
margarine and other items. Are we going to starve before our troops reach
us. Are they going to be a long time? The bridgehead, it seems, was just a
'windfall'. Our people are not yet ready to advance while we wait and wait
and it's hell. But we know we are being unreasonable!

Sunday 11th March

I think I may have influenza... aggravated by hypochondria! This morning
my head thumped and my bones ached. I got into bed early this afternoon
and I've been here since. I still feel very wobbly. Lack of food is really our

problem and I think we're all terrified of pneumonia. We come on a new
ration cut tomorrow. None of us could have envisioned conditions becoming
so bad. We dream of food from morning till night. And during the night
I dream of it: bread, butter, cheese, jam! Just simple items, but the items
we lack most here. Will we exist during the worse days to come. Usually I
write to Evelyn on Sundays but I shall have to put off today's writing until
tomorrow.

Monday 12th March

I'm still feeling wobbly but I'm not staying in bed today. After breakfast I
walked around the camp with Jimmy Brown. We talked of holidays. He has
his mapped out for some years to come: the Lake District, Cornwall, Norfolk
Broads, Scotland... He will then spend them nearer home and have a family.
Later I was talking to Basil Webb, a South African. He was enquiring about
my health. I told him how the cold nips me and he advised me to go to South
Africa after the war. He has given me his address.

Tuesday 13th March

I've just received a letter from Evelyn. She says they have been told to have
their letters to prisoners of war... (*diary illegible*)

Wednesday 14th March

The lights went out last night as I was writing. Our bombers seem to come
over every night at the same time. Evelyn's letter was intended to reach me
by Christmas. Perhaps so had I still been at IVb. It is a special letter meant
to take my thoughts back to Christmas 1940. She asks me do I remember?
As though I'd ever forget! It is wonderful to feel that she wants me. But how
much longer must she wait for me?

We've been given the report of the officer who went to Luebec.
Apparently there are lots of parcels and some trucks in which to transport
them but instructions are awaited from Götberg before any parcels may be
dispatched to camps. But he brought back with him 200 American food
parcels. The cigarettes have been removed from these and issued to us at the
rate of 6 per man, while the parcel distribution will work out at 3 parcels per
24 men. Perhaps in a week or so there'll be sufficient parcels from Luebec
for an issue of one per man.

The news is very quiet. The lull before the storm, we hope!

Thursday 15th March

According to a notice outside the camp office the power station at Hanover
has been hit by a bomb. We've been warned that our lights will be off for an
indefinite period. It must have happened yesterday afternoon. Oh well, we've
not been having more than two hours lighting any night. Perhaps the RAF

will drop another bomb on it as soon as it's been repaired. Rumours are rife this morning. I wonder how the lads conceive them on such meagre rations?

One of the rumours has it that there has been a big German collapse in the west. A German officer is said to have confided this to a feldwebel (I didn't know that German officers spoke to their sergeants). Another has Stockholm Radio stating that we have three more bridgeheads across the Rhine. And, of course, there's the big German collapse! It seems we've won the war and nobody's told us! But we've been having these rumours for weeks now. The British 2nd Army breaks through at Wessel every night! Actually, I don't think they have reached Wessel yet. But it will happen soon – I hope!

I am more hungry now than ever. I spend most of my time dreaming of food – don't we all?

Saturday 17th March

A very unpleasant morning of intermittent spells of heavy rain. There is a continuous strong wind. I am writing this in bed – not because I'm ill but because it's the least unpleasant place. The soup last night was awful. It was only water and beetroot, and not a lot of the latter. Worse and worse! and worse to come. Apparently the materials for breadmaking are some weeks overdue. If they don't arrive during the next two weeks our bread ration is to be cut to almost half of the present issue. Bread is the only solid item of food we are getting and that amounts to very little. We are going to be very weak specimens indeed when the end of the war finally happens – if we live that long!

The news is almost nothing. The bridgehead over the Rhine has been extended very little and is only 12 miles wide by 6 miles deep. It seems our people want first of all to clear the western side of the Rhine in the northern sector. The Germans are putting up a hard fight for it. But when is the 'final' push going to start? If it doesn't start soon I can see it being put off until spring next year! Quite simply, in that case, we in this camp will die before it happens. This is cold commonsense reasoning. Quite literally we are starving to death.

A bloke has had a letter from home which tells him that meat, butter, cheese and sugar are no longer rationed. But this is sheer fantasy!

Sunday 18th March

I've had another hot bath this morning but I had to go for it at 7a.m. I've written a lettercard to Evelyn and postcards to Margaret and Dad. I managed Evelyn's letter alright but found the other two rather a problem. Writing letters is a one-sided business when no letters are coming in.

Things seem to be moving again in the west. Are they, again, getting ready for the 'BIG' push? We're hoping.

Monday 19th March

Just received a letter from Sheilah dated 7th January. The first of such I've had. But what I want is a recently written letter from Evelyn.

Today the Germans demanded to know our trades and ages. As a regular soldier I can afford to tell them the truth. I could, of course, have said electrician or miner but I have no intention of working for them if I can avoid it. That would be as bad as fighting for them since it would free a German to become a soldier.

There is nothing spectacular in the news but spring starts officially on Wednesday 21st. But will our offensive start with it? Our spring offensives usually start in summer but I'm hoping our expected offensive to start in May. Then is it too optimistic to expect our troops to cross Germany in a few weeks? There would seem to be nothing to stop them but we've had lessons on unjustified optimism in the past. Now, I'm cynical and just hope! However, at my pessimistic worst, I think the war must end this year. Really, our worry is what may happen to us prisoners in the meantime? We are really starving. Malnutrition has already taken a heavy toll and obviously many more will follow before we are relieved. It is showing in swollen faces and limbs. So far, I can't see it in myself yet. I am weak, of course, but I don't think I look ill and I'm sure there's hope for me if the war doesn't last much longer and our rations are not cut any more. But if they are diminished further, 'what will the poor little Kriegies[11] do then, poor things?'. It looks as though a lot of Germany could be forever England! But I'm getting morbid again.

Tuesday 20th March

Another letter direct to this camp. It's from Jenny and dated 12th December. When she wrote it she said Bella was on leave. Bella always seems to be on leave. She quotes Bella as saying Evelyn is a lovely girl. I know! But Jenny: she's as affectionate as usual and mourns the scarcity of young men. There are many here who would be happy to accommodate her. She hasn't yet sent me the photo she promised to send last year. She hasn't had it taken yet! Faithfully, she promises to send one to me as soon as she has been photographed. My pretty cousin is a vain girl, I think. She asks, is her 'handsome cousin' keeping well? Considering the circumstances, he is quite well, but he is starving and a little moth-eaten. When she saw me last I was a fresh-faced boy of twenty-five just back from India. Now, I'm thirty one and have been through hell. Well, through hell – I'm still in it! – and waiting to be rescued by our victorious advancing army which hasn't yet started to advance. Any time now!

I've answered Sheilah's letter today but only on a card. Today I wrote a long letter to Evelyn. However, I don't suppose she'll receive it until after

---

[11] Our abbreviation of Kriegsgefangener – German for 'prisoner of war'.

I've been repatriated. The poor girl will wonder what she's got when she receives it. I've advised her to banish the 'ideal' me she is visualising and to resurrect the 'real' me. It's a rambling sort of letter showing my opinion of the Germans and my love for her. I hope it doesn't frighten her. Perhaps, of course, she may not receive it. That depends on how much longer the war will last.

Eisenhower has advised the people of western Germany to evacuate their towns and to billet themselves in the country. He says they should not join the Volkstürm (similar to our own home guard) as this would mean the useless loss of their lives in the last weeks of the war. 'The last weeks of the war!' But that is an American statement! But I hope it is so!

Wednesday 21st March
Last night a batch of evacuated prisoners was brought in. They are from Stettin. Five of them are in our hut: two Americans and three British.

Today is the first day of spring. It started well this morning with a sunny sky but there was a cold wind blowing. However the sky clouded over about 10a.m. and we've had an arctic temperature since.

The news is improving. We've now got Saarbrücken and our bridgehead over the Rhine is 25 miles wide. It seems there is utter chaos amongst the Germans on the west bank of the Rhine. It is said that German prisoners are pouring in. There are still many Germans cut off. They, I suppose, will be collected during the next few days. I am a little more optimistic today and it wouldn't surprise me to see the really big push by the Russians and us to start any time now.

We've been told that 22,000 Red Cross parcels have been allotted to this camp! Our receiving them, of course, depends on there being available transport! Happy days are here again – well, approaching!

Thursday 22nd March
The most beautiful day we've had since coming to this camp. The sun is shining brilliantly from an absolutely clear sky all day. With a few weeks of weather such as this our troops and air forces ought to cut through the Germans like a hot knife through butter. Today's news is very promising: the Russians appear to be preparing for another offensive and Montgomery is concealing his activities behind a smoke screen. With a push from both sides it shouldn't take much longer. It has developed into a rush job because it looks as though there may be a famine looming in Europe for next winter. It seems one already exists in Germany.

There is talk of meat being further rationed in England. The previous, rumoured news of the relaxation of rationing must have been just that, rumour! This is a blow to us as we've all been looking forward to uninhibited gorging on our return to England. But I'm sure, even British rationing must be feasts ahead of our current diet.

Saturday 24th March

Our third day of glorious weather. The last three days have been like summer. What a change to be warm again! Now, I'm only hungry. Never satisfied. Oh, and I'm homesick!

The news is still improving. General Patten is over the Rhine but there is something fishy going on somewhere: our own news has not mentioned Montgomery during the past week but today the German newspaper *das Reich* 18th March, states that Wessel, Bonn, and Cologne were lost to the Germans. Why should our news be six days behind the Germans – I wonder why our news didn't claim this? I'm getting impatient. We're all getting impatient. And the Germans are showing humanity. They're going to send one of their own 8-tonners to Luebec on Monday to get some food parcels for us. With luck, we ought to have one parcel between four men next week.

Special bulletin! Montgomery crossed the Rhine yesterday evening! How long now?

Sunday 25th March

Our bombers have just passed over. Hanover appears to have been their target because there is a very heavy blanket of smoke in the sky and it seems to be blowing from that area. Perhaps they've hit an oil plant. We've heard more of the latest Rhine crossing. The 1st Canadian Army, the 2nd British Army, and the 9th American Army have crossed. Latest reports state that they are doing well. 50,000 airborne troops were employed.

I've written a lettercard to Evelyn and postcards to Pam and the Jameses.

Tuesday 27th March

Our 'Man of Confidence' has come back from Luebec this morning and brought with him a consignment of cigarettes. These were sufficient to make an issue of 48 per man. Jerry and I are trying to swop ours for bread. We've exchanged some for saccharine to supplement our sugar. The news is good but local conditions are getting rapidly worse. The margarine ration has been cut and the bread and sugar are to be further reduced. And the Red Cross food is even more remote than ever. There is no transport available owing to its being used to supply prisoners who are being evacuated from camps in the west. We've been told that there are two barges at Luebec which will be used to bring the parcels to us when diesel oil can be procured. But where is the diesel oil to be found? And there will be no more mail or parcels as they can't be brought from Geneva.

However, despite the fact that the food situation is grim everyone in the camp is optimistic. The average estimate seems to be that we will have been by-passed in a couple of weeks. But find my pessimism taking over. Of course it is feasible that the war could end any day. Our troops are well into Germany now and General Patten is in the outskirts of Frankfurt which is almost due south of this camp and our troops have taken Löhnberg which is NNW of Frankfurt. And Montgomery's troops are said to have broken through in the north. But if I'm not careful I'll be working myself up into a state of optimism! Not long now!

Thursday 29th March

Received three letters from: Evelyn, Bella, and Sheilah. Evelyn's was a November letter. The others were written in July. Old but better than none at all. I doubt if there will be many more if at all.

The news is really terrific. At their present rate our troops ought to have passed us in a couple of weeks. South of us they have actually passed us.

Some Red Cross food is expected soon. The Germans have agreed to put two trucks on to a passenger train leaving Luebec. A truck usually holds 2,000 so if there are 4,000 altogether it will work out at two parcels between five men as some more men arrived in camp today. Several of the last batch who arrived last week have died. There were two buried today. Weeks of marching on German rations is too much for the fittest of men. But what a shame so near the end. There is a tale going round that no more prisoners are to be moved after those in transit have reached their destination. That this may be incorrect is my only worry. Besides the physical hardship a move now when we would appear to be about to be released would break our hearts. And for Evelyn's sake as well as my own I want to be in England soon. She has been wonderful.

Friday 30th March

A red letter day! The expected parcels – 6,000 – arrived this morning and they've been issued one between two men. It seems too good to be true having real food in front of us again. Butter, jam, fish, meats, powdered milk, large biscuits – it's wonderful! And today's news is better than yesterday's. Our troops are only 60 or 70 miles away at the most. Of course they may be much nearer as there is a security blanket on their movements.

We've been ordered by our camp leader that we must not try to escape as this would be highly dangerous as the Germans are particularly trigger-happy at the moment. While we are in a prison camp the Germans are obliged to treat us according to the Geneva Convention but should they catch us outside a prison camp now that our troops are so close they would be justified in shooting us. Rumours are rife but it's impossible to tell truth from nonsense. But the news is so good that we can afford to ignore the stupid stories.

Tonight the Germans have asked us for a list of doors, windows, stoves, blankets, greatcoats, etc in every hut. What is this for? Does the new commandant – arrived two days ago – want written proof to hand over to our forces that he has treated us according to the Geneva Convention? The thought amuses me. But at the back of my cynical mind there is the thought that perhaps there is something sinister in this request. I can't see how there could be but prisoners tend to look for a catch in everything. I don't think I've been so excited before. It could end any day. But, oh how I'm hoping!

Saturday 31st March

I've just learned that yesterday was Good Friday, and a good Friday it certainly was! But last night there was a reaction after the good news and the parcels. No one could sleep. They were all too excited. I could have slept but there was too much noise. The lads were talking all night and there were also air raids. A bomb fell in the near vicinity – the local station, I think. But now, this morning, having had little or no sleep, I feel as though I've been working all night.

The other day Jerry met his fiancée's brother in law, Bobby. Bobby was already in this camp when we arrived and it's taken all this time to bring about a meeting. Bobby's a very nice bloke. He's lived in Wales all his life but although his father is Welsh, his mother is Japanese. But the latter fact doesn't make him love the Japs. In fact, Bobby was a Spitfire pilot when he was shot down four years ago. His mother in law is the mother of Jerry's fiancée and she owns a hotel. So Bobby and Jerry have invited Evelyn and me to go there for a holiday. I think, perhaps, that Evelyn would like this.

Today I've written cards to Dad and Betty. I hadn't written to Betty since I left Italy.

Sunday 1st April

I've written to Evelyn, but as with so many of recently written letters, I doubt if she'll get it. But I must, for conscience's sake, write to her every week. The news has toned down rather but is still good. Everything in camp is prepared for 'when the balloon goes up', as the lads refer to the near future. Well, I'm ready for its ascent.

Tuesday 3rd April

Another Easter gone! the Germans relaxed to the extent of having only one roll-call each day, Friday, Saturday, Sunday, and Monday. We are still rather in the dark regarding the tactical situation. Our latest news tells us that about 100,000 Allied prisoners have been released. Lucky fellows! I wonder does Evelyn think I may be one of them. Poor girl, she's waited so long.

We're rather worried about our own situation. We feel sure the Germans will move us if they can. And our troops are still about 80 miles from us. Very few of my comrades think we will be moved but prisoners are ever optimistic. Their reasoning is that the Germans won't want their roads to be congested by moving prisoners. But I think they'll cling to every bargaining counter available to them. I believe they will move us if practicable and as our troops appear to be still some distance from us they may consider it if only to be bloody minded. Feeding us on the move may present a problem but they don't appear to be worrying much about feeding us at the moment.

Wednesday 4th April

The weather appears to be changing. It has been horrible during the past few days. We've had strong winds and rain and it has been very cold.

The news is good but our troops are a long way from us. A current rumour that Hanover, 31 miles south of us, and 25 miles west of us, has fallen to the Allies. But the power station which supplies this area is in Hanover and our lights are on as usual tonight. Our troops wouldn't overlook the fact that lots of small factories are powered from there. Just another silly rumour it would seem!

Tonight I've packed my kit and have weeded out everything I've considered unnecessary. Everything I want to keep I've packed in my haversack. It grieves me to abandon anything but if we have to march I don't want to burden myself with anything which is unnecessary.

Thursday 5th April

I've written a lettercard to Bella but don't entertain the faintest hope that she'll receive it. Hardly any of the chaps are bothering to write these days as no one believes that any letters leave the camp. The Germans are in a bad way in this area. According to the latest news our troops have crossed the Weser and are only 37 miles from Hanover. Apparently they are going all out for Emden, Bremen, Hamburg and Hanover. It is hard to believe that while I'm writing this, Allied troops are fighting a mere forty miles away. The Germans here seem to be in a frenzy preparing positions and digging in guns. We are hoping our troops will break through somewhere other than here because we believe we stand a much less chance of being moved if they do. All the food from the outside food-dumps is being transferred to this camp. This baffles me! Surely they don't mean to make a fort of the camp. If this is their intention it means that we are to be moved. But if we're to be moved why are they bringing more men into the camp? Does the German left hand know what its right hand is doing? Some men were brought from another camp yesterday and more have arrived today. Yesterday's batch came from an NCOs' camp while today's lot are – were – officers' servants.

And our Man of Confidence is trying to arrange another visit to Luebec and transport seems to be the only difficulty. If he's successful he'll go tomorrow and return on Saturday. But if he goes will he bring back food and cigarettes? But our immediate worry is not so much food as 'will they move us'? The news is so very good that some of the blokes think it's only a matter of hours before our troops will be here. My optimism doesn't reach this altitude though I'm reasonably confident that our troops will be here in a few days. But will we be here to welcome them? The philosophical view would be that the conflict can't go on much longer anyway. But many may die in the meantime and our worry is that we may be of that number.

The Russians are now fighting in the suburbs of Vienna and our most easterly troops (American) are only 80 miles from Leipzig. Germany is almost cut in two. There is a tale that Göring has been murdered by the Nazis. This could be true. He always appeared to regard himself as more important than his fellows.

A special order has been read out to us. The Germans have intimated that this area will be defended! In the event of there being any fighting in the vicinity we are warned that we must stay in our barracks unless ordered otherwise. However, our camp staff is of the opinion that the Germans will show little, if any, opposition. There are, however, some anti-tank units here who may fight it out. The German officers have told our leaders that they think it unlikely that we'll be moved but they've promised to give us as much warning as possible. I set no store by the officer's opinion that it's unlikely we'll be moved. They'd tell us that anyway to maintain our docility. 11,000 panicky men would present a problem! Optimistically, our staff have told us that if the Germans suddenly move out and leave us, a rigid discipline must be observed by all of us. This strikes me as commonsense but some fellows are always ready for a bit of mischief. The suspense is awful. Will they? Won't they? How long? We don't know!

Friday 6th April

They will! I was right. We are to be moved. RAF prisoners have been standing by to move since 9 a.m. but it is now 1.30 and they are still here. The Germans are trying to get them away but the RAF lads are being as awkward as possible. We others, while happy to see the Germans frustrated, are worried that the Germans may use their weapons and start shooting. In the meantime, we Army prisoners are hoping as we've never hoped before, that our troops will get here in time to prevent our being moved. A vain hope. As far as we know, our nearest troops are at Nienberg, about 25 miles from here.

But we've just had some letters delivered: Pam and Bella, November letters, and one from Evelyn dated 1st December. Pam has decided to take my advice to stop writing to me. I believed it was making her unhappy. I can't answer her letter – in fact, I can't answer any more letters as a prisoner. No more letters! And, really, that's all we had! How much longer?

5 pm and still here but with no more hope than I had this morning. At last the RAF chaps are moving out. But they are moving very slowly and the Germans appear to be half-hearted about it, understandably, they were reasonably safe as camp guards. But the RAF lads are moving. The Germans really mean to take us away. But I doubt if we Army prisoners will go until tomorrow.

We've had the BBC 3 o'clock news but although our troops are doing well they don't appear to be moving in our direction. They are reported to be 35 miles from Bremen and the threat to Hanover increases hourly. Both of these towns have been evacuated of civilians.

I've swopped addresses with Jerry lest we be separated when we're moved. In the distance I can hear gun-fire and, periodically, we can hear local explosions as though the Germans are doing a bit of demolishing.

6 pm There seems to be another hold up and I can still hear the distant gun-fire. It's infuriating to know that our people are so close to us and we are so helpless.

7.45 pm Our troops are 19 miles from Bremen and 16 from Hanover. This is getting exciting. Just like an American film. Apparently our forces have started on their drive towards Leipzig and are intent on linking up with the Russian, Marshal Jukov. This situation is sure to be to our advantage if the Germans continue to move us. And the local guns appear to be pounding away merrily. I don't think we'll move tonight.

Saturday 7th April 8 am
A sleepless night. Very few went to bed before midnight and most were up before 5 a.m. Everyone was too excited to sleep but I do wish they could show their excitement more quietly. The RAF did a fair amount of bombing during the night. Late last night we were given our rations for a week: a kilo loaf of bread and some margarine. I think there is more to come. The remainder of the RAF prisoners are moving out now and it is expected that we Army prisoners will be taken later this morning. There seems no hope that the Germans will leave us.

7 pm I've just received another letter from Evelyn! A wonderful letter but it's made me very love-sick. It grieves me not to be able to answer it.

The news is good tonight but it seems this will be our last night here. There is part of B compound still to move out tomorrow and then we, A Compound, are to follow them. This is, if the military situation is conducive, say the Germans. But I think they are taunting us even though our troops are so close. They are 12 miles from Bremen and 10 from Hanover. Prison camps all over Germany have been relieved by our troops. And we are unlucky.

Sunday 8th April
A rude shock this morning. We were awakened by the guttural voice of a German interpreter informing us that it was 6 a.m. and that we would move out of the camp at 7 a.m. Some fellows have already gone and those of us who are still here are due to move very soon. Our hope was vain. Now, we shall, after all, have to wait until Germany is absolutely crushed before we will be released. It must happen. May it happen soon!

Monday 9th Mid-day
We marched about 20 kilos yesterday, but owing to our very slow pace, plus a few halts, we did not arrive until 9 pm last night. We are in a small farming village and billeted in batches of 50 in barns. No food has been issued to us

but in good old soldier style we have helped ourselves to potatoes. Even a chicken and a small pig were recruited. I feel quite fit today but soon after the start of our march yesterday something went wrong with my stomach. Perhaps it was my own fault for eating too much barley and peas. I had to make an emergency stop to relieve myself because the pain was such that the presence of three German service girls couldn't in the least deter me. But, in the circumstances, why should it? I'd just seen one of the girls come from behind a quite inadequate bush, tucking her shirt into her trousers. She smiled and appeared to be quite at ease. We are due now to move off in about an hour. The Hanover-Hamburg Autobahn is only a couple of kilos away. It is believed that after we've crossed it, there will be no hope of our troops cutting us off.

Tuesday 10th April 1 pm

Our present billet isn't as good as the last one, there being too many of us. Owing to a mistake by the Germans who were in charge of us we were first of all taken to the wrong billet and, by the time they had found the right place, it was almost dark. We were very crowded, there being 120 of us in a place intended for 60. However, after a not too unpleasant night, we are beginning to feel at peace with the world today. For some reasons not yet explained to us, we are having today as a holiday and we have no marching to do. It is a glorious day and we are living like gypsies. We are all brewing tea or cooking stolen spuds and some canned meat which was given to us last night. The latter was issued at the rate of a kilogram between two men, and that's almost 1lb each[12]. We are feeding better now than we were at IVb. The front line appears to be rather close. There are lots of track vehicles and very young soldiers here. We've no idea at all of what the military situation is but it's obviously an important area because there are so many of our tactical aircraft in evidence.

Important – We've just been informed by the Germans that we are to go back to our camp tomorrow! It would seem that our troops have cut us off! We hope so.

Wednesday 11th April

One of the hardest days of my life. We have done the march back to Stalag 357 in one day but at last we are back. The Germans were very easy with us and anyone could have escaped. Some fellows stopped at a stream and actually had a bathe. The leniency of the Germans surprised me at the time but now I realise that they were actually prisoners themselves. Our troops have cut us off and our camp is in a pocket still held by the Germans. But the main thing is: WE CAN'T BE MOVED! But we've been lucky! All of those fellows who were marched out of this camp before us on Sunday were

---

[12] It's actually a little over 1lb each.

got away by the Germans. We've been saved by a matter of hours. We are not 'out of the wood' yet but we are hoping that this little pocket of German resistance will soon be liquidated.

The camp is in an awful state. After we had left, thousands of European displaced people were moved in and obviously went on the rampage: doors have been torn off and all of the windows smashed, everything which could be broken has been broken. We shall have to sleep out in the open but we can do what we like inside the camp.

There is a hint of a possibility of an American Red Cross parcel issue of one between two men. We hope to have these tomorrow. The short time we have been out of the camp has been enough to show us what an awful state the Germans are in. And the RAF and the American planes seem to be able to do anything they want. As we marched back here we saw Soltau being bombed. We're quite close and most of us, I think, felt awful as we watched the terrible destruction of that town.

Wednesday 12th April
Each of us got a half-share of a Red Cross parcel today. I've just seen a newspaper dropped by our aircraft for the German troops, informing them of the military situation of the moment: Hanover has fallen, and there is street fighting in Bremen. Soltau is occupied by the Americans. (They must have moved in after it was bombed yesterday.) The Russians are in the outskirts of Berlin. There was also general world news, including the death of Roosevelt. I thought it was sad that he had died just before victory. But he must have known that victory was imminent. I'm beginning to feel that we are safe. Soon we shall be free men. At last I'm going back to my Evelyn!

Friday 13th April
Four blokes of our old group have cleaned out a hut and invited us, Jerry and me, and two other fellows we've teamed up with, to move in with them. We've done this and are quite comfortable now. We've put some tables together to make a bed for four of us. We've had a big issue of spuds, so many that we hardly know what to do with them. Bremen has fallen and the Americans are moving up the Hanover-Hamburg Autobahn. And the Americans have also crossed the River Elbe at Magdeburg. Allied troops are, literally, all over Germany. And we're living well now. All we lack is bread but, as they say, you can't have everything.

Saturday 14th April
We got some more food today: peas, oatmeal, sugar, and a loaf between four men. This food is to serve us over an indefinite period. But we're to get an American food parcel between two men every three days. If this is so and we get bread a little more frequently we shall live very well indeed! I haven't

heard any definite news today but we believe our troops to be only 15 kilos from us but it seems the Germans are offering some very stiff resistance.

Sunday 15th April

Still waiting for our troops to reach us. According to a late report they have taken Bergen, the small farming village in which we were billeted last Sunday night so we know they are not far away. But ever since we returned we have heard the continuous thundering of guns. And last night and this morning some fellows reckon they heard what they believed to be Bren-guns, a British Army weapon. If this is so, our troops can't be more than a couple of miles away!

We fellows ought to be excited but we're not! Perhaps it is the relaxation after the worry. But it's nice not to have the blasted Germans to contend with. There aren't any inside the camp and those in the sentry boxes and at the gates are very mild indeed. Those at the gates are no more than commissionaires – they open and close the gates for us.

But, despite this easy living I'll be happier when we are really released. The people at home must be worrying until they know positively that we have been released. I suppose they must know that we are in a contested area. I wonder what Evelyn is thinking? I can hardly believe that I shall be going back to her soon. After this seeming endless wait we are at last to see each other again. I am still undecided whether to go to her first or to go home first. There is no question about wanting to go to her first but I'm wondering, because of my poor physical state, might it not be better to go home and spend a few days there to cover my bones with a few pounds of flesh before letting Evelyn see me. I'm so appallingly thin I feel ashamed to let her see me as I am. I'm sure I look so weak and ill that the poor girl would have reason to fight shy of me. But perhaps there will be time to improve myself physically before we are moved away from here. All we lack at the moment is bread.

Monday 16th

It was my turn to make the early morning tea. It was about 7.30. 'Taffy' Lewis, near me was doing likewise, heating his can on a little fire between two bricks. Absently, we heard a machine gun. 'Taffy' stood, silent for a moment, he'd been a machine-gunner, perhaps his mind was doing a recapitulation of the sound. Then he turned to me.

"Dave," he said, almost in a whisper, "wasn't that a Vickers?" (Vickers machine-gun, British.) Doubtfully, I agreed. Then there was another burst. There was no doubt in Taffy's mind now. He kicked over his fire and can of water, shouting at the top of his voice: "They're here, They're here, Our lads are here!" And as the gun continued its merry chatter, I thought: at last! We're free at last. For us the war has at last ended! But the local battle was still in progress and in the distance we could see our tanks on the skyline.

Somebody said, "They're Crusaders," but to me, and, I suppose, most of those about me, they were just British tanks and that was all that mattered. We took for granted that the war for us was ended. Selfishly, that was all that mattered to us. At 10 am we unarmed the Germans in the camp. The German flag was pulled down and the flags of other nations went up. British, Dominion, and Americans were all comparatively calm, but the French, Yugoslavs, Russians, etc. went wild. They ran around shaking hands and kissing and hugging one another. I boiled some spuds and peas for my dinner – Jerry is still off his food. His stomach is out of order. A little later, a couple of tanks and an armoured car came into the camp.

The lid of the armoured car opened and an officer poked his head out and bawled in his public school accent "Morning, chappies. Just a social call. Can't wait. Monty's just down the road. Cheerie bye!" and they left us. And I thought, the people at home will know now!

5 pm I've just had a gentle amble around the camp with Jerry. He's been ill a couple of days and he's obviously very weak, not having eaten anything and he can't yet bear the sight of food. He felt he needed a little fresh air so we went to see what was happening in the camp. We've seen a British Movietone Film Unit. They were filming but Jerry and I didn't go near the front. The 'movie' team passed bottles of beer amongst us.

There are some conflicting reports regarding what's going to happen to us. There's a tale that we're to be flown back to England in troop-carrying aircraft and bombers. How soon will I be back in England? Perhaps in a few days! Oh, my Evelyn, soon I'm going to hold you.

Tuesday 17th April
Our first British rations have just been issued to us. Bread: pure white, tea and cigarettes. Real English bread! It's like eating cake after the German stuff we've been having.

But what a state the country is in according to what we've been told. The slave labour of Russians and eastern Europeans, it seems, have been creating havoc while unchecked during the last couple of days. There's a lot of looting, destruction , and much worse. They are reacting vengefully and aren't human in their present state. I have no reason to have any love for the Germans but this venting vengeance on the homes of women and old people, unprotected as they have been while their men-folk are away, is simply criminal. But our forces are rapidly restoring order.

Wednesday 18th April
This morning we filled in forms for our repatriation. Some fellows have already gone. Priority is being given to those who have been prisoners longest. Of course, as was to be expected, some 'clever lads' who were captured comparatively recently have claimed that they were captured at Dunkirk. There is no way of checking these claims. The Germans have left

no records in the camps. This is very unfair to those of us who have filled in our forms truthfully. We've been told to take with us only our necessary kit plus one blanket. I wonder are we to be flown home?

I wonder what has happened to Terry Bray and Jimmy Brown? They were with a party of 300 who were sent in the opposite direction when we returned here last Wednesday. I wonder did the Germans manage to get them away?

Friday 20th April
I feel awful. The good food has upset my stomach and I've paid several visits to the latrine during the night. I've been in bed all day and I've eaten nothing. I'm weak, dirty, and in an awful state. I've written to Evelyn but I hope to be in England before she receives it.

Saturday 21st April
I feel much better today though my stomach is still a bit uncertain. I must be careful with the food I eat. I've been starved too long! There is a hitch in the departures from here owing to bad weather. The repatriation people say it is too dangerous for flying. It looks as though I shall be here for some time yet. Next Tuesday, perhaps? I've written a lettercard to Dad. He ought to receive it before I arrive in England. I shall write again to Evelyn when I get another lettercard or a sheet of paper. We are on full British Army rations now and have more food than we know what to do with. We've almost forgotten about eating!

We are being inundated with cigarettes, tooth brushes, tooth paste, shaving cream, soap, etc. Our troops are treating us very well and were horrified when they saw our conditions.

Sunday 22nd April
Gerald Stehr and Len Hensman have gone today, lucky people! Now Jerry and I are on our own again. The weather has been unpleasant all day but the sky is clearing tonight. Perhaps we shall have fine weather tomorrow. If everything goes as expected, Jerry and I expect to leave here on Tuesday, fly and arrive in England on Wednesday, and, possibly, go on leave on Thursday or Friday. Six weeks leave in England! It's going to be wonderful as I shall spend most of it with Evelyn. I wrote to her today and I've told her how the Germans tried to get us away but how they failed with 30% of us. I wonder is she worrying about me? I wish I could have sent her a telegram!

Monday 23rd April
If everything goes well this will be my last day in this camp. According to today's orders, my group must parade at the main gate tomorrow for disinfestation prior to being taken, by truck, to the airport where we will stay tomorrow night. I intend to have a very light breakfast of toast and milk tomorrow. I daren't risk upsetting my already none too sure stomach when

I'm going on a long journey in a motor truck. In fact, I intend to eat very little tomorrow. I want to have my stomach properly in order before I arrive in England.

A few weeks ago when our secret radio informed us of the San Francisco Conference I wouldn't have believed that I would be flying, a free man, to England on that day. I suppose I ought to be excited that this will be my last night in this camp but, somehow, I'm not. Perhaps I've been numbed by the shock of our relief. Today Jerry asked me shall I get married on my first leave. I wonder? I think I'm beginning to get stage fright! But Evelyn can decide. I want to marry her as soon as possible even though I'm afraid of 'the frills' as she calls them but I'd go through much more than 'the frills' to get her. Six weeks is a long time so perhaps I shall be married before the end of my leave.

Tuesday 24th April

We are at the Prisoner of War Reception Camp. I've forgotten the name of the place but it is 120 kilos from Stalag 357. It's very well organized and we're being shown every consideration. There are a few Air-force girls here but I haven't spoken to any of them although I have heard them talking. They're the first English speaking women I've heard in more than three years. We hope to fly tomorrow but we're uncertain whether we'll fly direct to England or stop for a day at Brussels. Obviously we'd prefer to leave out Brussels!

Wednesday 25th April

We stopped at Brussels and have been taken by train to Ostend.

Thursday 26th April

In the Channel: Coincidence! This ship, The Viking, is the ship which took me to France, Sunday 10th September 1939. There are three ships carrying us ex-prisoners back to England: Viking, Bruge, I can't see the name of the other one. We are being escorted by a destroyer lest there be submarines lurking in the depths. We've been told that we are bound for Tilbury.

The destroyer has just signalled: 'Viking and Bruge to go ahead independently'. Apparently we're considered to be in a reasonably safe area and Viking and Bruge are much faster than the other ship so we are being allowed to ahead.

To be continued in England.

Friday 27th April

We disembarked at Tilbury on the night of Thursday 26th April. We were taken to large marquees where a colossal meal had been laid on for us. The place was strewn with bunting and fancy lights. There were girls in abundance to serve and to talk to us: girls of the three services and also of the Land Army and the Salvation Army. Many of us over-ate, and some – not I – were ill! After the meal we were taken by lorries to the nearest railway station where each of us was given a blanket and put on the train for Crawley in Sussex. We were taken by road to a prepared camp – nissen-huts. Although beds had been prepared for us and though we needed them – we'd had no sleep since Tuesday night – this was not to be. Our clothes were taken from us. We went through showers, passed doctors, dentists, radiographers; completed questionnaires concerning our treatment as prisoners, were paid, allowed to send free telegrams and given travel warrants. It was Friday evening before we were free. We were being allowed to go on leave.

Saturday morning 28th April

Initially, I had intended to go to my dad's home near Chester-le-Street, County Durham because of my poor physical state but on Saturday morning I phoned Evelyn at her Inland Revenue office. She convinced me that I should go to her first. I did. We were married by special licence the following Friday.

And they all lived happily…

Postscript

I shall be 89 next birthday, Evelyn 80, and in common with most of us I often wonder what might have been. If! If only…

But as was said in those distant barrack rooms in India so long ago: If your Aunt Sally had had testicles instead of tits she might have been your Uncle Bob…!

I left the Army at the end of the war but, after three years as an electrician, in desperation to have a home of our own – we had been living with Evelyn's parents and we had a baby – I decided to go back to the mining industry. The offer of the National Coal Board seemed to be that an ex-miner could go to the mine of his choice and the type of work of his choice. I would go to a mine in Durham and I would be an electrician. Unfortunately, the offer held good only so far as it suited the requirements of the Coal Board. I was directed to Silverhill Colliery near Mansfield to use a pick and shovel. For a few weeks I lived in lodgings, then Evelyn and our baby joined me and we bought the house in which we now live.

And that's my lot!